DOING EXCELLENT SOCIAL RESEARCH WITH DOCUMENTS

In today's society we increasingly create and consume written content and images. This includes a range of sources, from social media posts to records held within organisations, and everything in between, including news articles, blogs, shopping lists and official government documents. Critically reading these 'documents' can help us to understand a huge amount about society. *Doing Excellent Social Research with Documents* includes guidance on how to 'read between the lines' and provides an overview of six research projects which use documents as data.

The substantive chapters are organised in two sections, with each chapter focused on a specific type of data. Section I focuses on documents that are found in isolation from their authors, including official and historical documents, traditional media, diaries and online content. Section II focuses on using documents in addition to existing data from primary research, including the role of documents in ethnography and visual research methods. In each chapter, you will be guided through the process of:

- Developing research questions, and how this impacts which documents are selected;
- Considering aspects of bias and quality within the documentary sources;
- Undertaking analysis, using six different strategies including thematic analysis, framework analysis, content analysis, discourse analysis and narrative analysis.

Drawing on research projects that reflect real world situations, you will be methodically guided through the research process in detail, enabling you to examine and understand the practices and value of documentary analysis. *Doing Excellent Social Research with Documents* is a practical how-to guide for students (final year undergraduates onwards) and researchers using documents as data.

Aimee Grant is a Qualitative Researcher at the Centre for Trials Research, Cardiff University. She undertakes research on health, pregnancy and motherhood, drawing on a range of disciplinary fields including critical public health, sociology, human geography and cultural studies.

DOING EXCELLENT SOCIAL RESEARCH WITH DOCUMENTS

Practical Examples and Guidance for Qualitative Researchers

Aimee Grant

Routledge
Taylor & Francis Group

LONDON AND NEW YORK

First published 2019
by Routledge
2 Park Square, Milton Park, Abingdon, Oxon OX14 4RN

and by Routledge
711 Third Avenue, New York, NY 10017

Routledge is an imprint of the Taylor & Francis Group, an informa business

British Library Cataloguing-in-Publication Data
A catalogue record for this book is available from the British Library

Library of Congress Cataloging-in-Publication Data
Names: Grant, Aimee, author.
Title: Doing excellent social research with documents: practical examples and guidance for qualitative researchers / Aimee Grant.
Description: Abingdon, Oxon; New York, NY: Routledge, 2018.
Identifiers: LCCN 2018025981 | ISBN 9781138038653 (hardback) | ISBN 9781138038660 (pbk.) | ISBN 9781315177274 (ebook)
Subjects: LCSH: Qualitative research—Methodology. | Social sciences—Methodology. | Government publications.
Classification: LCC H62. G7167 2018 | DDC 300.72/1—dc23
LC record available at https://lccn.loc.gov/2018025981

ISBN: 978-1-138-03865-3 (hbk)
ISBN: 978-1-138-03866-0 (pbk)
ISBN: 978-1-315-17727-4 (ebk)

Typeset in Bembo
by codeMantra

Printed and bound in Great Britain by
TJ International Ltd, Padstow, Cornwall

For Margaret and Nick

'Grant's text offers an excellent overview of the practicalities attendant on the use of documents in social research. It will no doubt prove to be an indispensable guide for both novice and practiced researchers, and is worthy of a prime slot on the bookshelf'.

Lindsay Prior, Emeritus Professor of Sociology and Honorary Professor, School of Public Health, Queen's University of Belfast

'This truly is an Excellent resource for both students and fully-fledged academics seeking to get their teeth into documentary research. Aimee Grant's style is clear and accessible, whilst also unflinching in its approach to dealing with the nitty-gritty of the practicalities of accessing, sampling and analysing documents for effective scholarship. The "how" of documentary research is clearly underpinned by the 'why', tutoring the reader in the theoretical and ethical context of research with documents. The practical approach, complete with hands-on activities and detailed examples, makes this an essential resource for anyone looking for a step-by-step guide to doing documentary research'.

Nadia Gill, Lecturer in Human Geography, Lancaster University

'Documents, be they digital or paper, are central to our social life, yet they often receive little attention. Aimee Grant's excellent book really helps us think about the practical and conceptual issues we can face when working with documents. She shows us, through a range of really useful examples, the wonderful possibilities of doing social research with documents'.

Tim Rapley, Professor of Applied Health Care Research, Northumbria University

'This book makes a compelling case for why documents make great data for social science research. *Doing Excellent Social Research with Documents* is an accessible guide and a very welcome addition to the methods literature'.

Amanda Coffey, Pro Vice-Chancellor, Student Experience and Academic Standards, Cardiff University

'This is essential reading for anyone using documentary analysis in their research – I only wish it had been available during my doctoral studies! It is interdisciplinary in nature and, as a socio-legal scholar using documentary analysis in researching the influence of non-governmental organisations in international human rights law, I found much of the content to be really valuable. The author notes that many researchers may have been improvising up until now. Improvise no more, the handbook for documentary analysis has arrived'.

Fiona McGaughey, Director of Higher Degrees (Coursework), University of Western Australia Law School

'This fantastic text will support those conducting research with documentary sources, especially through its practical examples and guidance. The author skilfully discusses both historical and contemporary documents in this lively, engaging and accessible text for researchers and students'.

Sarah Mills, Senior Lecturer in Human Geography,
Loughborough University

'This is a well-written and highly useful book. It covers theoretical and empirical issues in an accessible way, and enables researchers to improve the quality and impact of their work'.

Kirstein Rummery, Professor of Social Policy and Co-Director of
Centre for Gender and Feminist Studies, University of Stirling

CONTENTS

DETAILED TABLE OF CONTENTS

FIGURES

TABLES

BOXES

FOREWORD

I am very happy to have the opportunity of writing this foreword to Aimee Grant's book. Documentary sources comprise some of the most widely used sources for social scientists, yet they receive far less attention in textbooks on research methods than is the case for survey methods and ethnography. This absence of significant discussion is especially striking in a period when there is an increasing reliance on visual and digital documentary sources in a variety of areas of sociology. Aimee's work fills a real need in the literature by providing an overview of the various types of sources and their uses and illustrating these with concrete examples drawn from her own research practice.

The author presents an interesting overview of types of documents and how these relate to other sources of qualitative data, showing that documentary methods must be firmly embedded in an overall strategy of social research. Each type of use is complemented by a reflexive case study that demonstrates the power of the sources. Aimee Grant is based in a School of Medicine and has a clear grasp of the wide interdisciplinary relevance of these methods. Her own empirical research ranges over health and wellbeing and includes an investigation of smoking and the tobacco industry, studies in pregnancy, parenthood and child care, and enquiries into illnesses and the actions of medical staff. All of these interests are brought to bear on the questions that arise in the use of documents as sources of research data.

It is this personal involvement in research that brings Aimee Grant's text to life. Documents are considered not simply as topics of study but for what they can tell us about the richness of the lives of individuals in a variety of social situations. Documents and research are brought together in relation to key theoretical issues, and wider implications and consequences are shown. The book is focused on examples of how to actually do documentary research, with sufficient guidance for the reader to be able to go away and handle the material for him or herself. Throughout the various chapters, there are illustrative extracts and examples that expand the analysis and inform the reader.

The book is topical and relevant in its examples and will have a wide appeal to researchers in all areas of social research. Its focus on the combination of ethnographic and documentary sources as qualitative methods will form an essential counterpart to the equally important focus on quantitative methodology found in other texts. This is a genuinely student-friendly textbook that doesn't talk down to its readers but treats them as equal participants in the great project of sociological understanding. I am sure that you will enjoy reading Aimee Grant's book and that it will find a permanent place on your bookshelf.

John Scott
Cornwall, UK

ACKNOWLEDGEMENTS

This book has benefited from the input of a number of organisations and individuals. First, I have received funding from the Cardiff University Respiratory Bequest Fund (Chapter 5), the Economic and Social Research Council (Chapter 7) and the Wellcome Trust (Chapter 8).

Second, many people have worked alongside me to explore topic areas or undertook parts of the analysis described in the case studies. These include discussions around Actor Network Theory with Davina Allen, Amy Lloyd, Nina Jacob, Yvonne Moriarty and Heather Strange (Chapter 2). In relation to the exploration of the London Riots (Chapter 3), Berit Bliesemann de Guevara, Catrin Fflur Huws, Yvonne McDermott Rees, Cheryl Allsop, Nick Davis and I were fortunate to be funded by the Welsh Crucible to look into this incident, from a different point of view. I learned a lot about undertaking analysis of media articles when working with Louise Hoyle on an analysis of treatment targets in Accident and Emergency departments. In relation to Chapter 5, the majority of the analysis was undertaken by Hannah O'Mahoney who developed methodological insights as part of this work. Alongside my analysis of the infant formula industry documents in Chapter 6, Hannah Williams undertook a full set of independent double coding for her BSc dissertation. The data presented in Chapter 7 were part of my doctoral research, supervised by Mark Drakeford and Gareth Williams. The research that forms the case study in Chapter 8 involved data collected by Melanie Morgan and Dunla Gallagher, with input into research design from Dawn Mannay.

More practically, I received comments on drafts of chapters from many colleagues and students, who were very helpful in refining the argument and, later, in making the book more reader friendly. They include Jessica Baillie, Marita Hennessey, Phil Smith, Maria Pournara, George Jennings, Kate Boyer, Bethan Pell, Rachel Williams, Rachel Waters, Nadia von Benzon, Claire Sedgwick,

Beth le Roux, Maria O'Brien, Erica Bowen and Beverley Pickard-Jones. Matthew Arthur undertook additional proofreading. Any mistakes are, of course, mine. Alongside the practical support, Sara Delamont has been a constant source of helpful advice throughout my career.

I would also like to acknowledge the important contribution of Margaret Wade and Julie Osborn. Margaret and Julie are dyslexia study skills coaches. Margaret provided study skills training during my undergraduate and post-graduate degrees funded by the Disabled Students Allowance. As an employee, I secured funding through Access to Work in order to spend 12 hours with Julie during a period of severe disablement related to dyslexia. Within this time, Julie provided new coping strategies which enabled me to return to working at the level required to not only do my day job, but to write this book. I must, of course, also thank the UK Department for Work and Pensions for providing funding through the Access to Work scheme and also urge them to maintain support for disabled workers.

ABBREVIATIONS

API	Application Programming Interface
B&B	Bed and Breakfast
CAQDAS	Computer Assisted Qualitative Data Analysis Software
CDA	Critical Discourse Analysis
CMP	Condition Management Programme
DIN	Document Identification Number
ESA	Employment and Support Allowance
GCSE	General Certificate of Secondary Education
NHS	National Health Service
RCUK	Research Councils UK
UK	United Kingdom
URL	Uniform Resource Locator
USA	United States of America
WHO	World Health Organization

1

INTRODUCTION

Documents, documents everywhere

Summary

This chapter opens by considering if this book will be relevant for your research. Next, I provide an example of the documents that I engaged with on one particular day. This supports the conclusion that documents are everywhere in developed societies and can therefore help us to understand a wide range of phenomena. Following this, I explain the need for this book and the way in which it varies from other books that are available. Finally, the chapter ends with a description of the structure of the book and provides a detailed outline of the remaining eight chapters.

Is this book for me?

Doing Excellent Social Research with Documents is intended for those of you who are about to begin a project using documents as data, including students and faculty, as well as those of you supervising students who are doing research using documents. The book may also have value for those of you who already have experience in doing research with documents, particularly if you feel that you have been 'improvising' methodologically. At a broader level, this book will have relevance for teaching research methods at undergraduate and postgraduate levels, where students are already versed in the basics of qualitative research methods. This book is not bound by any one academic discipline and aims to be accessible to any discipline using documents as data. If you are a historian, however, there are other books that describe doing research with historical documents in more detail, and you should consult them too (see, for example, Brundage 2018).

Once you have identified a topic area of interest for your research, this book will provide tools to help you think about refining your **research questions** to fit the documentary data source(s) available to you. It also outlines a range of analysis techniques, providing a breakdown of the processes that need to be undertaken and refers to more detailed sources that can provide further help. This should help you to think about the aims of your research project and which analysis strategy would, therefore, be most appropriate.

I understand that not everyone will have time to read a whole book, particularly when you are keen to get 'stuck in' to analysing your documents. If you are short of time, it is recommended that, before planning your project, you read Chapters 2 and 9 and at least one chapter from Section I (if your research uses documents found away from their **authors**) or Section II (if you use documents to triangulate knowledge or use **visual methods**). If you have already started your project and you find yourself feeling a bit methodologically unsure, I would also suggest reading those chapters. That said, if you can find the time to read the entire book, you will benefit from reading all six case study chapters (Chapters 3–8) in order to better understand how **research questions**, data sources and analysis strategies can be planned when using different types of documents. In Chapter 9 (pp. 175–177), a checklist is provided that will help you to think through how to do your research at each stage of the project to ensure considerations relating to **research questions**, quality and **bias** within data sources, analysis strategy, ethics, write up and impact are addressed. Also, a glossary is provided to help remind you of the definitions of key terms used throughout the book; words found in the glossary are in **bold print**.

By using this book, you should avoid some of the pitfalls and mistakes that could otherwise cost you valuable time and effort. A considered approach to your research with documents is also likely to improve the quality of your research, and thus your likelihood of a good grade, a paper being accepted by a peer-reviewed journal or your research having an impact on policy and practice. This chapter now moves on to consider where we find documents in everyday life.

Documents, documents everywhere!

I think documents are great data, but you might not (yet!) be convinced that you should use documents in your research project. One reason that documents make great data is that they are literally everywhere in developed societies and can therefore tell us a lot about a broad range of phenomena. Alongside the paper documents we produce in vast quantities, our increasingly digital lives mean that the volume of 'documents', if we include digital content, is still continuing to increase year-on-year. In order to understand the potential of including documents in your research studies as data, I have listed the documents that I have interacted with or produced today (a Sunday, over a public holiday weekend). I have:

- tweeted and shared the tweets of others
- commented on photos posted by friends on Facebook

- shared posts related to the forthcoming UK general election on Facebook
- emailed multiple colleagues, catching up on the previous week
- written a shopping list
- exchanged a long conversation via a messenger application with my sister
- taken digital photos of DIY projects and shared these with my parents
- drafted a press release to go alongside a piece of research I led which will soon be published
- completed an application form to enter a half marathon
- written a to-do list for the forthcoming month
- edited and finalised Chapter 7 of this book
- commented on a draft journal article written by a colleague of mine

Each of these documents had a very different purpose. This was related to their intended audience and subject matter. For example, my use of social media is polarised. My Twitter account is exclusively academic, whilst my Facebook profile is around 90% non-academic, consisting of friends and family. When I post to Twitter, I undertake various roles. I show that I am a member of Cardiff University and promote our successes. I also undertake (sometimes shameless!) self-promotion in order to spread the findings of my research as widely as possible. Even more shamelessly, I have tweeted that I think it is a 'genius idea' for me to highlight the importance of documents in social life, by describing my own interactions with them. By their very nature, we expect the things that we write on social media to be viewed by others. In contrast, I expect that my shopping list and to-do list will remain largely private. Likewise, the conversations that I have with my family and the emails to colleagues I expect to have a much more select audience.

As the expected audience varies by each of these data sources, we might expect that the **author**'s rationale for writing in particular ways would vary. In my example above, when I email colleagues, I may use varying levels of formality, depending on my pre-existing relationship with the individual, whether I feel that it may need to be copied in to somebody more senior at a later date or if I also have a non-professional relationship with that person outside of work. Some of my most long-standing colleagues are close friends, and I may dispense entirely with formalities and even use 'kisses' at the end of emails about work-related matters, but if I were to add a second colleague to these emails, they would return to the standard, accepted level of formality, regardless of the pre-existing friendships. This is because we present different versions of ourselves depending on the anticipated audience. For example, it has been shown that on some social media platforms, individuals present an idealised form of themselves, as will be discussed in more detail in Chapter 5.

To wrap up this section, I would suggest that documents are, like love in the 1995 Wet Wet Wet[1] song, literally all around us in contemporary developed societies. The extent to which one interacts with documents may vary by age, occupation, education level and health status. However, most people in developed, and many developing, societies will interact with at least one document every day. As you are reading this book, I imagine that you will also have read and/ or created at least ten documents so far today (or yesterday, if you're reading this over breakfast). By delving into the relationship between individuals, documents and society, we can learn about society in ways that we may not be able to through other qualitative methods.

Exercise: considering your interaction with documents

Now maybe an opportune moment for you to make a list, or a mental list, of the documents that you have written (including digital content), read or interacted with in some way over the past day, and to think about their purpose in your life. There is no right or wrong answer here, but you may feel that there were some documents you assume would be public and others that you assume would be relatively private. This may help you think about the way that you write for yourself and the way you write for a range of broader audiences.

Why there is a need for this book

I decided to write this book for several reasons, the most important of which is that I have discovered that documents are excellent data to understand society. Alongside this, they are very accessible to those who need quick and easy access to some data for a dissertation or suchlike. As many students and researchers use documents as data, but very few people are (academically) talking about how to do this, I thought that I should share what I've learned. This book comprises lessons from existing books and articles and my own strategies for doing research with documents.

Despite the benefits of using documents as data, I also have first-hand experiences of the challenges of using documents as data. I used documents as data during my doctoral research (Grant 2011a), which reported on the experiences of benefit (welfare) claimants (Grant 2011b; Grant 2012), welfare advisers (Grant 2013a) and National Health Service (NHS) health professionals (Grant 2013b) who were involved in the rollout of the Welfare Reform Act 2007. My PhD research utilised an interpretivist ethnographic approach. I undertook periods of non-participant observation within welfare offices, and (electronic) documents were used extensively by the welfare advisers prior to, during and after each meeting with a claimant. Alongside this, some claimants gave me permission to access their case files from the NHS back-to-work programme they attended (as will be discussed in more detail in Chapter 7), and I drew on policy documents extensively to contextualise the experiences of claimants and workers.

Together, these data sources provided a well-rounded account of how the policy was implemented in practice. However, when it came to the case files, I didn't know *what* to do to analyse them. I read the two core texts recommended by my supervisors (Scott 1990; Prior 2003), which provided important information in terms of quality and **bias** within the documents (Scott 1990) and helped to contextualise the way the documents shaped the behaviour of those responsible for implementing the Welfare Reform Act (Prior 2003). I also consulted a four-volume collection of examples of documentary analysis in a wide variety of settings, which opened my eyes to a broad range of data sources and analysis strategies (Scott 2006). But I still felt confused as to exactly what practical steps were required to analyse my documents in a rigorous way. I was also unsure how I should report my findings as they came from differing sources, all of which were affected by varying forms of **bias**. This was in contrast to interview data, of which there were considerably detailed accounts available that explained *how* to do analysis.

I was fortunate to have the opportunity to present this data to the Qualitative Analysis Research Group, hosted at the School of Social Sciences, Cardiff University, which was chaired at the time by William Housley. I took one of the case files, the smallest file, to the group. In my field notes from that day, I noted that the data had been described as "fascinating", "rich", "illuminating" but also "overwhelming". In order to complete my PhD on time, I undertook a relatively superficial analysis of the documents. This was in contrast to the rest of my data, which I had very thoroughly analysed.

Over the next six years, I returned to the case files periodically. I knew that they contained rich detail and could provide further insight into not only the lived experience of the back-to-work intervention, but also the way in which health professionals documented their work within the UK NHS. I also spoke to others about my struggle. A professor mentioned that her students regularly collected documents in **the ethnographic field** but that she did not have a good source to direct them to in terms of analysis. As I began to confide my fears that I had not done full justice to this data to a wider range of colleagues, other researchers shared their stories of undertaking superficial analysis of documents as part of wider studies, where interview and ethnographic data were analysed more comprehensively.

It seemed as though there was a gap for a methods text that really focused on *how* to analyse documents. But the need was bigger than that: the entire process of researching with documents needed describing in a way that was more accessible to the novice researcher. I also felt that there was a need for documents to be brought alive as data, so that researchers who were not routinely using documents in their own research could understand their potential value. I hope that I have gone some way towards meeting these aims.

Structure of the book

Within each chapter, I draw on a broad range of literature, crossing disciplinary boundaries. Chapter 2 is a stand-alone chapter and provides a general overview of doing research with documents. Chapters 3–8 are case studies of documentary analysis that I have undertaken, and describe the process of research from designing the study through to analysing the data. In each chapter, there is a review of literature that is relevant to undertaking research using that particular type of document as a data source. In each case study chapter, I then move on to describe the context of the case study and the research design – including sampling and analysis. Practical challenges in undertaking research using that type of document are also presented. At the end of each of these six chapters, new data is presented alongside an exercise to let you practise the analytical skills used within the case study. It is intended that any one chapter can stand alone as a case study of a piece of documentary analysis. Moreover, the analysis strategies described may also fit with alternative sources of data, and these can be read in isolation. The book closes with Chapter 9, which aims to help you consider if documents can be used as a source of data to answer your **research questions**. A more detailed breakdown of the contents of each chapter is provided below.

Outline of chapters

Chapter 2: How to do excellent research with documents: general principles

In Chapter 2, I give an overview of what documentary analysis is. This includes describing what a document is, **epistemological** concerns when using documents, and an outline of the practical steps to undertake in order to ensure good quality research. The practical steps I describe include how to access documents, record keeping and assessing quality and **bias** in documentary sources. Alongside this, I compare research that uses 'found' documents, which have been written in isolation from the researcher, and 'researcher-influenced' documents, which have been generated as part of a research study. If you have never done any research with documents, I would advise that you read this chapter first.

Section I: Documents found in isolation from their authors

In this section, I guide you through three case studies where I have analysed 'found' documents. At the end of each chapter, I describe some of the possible pitfalls of the data source, and provide additional documents and a data analysis exercise, so you can practise doing the different types of analysis.

Chapter 3: Traditional media: investigating the construction of societal norms

In the first of the case studies, I introduce existing research that shows that media coverage of social issues can create a 'moral panic'. I then provide an example of this sort of research based on UK **tabloid newspapers** reporting of the 2011 London Riots. Through this worked example, I describe how **research questions** were formed in order to match with the available data. I also outline the first of the six analysis strategies to be detailed in this book: **thematic analysis**.

Chapter 4: Historical and official documents: moving beyond simple interpretations

In this chapter, I draw on two types of documents: historical documents and contemporary **official documents**. I chose to combine these two sources as sometimes the same phenomenon can be investigated over time through the use of multiple sets of data. The topic under investigation is the way in which people living in poverty are provided with financial support, and what this tells us about power relations. I used historical documents focusing on the implementation of the 1834 UK Poor Law Amendment Act and contemporary **official documents** in relation to the UK Welfare Reform and Work Bill 2015. The analysis strategy I use to compare these two data sets is **Critical Discourse Analysis (CDA)**.

Chapter 5: Documents created by individuals: collection and analysis of multi-modal content

In this case study, I describe a research project that examined how individuals reported their waterpipe (also known as hubble-bubble, hookah, shisha) smoking on Twitter. Unlike in the first two case study chapters, in this chapter I consider how words and images can be combined to create a more detailed understanding of **meaning**. Alongside the two types of data, I chose to use three analysis strategies with the complex data set: a basic **semiotic analysis** and **inductive thematic analysis** of the textual elements and a **content analysis** of images.

Section II: Documents as an addition to existing qualitative research methods

Documents are often used alongside other sources of qualitative data in research projects to create a greater understanding of a phenomenon. This is one type of **triangulation**. In this section, I present case studies from three research projects where I have undertaken documentary analysis either alongside interview or ethnographic data or to triangulate findings from an earlier study.

Chapter 6: Triangulation of findings from primary research: things we might not have otherwise been able to establish

In this chapter, I introduce the concept of **triangulation** as something that can strengthen research. The original research project involved focus groups with new mothers to understand their preferences and needs for information regarding their babies' health. Mothers highlighted infant formula companies as a source of information. Following this, a secondary research project was undertaken to analyse infant formula marketing materials against a Code of conduct that infant formula companies are supposed to abide by. As there was a clear list of **deductive** codes to analyse the data against, **content analysis** was the analysis approach used within this project. I also report on how I coded the data without the use of a specialist **CAQDAS** computer programme, providing insight for those of you coding your data 'by hand'.

Chapter 7: Documents in ethnographic research: things we might not have been able to observe

Ethnography includes the use of observation, interviews and the analysis of any other available information to understand a phenomenon. Documents can be particularly useful data to an ethnographer. I present a case study of a back-to-work programme for the long-term sick in the UK through the use of interviews, observations and case files. Consideration is given to how to prepare organisational documents ahead of analysis. I describe how I made use of **framework analysis** to analyse the case files alongside interview data and how I compared the two data sources.

Chapter 8: Participant-created documents as an elicitation tool: things we might not have otherwise been told

Visual methods have become popular in qualitative research. They often include the participants preparing a written or drawn document, followed by an **(elicitation) interview** based on the participants' documents. In using this approach, it can be argued that we create space for participants to tell us what they think is important, rather than relying on our predetermined ideas and a topic guide. Alongside this, we can ask the participants, the **authors** of the documents, to elaborate on the documents they have created, in order to enhance our understanding of **meaning**. The case study I draw on in this final empirical chapter focuses on women's experiences of health during pregnancy, which I asked them to consider through the use of a timeline. I describe in detail how I analysed the data using **narrative analysis**, which is well-suited to chronological accounts.

Conclusion

Chapter 9: Reviewing and applying concepts to your research project

In this final chapter, I recap the types of documents that can be used in research projects, the ways in which quality can be assured in documentary research and the common pitfalls you should try to avoid. I provide a range of checklists, questions and topics to consider when designing your own studies.

Feedback is always welcome

This book is a first edition that has been developed through my experience in research using documents, as well as through feedback from colleagues who have undertaken research in this area. Although I have thought about this a lot, read a lot about this method over the last decade and added new concepts from colleagues, I may have missed something important. Please do let me know if you feel there is something missing or that could be explained better. Likewise, if you've found this book helpful, do feel free to tell me. You can find me on Twitter (@ DrAimeeGrant).

Note

1 Wet Wet Wet are a Scottish band that was formed in 1982 and led by Marti Pellow. See: http://wetwetwet.co.uk/ for more details

References

Brundage, A. 2018. *Going to the sources: a guide to historical research and writing.* London: John Wiley & Sons.

Grant, A. 2011a. *New Labour, welfare reform and discretion: pathways to work for incapacity benefit claimants.* Cardiff: Cardiff University.

Grant, A. 2011b. Fear, confusion and participation: incapacity benefit claimants and (compulsory) work focused interviews. *Research, Policy and Planning*: 28(3), pp. 161–171.

Grant, A. 2012. Barriers to work for incapacity benefit claimants in Wales. *Contemporary Wales*: 25, pp. 173–190.

Grant, A. 2013a. Welfare reform, increased conditionality and discretion: Jobcentre Plus advisers' experiences of targets and sanctions. *Journal of Poverty and Social Justice*: 21(2), pp. 165–176.

Grant, A. 2013b. The effect of the use of discretion on occupational therapists' identity. *British Journal of Occupational Therapy*: 76(9), pp. 409–417.

Prior, L. 2003. *Using documents in social research.* London: Sage.

Scott, J. 1990. *A matter of record: documentary sources in social research.* London: John Wiley & Sons.

Scott, J. 2006. *Documentary research.* London: Sage.

2

HOW TO DO EXCELLENT RESEARCH WITH DOCUMENTS

General principles

Summary

This chapter introduces key principles of using documents as data in social research. It is divided into the way that documents are used in developed societies and practical tips for undertaking research with documents. First, drawing on a range of existing literature, the chapter opens with a discussion of what documents are, including online sources. The chapter also describes the way that documents are used in society, through discussion of **authors**, **readers** and the way that they interact. The second part of the chapter reviews existing literature to understand how to carry out high-quality social research with documents. This includes ensuring fit with **research questions**, accessing documents and sampling to ensure that the data available answer the **research question**. Alongside this, ways in which to consider quality and **bias** in documentary sources are noted. **Epistemological**, ethical and practical concerns are also described. Whilst the literature to date on documentary analysis tends to focus on 'found' documents, the chapter also considers these elements from the point of view of 'researcher influenced' documents, which have been generated as part of a study using visual or creative research methods. Finally, the chapter includes signposting to potential analysis strategies. The topics in this chapter are returned to in the final chapter of the book (Chapter 9), in order to build on the lessons learned through the six empirical chapters and to provide more practical guidance on how to design your research study in a methodologically robust way.

Key learning points

- What a document is
- How documents are used in everyday life, and what this means for research
- How to assess documents for quality and **bias**
- How to choose a **research question** and data for your project
- How to plan a project that fits the time and resources you have available
- What ethical issues you should consider in your research
- How to ensure you don't lose your data

Documents and everyday life

So, what is a document?

Whilst we might think that this is quite a straightforward question, like many areas when it comes to research, there is a level of debate. In 1990, John Scott stated, "a document in its most general sense is a written text" (Scott 1990, p. 12). However, Scott's text-based definition could exclude documents that are largely graphic in their construction. A more recent definition of documentary analysis extends the idea beyond written text: "...it is quite artificial to restrict analysis of documents to text" (Prior 2003: 5). In today's increasingly digital society, we often see written text alongside graphical or pictorial content. In recognition of these challenges, Lindsay Prior also notes "it is no easier to specify what a document is than it is to specify, in abstraction, what is and what is not a work of art" (2003, p. 1). Accordingly, I would define documents as:

> content or objects which include written, graphical or pictorial matter, or a combination of these types of content, in order to transmit or store information or meaning.

For me, the intended use of the document, that it is transmitting information or **meaning**(s) either to the **author** or to an intended **reader**, is important alongside the genre of the content. In using my definition, we can say that documents encompass a very wide range of materials, both those in hard and digital copies, and formal and informal documents, ranging from official case files to tweets, letters or even Post-it® notes. To think briefly about how these documents vary, we can consider how much time is spent in making the content understandable to others. Whilst a letter needs to be largely understandable by its recipient, a Post-it note is often only written for the **author** to consult again at a later point (and if enough time has passed, the note may fail to have any **meaning** to the **author**). These sorts of issues can be understood by considering how documents are used in contemporary developed societies.

How documents are created and used

As was mentioned above, an **author** is one of the key elements in document construction, but it is important not to forget that **readers** also help to shape **meaning** when they read or consume documents. For Prior (2003: 2) and myself, documents are not "stable, static and pre-defined artefacts". What this means is that they have uses in society, and that their use and **meaning** may vary over time depending on the **author(s)** and **reader(s)** interpretation of situations and language. If this sounds complicated, and makes you want to hide the book in the freezer,[1] don't worry. There are examples given below, so you can think about this, and apply these theoretical concepts to your own lived experience as a writer and consumer of documents. Following this, the way that documents fulfil functions in society is considered in relation to **Actor Network Theory** (Latour 2005). Again, this section has examples to make it easier to understand the key points. For those of you who have to write a section on **epistemological** concerns in your dissertation or report, this section will provide a foundation to enable you to explore this issue in more detail. At this stage of the book, discussion is largely abstract, but we will return to these concepts in each of the six empirical examples, to critically consider the purpose of the document as part of the analysis, further bringing these concepts to life.

Authors

When we think of **authors**, we may think of someone carefully composing a paper, a book or a thesis, but as we considered in Chapter 1, we are all **authors** almost every single day. We write text messages to friends and family, shopping lists and, if you are anything like me, lots of emails and 'to do lists'. When I am writing these different documents, in the very back of my mind, I am considering the intended use of the document. One key element of my (and all **authors'**) consideration is the document's intended audience. Do we imagine that this will be private, between ourselves or ourselves and some close trusted friends and family, or public, to be read by those at the furthest reach of our social networks (or even beyond)?

In order to conceptualise this, consider the different ways that you would communicate with a close friend, compared to one of your lecturers, supervisors or your manager. Or think about the last time you agonised over the wording you used, for example, in an essay, an email to someone important or on your social media accounts, drafting and redrafting until you felt that there was no way your **meaning** could be misinterpreted. You may realise that often we change the way in which we speak and write to suit both the occasion and the audience. Things may change further depending on whether you are writing the document for somebody else, particularly if it is part of your job or important to your identity in some way.

Moving beyond our own experiences, we can apply a **theoretical** lens to this: we could say that documents are a **social construction** (Thomas 1966).

That is, when you or I or any other **author** creates a document, we apply rules in order to meet social expectations and to jointly create knowledge with the (anticipated) **reader(s)**. In being an **author**, we may follow imagined rules, informal understandings or even explicit instructions we have been given. Imagined rules may include the formal tone of language used in job applications or academic essays and publications. By contrast, when you are given a form to complete and it contains boxes for your responses, the size of the boxes gives an indication of how much information you should include. At other times, a form may explicitly tell you not to write more than, for example, 250 words. As such, the **author** of the template and the **author** of the responses work together to create knowledge following a set pattern.

It is also worth noting that in many instances there is not one single **author** of a document. In the workplace, teams may be involved in developing content orally that one person (who is later defined as the **author**) is given responsibility for writing down. In other situations, **editors**, proofreaders and critical friends are involved in helping to refine the core **meanings** or language so that they are clearer. In doing so, they may add points that were previously excluded, or they may change **meanings** in the document that they feel are unsuitable.

In our research, it is important that we move beyond considering only a document's content. If we do not consider the conditions under which the document was developed, we fail to understand why particular formatting, length and language may have been used. We may also misinterpret some of the subtle **meanings** in the data. It is for this reason that we may benefit from the expertise of those who authored the documents to help us interpret them, although this is not always available. If it is not possible to access the individual **author**, a similarly qualified individual may also be able to undertake some level of **validation** of interpretations. Otherwise, by reading widely around the social context in which the documents were constructed, you can consider the latent **meanings**. For example, in the case study presented in Chapter 7, I was able to discuss the general principles in case files during interviews with staff. However, it was also important to consider latent **meanings** around health and deservingness (Bambra and Smith 2010).

Readers

Whilst we may routinely consider the **author** of the document in our analysis, it is also important to consider the anticipated **reader(s)** in order to understand **meaning**. A single document may have one or more intended **reader** or groups of **readers**, including of course the **author** as a **reader**. Each of these **authors** may take away a slightly, or even vastly, different interpretation of the document's contents. This is related to their existing knowledge of the topic which the document addresses, their belief in the robustness of the **author**'s information and their entire social background, including how they were socialised and educated, as either passive recipients of information or active challengers of information.

As well as simply transmitting information, documents may also seek to change opinions in the **reader**. This is the case in advertising (as will be considered in Chapter 6) and the media (see Chapter 3). Advertising, of course, seeks to convince the **reader** that they *need* the product being sold, whilst the media is linked to politics and powerful agencies in society in a complex web. At the time of writing, 'news' stories which were inaccurate or sometimes entirely made up were regularly being read (and shared) on social media platforms by **readers**. We can imagine that the **authors** of these 'fake news' stories thought that a sufficient volume of **readers** would uncritically believe the stories, in order for their writing to be worthwhile. The purpose of these 'fake news' stories was to change political opinion. Unfortunately, it worked (Tait 2017).

To bring this concept to life, let us consider the **authorship** and **readership** of a letter sent *en masse* to many individuals at their home addresses by a charity. The letter may have multiple purposes. Although the stated purpose may appear to the **reader** to be to elicit a donation, the charity may also be hoping for an opinion change in the **reader**. Perhaps this might encourage the **reader** to sign a petition, **lobby** a politician or take some other form of political action, either at that point in time or at some point in the future. However, if two people receive the same letter, for example, about rising levels of homelessness and housing insecurity, they may interpret it differently. One **reader** may feel sympathy or empathy for the homeless, through their understanding of the structural causes of inequality in our (unequal) society. Another **reader** may feel that there is too much immigration, leading to housing insecurity, due to their regular reading of the **tabloid press** and exposure to anti-immigration politicians, who frequently propagate these views. Accordingly, the document's effect on the **reader** varies significantly depending on their prior views and experiences. **Actor Network Theory** provides a framework for helping us to understand how **authors** and readers are linked through **social construction**. If the thought of a 'theory' scares you, there is no need to worry: this one formalises the things we have already been thinking about.

Theorising the everyday use of documents: Actor Network Theory

Within **Actor Network Theory** (Latour 2005), you and I (humans) are considered 'actors', but so are all other living beings and objects that we interact with. This includes literally everything in your environment; for me that could include all of the people I work with, my family and friends, pets, furniture, computers and stationery. I could go on forever! In terms of producing a document, we would consider the physical spaces the **author** was in and the objects on which they might write a document, including mobile telephones, computers and notebooks. Together these human and non-human actors collaborate to enable the **author** to decide what and when to write. This includes the **author**'s belief about the **readers'** competence.

If we consider a primary healthcare centre (a GP surgery in the UK), human actors would include patients, patients' families, doctors and nurses. Non-human actors could include the equipment used to undertake tests, and the charts and pens used to note the results. The network is completed when these human and non-human actors each take part in an activity. For example, the nurse takes a blood pressure reading from the patient. The nurse records the results using a pen on the paper record chart or electronically in the patients' notes. In doing so, the nurse uses a standard approach to notation that would be understood by nursing and medical colleagues. At a later point, the nurse or another health professional reviews the patient by taking the test again, looking at the records and comparing the two sets of results. In this example, we come to understand that different levels of evidence have different levels of status, and that some documents are very high status. A visual representation of this relationship can be seen in Figure 2.1. This approach to medicine, where a colleague's notes can carry more weight than a patient's report of their condition, has been interpreted critically (Foucault 1963; Armstrong 1995).

Prior (2003) states that documents have the power to influence human agency because of the ways we use them in developed societies. In the example of the GP surgery, the network around the document was completed when the document was used on a second occasion to provide information. If I, a non-medically trained individual with a background in social science health research, read this chart, I may well end up with a different understanding of what the issues were, compared to the understanding of somebody with medical training. That said, I have developed knowledge because of my research in this area (Collins and Evans 2007).

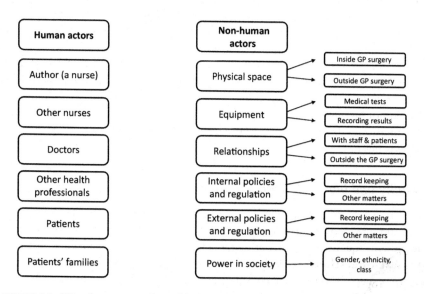

FIGURE 2.1 Visual representation of Actor Network Theory and the construction of documents within a GP surgery.

Alongside this, I may not understand some of the abbreviations and shorthand used, which may well be routine in either that profession or that organisation (see Source 1 in Chapter 7 for an example). Therefore, the **author's** belief in the competence, or lack thereof, of the intended **reader** will influence the document's content. In the next section, these theoretical concerns will be considered more broadly from the point of view of organisations, many of which keep expansive records (Lipsky 2010).

The use of documents in organisations: consideration of Actor Network Theory

Within organisations, the keeping of text-based records is common and may structure many aspects of work. This includes the use of routine forms, agendas and notes during meetings, and files for individual customers or service users (Smith and Turner 2014). Alongside this, written records may have legal standing or uses, and will normally be used by others within the organisation as well as the **author** (Coffey 2009). You may wish to consider record-keeping during a time you have visited a doctor or other health professional. During the encounter, your previous medical records are likely to have been consulted by the health professional, alongside your (oral) account of your health condition. During the consultation, the health professional may have written or typed elements of your account that they felt were pertinent to your diagnosis. If you are to be referred to another health professional, sent elsewhere for a test of some kind or given a prescription for a medicine, these will all be ordered in writing (or typing). If a follow-up appointment is necessary, the notes taken during the first appointment will probably be consulted. Organisations that deal in finances are also highly regulated, and forms must be completed to open a new bank account, complete a tax return, buy a home or register a new business. These documents have additional power and status compared to, for example, a notebook or digital document with details of your own finances, due to their legal standing. The language used, and negotiations around what should or should not be included in documents, is of particular interest to those studying organisations ethnographically (Eastwood 2014). We return to, and expand on, these issues in Chapter 7.

Quality and bias within found documents

We can assess the documents in our research for **bias** by considering authorship and intended readership. The authorship and audience might also affect the documents' quality, in terms of being able to answer our **research questions** (**research questions** are dealt with in more detail in the next section). There are two specific sources for considering issues of quality and **bias** within research on documents, from Jennifer Platt (1981a, 1981b) and John Scott (1990). Platt divides her consideration of quality into two sets of problems: those which impact documents alone (Platt 1981a), and those which are shared with other research methods (Platt 1981b). For Platt, five factors are relevant to the study of documents:

- **Authenticity**
- Availability of documents
- Sampling problems
- Whether the document contains 'the truth'
- What inferences a researcher can make (Platt 1981a)

Alongside these factors which affect research using documents, the researchers' interpretation of the data and presentation of findings should be considered as adding a second set of **biases** (Platt 1981b).

Alongside Platt's analysis, within Scott's (1990, 2006) work, four elements are included for understanding the quality of found documents. These are **authenticity, credibility, representativeness** and **meaning**, and are summarised in Table 2.1. In terms of **authenticity**, the researcher should consider whether the document is an original text, and whether it is available in full. Alongside this, **authenticity** refers to whether it is possible to identify who the **author** was, including consideration of the possible involvement of others in drafting elements of the text. Scott's second criterion, **credibility**, refers to whether the **author** reported their sincere views of events as they experienced them, or distorted the events or their views. The third criterion Scott describes relates to **population** and **sampling**; researchers should consider how **representative** the available data is of all documents in that **population**. Availability is subdivided into surviving documents and those which are made available to researchers (i.e. those which are not in closed private collections). Finally, Scott considers whether researchers are able to

TABLE 2.1 Summary of Scott's criteria to assess documentary sources (1990, pp. 19–35)

Scott's criteria	Scott's definition
Authenticity	• Original document or high-quality copy • Full text available • Clear who the author was, acknowledgement of others involved in writing (if relevant)
Credibility	• Author reports sincerely on their experience (contrast with presentation of self) • Author describes an accurate narrative
Representativeness	• Survival of a representative sample of the original population • Availability of surviving documents to researchers
Meaning	• Ability to understand the language, meaning of individual words in social context and decipher the handwriting • Ability to combine document with understanding of context to interpret likely meaning

understand **meaning** within the text. This can be considered in two ways. First, if the source was written in a foreign language or in handwriting that is difficult to decipher. Second, if the document and our knowledge of the wider circumstances allow us to interpret what the **author** meant. These factors will be utilised through this book in order to assess quality and **bias** in the sources in each of the six case studies.

It has been argued that being overly prescriptive of what quality *is* may be detrimental to research quality. This is due to the broad range of methodologies, **theories** and **epistemological** approaches used by qualitative researchers (Hammersley 2007). Accordingly, it can be argued that qualitative research is a craft and a skill, and thus researchers should aim for 'methodological awareness' at all times to enhance quality as far as they are able at that stage in their research career (Seale 1999). It is for this reason that this section focuses most strongly on the criteria found within Jennifer Platt's (1981a, 1981b) and John Scott's (1990) work, rather than presenting more specific guidelines. It is worth noting that issues relating to data quality should be identified and described in your report or article. It would be very rare for data sources to be entirely discarded due to high levels of **bias**, but the strength of your discussion and conclusions should be tailored to any identified weaknesses in your data.

Quality and bias within researcher-influenced documents

Although we often think of documents as being produced externally to the researcher, qualitative interview methodologies are increasingly asking participants to create documents, either prior to the interview or as part of it (see Mannay 2016 for an excellent account of these approaches). In research projects that use these methods, it is necessary to consider the research encounter as part of the **social construction** shaping the document the **author** produced. Therefore, these documents should not be seen as an objective insight into the participants' lives. The content of the document would be influenced by many things, including the participants' interpretations of what the researcher requested, how much a given participant felt they wanted to share with the researcher on the subject under study, and the amount of time and enthusiasm the participants had for completing the task (Rose 2001; Packard 2008; Reavey 2011; Lomax 2015; Mannay and Morgan 2015). When interpreting such data, we may wish to include our own interpretation of the documents alongside the interviewees' descriptions or even to co-author the document during the interview (Sheridan et al. 2011). These are all important elements of research design that should be carefully considered prior to data collection.

Practical tips for your research with documents

In this section, I move on to outline the key factors that are of relevance when you are designing a study that uses documents as data. In doing so, I use a broad range of sources, some of which you may find useful to read yourself. Seven key topics are described:

• Identifying a research topic and writing **research questions**
• Time and financial considerations
• Selecting a **sample** of documents
• Ethical considerations
• Data management
• Data analysis
• Dissemination

In Chapter 9, I return to these key areas and reflect on the additional learning from the six empirical chapters presented in this book (Chapters 3–8). Moreover, a checklist of key considerations in designing your research study is included in Chapter 9. If you are about to design your study, or have already begun your study, I suggest that you read this chapter alongside Chapter 9 and appraise your study against the checklist sooner rather than later.

Identifying a research topic and writing research questions

If, like me, you are interested in lots of areas of social life, it might be hard to pin down a single area to focus on. But this is the first thing you need to do, if you are ever going to get your research done. Bell and Waters (2014) suggest that if you are struggling to decide on a single research area, you should write all of the possible topics down in a list, assess if they could hold your attention over time and discuss your ideas with supervisors and peers. When you have one or two ideas, search to see if your project has already been done. This is known as 'gap spotting', and is a valuable approach for novice researchers and students who know that they will add to existing knowledge. At this stage if more than one question still looks relevant, the second most interesting question should become a backup (Bell and Waters 2014).

In designing your **research question**, it is essential to ensure that it is one that can be answered using social science methods, that is, it has high "research-ability" (White 2009, p. 59). Researchability relates to an ability to be inves-tigated through social research methods in principle, but also more practical aspects, such as the size of the project and its relation to the time and resources available. Nicola Green provides a more detailed framework and suggests that **research questions** should have six key ingredients: interesting, relevant, fea-sible, ethical, concise and answerable (Green 2008). Not all of these relate to quality in the usual sense. For example, the research should be of importance to the researcher, or they will struggle to complete it, and to the broader research community, or it holds no purpose. The question of whether the research is feasible is linked to whether the question is concise whilst also containing all necessary detail. In terms of being 'answerable', Green (2008: 50) asks, "Can the data source you are considering answer your question?" Finally, the ethical code of conduct for your professional discipline must be considered as your guiding source on ethical matters. Alongside this, you may wish to consider aspects of **theory** in your question (Alvesson and Sandberg 2013), if you are unsure, discuss this with your supervisor.

In order to finalise your **research question**, you will need to carefully consider your entire methodological approach. This can be described in terms of the "What? How? And Why?" of your project (Punch 2016), where you are able to describe:

- *What* your research is seeking to find out
- *How* it plans to do this, with reference to methods
- *Why* the research is important enough to warrant doing (Punch 2016)

The process of moving from an area of interest to a **research question** can be seen throughout the six empirical case studies later in this book. For example, in Chapter 3, we consider the way in which the media portray those involved in civil unrest (the *What*). However, the initial topic area limited this to one particular instance (the 2011 London Riots) and then further still to the analysis of particular news sources over a defined period of time (the *How*). Finally, this is justified as important research through reference to the **theory** of moral panics (the *Why*). Excellent guidance for novice researchers on how to formulate **research questions** can be found in Green (2008, pp. 50–57) and Bell and Waters (2014, pp. 29–32). More detailed guidance, aimed at graduate students and beyond, can be found in Punch (2016).

Should you find that you have several (linked) **research questions**, it is good practice to prioritise the question that is most important. That can either be because it is most interesting to you, or most relevant to funders or policy makers. Overall, Patrick White (2009) suggests that studies should have no more than four questions unless they are very large (certainly not an undergraduate or master's dissertation), in order to ensure the questions can be answered in sufficient detail. In order to keep questions answerable, they should be written clearly and concisely including all of the main details, but they should not usually be longer than one sentence.

Selecting a sample

Identifying a population to answer your research question

A **population** is every piece of data that could answer your **research question**. A **sample** is a subgroup of your population. For example, if we were interested in how women's magazines in the USA have changed their discussion of food and diets over a 50-year period, every article within a women's magazine in the USA which had discussed food or diet within the 50-year period would be our population. It is likely that we would be able to identify the names of women's magazines quite easily, but we would need to check that we were able to access every issue for the entire time period. We may find that we have too many articles to include if we consider all of the magazines, so we might choose to **purposively sample** the magazines with the highest readership, for example, to reduce the number of documents in the research and make it feasible.

Within social research methods, considerable importance is given to **sampling**, as it has a major impact on the results found, and if they should be considered as applying to the population as a whole (Schutt 2015). Within many research methods textbooks, the unit of data is a person, but it could just as easily be individual documents, such as advertisements, policy documents or **blog** posts. Two approaches to sampling exist: **probability (or random) sampling** and **non-probability sampling** (including **purposive sampling**). One key concept is that you always need to be able to access every piece of data in your population to be able to do **probability (random) sampling**. There are instances where **probability samples** (including **random samples**) are taken from within a population (see, for example, Krauss et al. 2015). This is often when quantitative outcomes are being considered in order to draw inferences about significance from the whole population. **Non-probability** sampling is usually undertaken by using the documents available when you do not have access to the whole population, and comprises a range of types. A convenience **sample** is where you use the data that are available to you. A quota **sample** is another type of **non-probability sample**, where documents are selected because they are able to meet a range of different characteristics (such as a range of diaries written by people of different ages), but they are not randomly selected. If talk of **sampling** is new to you, there are definitions and case studies of **sampling** approaches in Walliman (2015, pp. 107–119) which might be of use.

At an early stage of planning your study, you should know which **sampling** strategy you are going to use. If you are going to use a **sample** from within your **population**, it is helpful to be able to say how much difference you think there is between pieces of data (that is, how **homogeneous** or **heterogeneous** the data is). If your **sample** is a **non-probability sample** that is not a problem, but this approach will need to be justified and acknowledged as a limitation. Whenever you are making decisions about **sampling**, it is important to keep good records of the decisions made, in order to be able to report on **bias** at a later stage.

Accessing found documents

Documents are often referred to as easily accessible in the research field (Prior 2003). With the advent of the Internet, many contemporary documents are present in the public domain and ready to be downloaded for analysis. Others exist in libraries and **archives**. The National Archives website provides a list of UK and international **archives** (www.discovery.nationalarchives.gov.uk/find-an-archive), and Niamh Moore and colleagues provide a how-to guide on the specifics of doing research in **archives** (Moore et al. 2016). The subject librarians within your university will also have useful knowledge, and it is often worth consulting with them after an initial Internet search, to identify possible **archives**. Once you have found an **archive**, you are often able to search within it using key words to identify relevant articles. The use of **Boolean operators**, such as AND, OR, NOT, among search terms enables a more refined search to be undertaken. This is particularly helpful if your initial search is returning too many results (many university libraries have guides to help you use **Boolean operators** if this concept is new to you).

In contrast to **archive** research, when researching organisations, there may be different issues to overcome when accessing documents. Many organisations have no obligation to share data with researchers[2] and may have concerns about client confidentiality or their reputation. Specific problems that researchers have reported include: delays in accessing documents from courts (Barlow 2016), lack of access to documents which should have already been in the public domain (Hughes and Griffiths 1999) and the need to be present on site to analyse documents (Scourfield et al. 2012). Prior to designing your research project, it would be sensible to consider these access challenges, ideally through discussion with somebody with experience of accessing similar data to the type you wish to use. This will allow you to consider if your planned project appears feasible within the time and financial budgets assigned to the study, which are described in more detail next.

Time and financial considerations

When considering the size of your project and how much time your research is going to take, the use of a **Gantt chart** or project timetable is advisable. If you are relatively new to research, assume that each activity will take longer than you anticipate and leave some spare time at the end of your timetable (a minimum of 5–10% is recommended, depending on how much time you have). Figure 2.2 shows an example of a **Gantt chart** which contains part of my current Wellcome Trust Fellowship project, with major headings for each part of the project, and a more detailed list of tasks and a timetable below these. In terms of data collection, if your data is available from an online **archive**, it shouldn't take too long for you to be able to access your data set, but it may still take time if each individual file needs to be downloaded, particularly if the **archive**'s website is slow. If you need to physically go to an **archive** or organisation to collect your data, or even to undertake all analysis of the data at the research site (Scourfield et al. 2012), this will take additional time. You should be aware of how much time data collection will ideally take prior to completing your protocol.

Alongside considering how much of your time is available, it is important to consider if any other resources are available to you, how much of them you have and when. For example, support from a supervisor, **archivist** or librarian, or somebody who can help support you use a new analysis technique can be invaluable. However, it is very important to know things like if your supervisor is on research leave for a month near your deadline! This can help you to plan your project timetable. You and your supervisor can then use the timetable to assess how well the project is progressing and if it will be necessary to reconsider the size of the **sample** in order to complete the project in time.

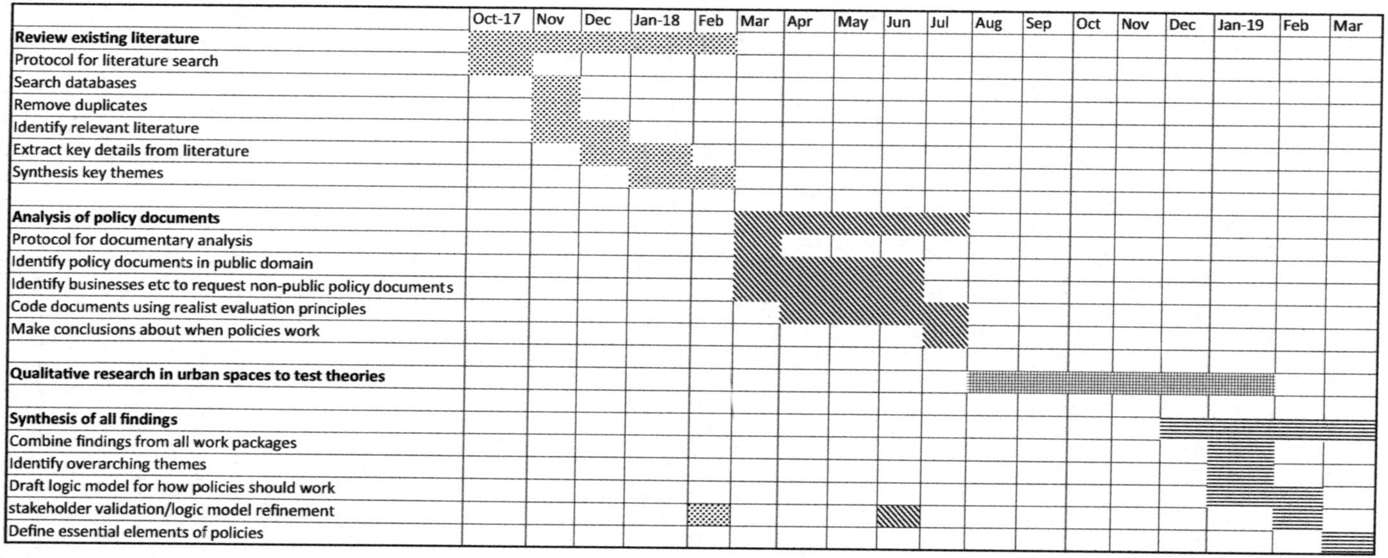

	Oct-17	Nov	Dec	Jan-18	Feb	Mar	Apr	May	Jun	Jul	Aug	Sep	Oct	Nov	Dec	Jan-19	Feb	Mar
Review existing literature																		
Protocol for literature search																		
Search databases																		
Remove duplicates																		
Identify relevant literature																		
Extract key details from literature																		
Synthesis key themes																		
Analysis of policy documents																		
Protocol for documentary analysis																		
Identify policy documents in public domain																		
Identify businesses etc to request non-public policy documents																		
Code documents using realist evaluation principles																		
Make conclusions about when policies work																		
Qualitative research in urban spaces to test theories																		
Synthesis of all findings																		
Combine findings from all work packages																		
Identify overarching themes																		
Draft logic model for how policies should work																		
stakeholder validation/logic model refinement																		
Define essential elements of policies																		

FIGURE 2.2 Extract from a Gantt chart showing research tasks and deadlines.

If you are applying for funding to run your study, there are a number of potential sources that may be of relevance to you. Research Professional is a portal that provides details of funding available from a wide range of sources; your university may have an institutional membership. Your supervisor or manager may also know of sources of internal funding available at your university. In many universities, research officers are available to help you adequately cost your research project. If you are undertaking unfunded research, such as a dissertation, it is even more important to consider potential costs at the outset in order to shape the **research questions** in a way that you can afford to carry out.

In the case of research, costs of using found documents as data include accessing documents from physical **archives** and costs for retrieval. By contrast, in researcher-generated encounters, costs may include incentives for participants and transcription of associated interviews (or time to transcribe the audio yourself). Alongside this, costs for travel and subsistence when undertaking data collection (if required) should be considered (White 2009). In terms of analysis, you may wish to consider budgeting for photocopying in order to annotate documents or the use of a **CAQDAS** programme such as **NVivo** or **ATLAS.ti** to facilitate computer-based analysis (Bryman 2012), although you may be able to access **CAQDAS** programmes for free or a reduced rate through your university.

In Table 2.2, I show the non-staff project expenses for a research project using participant-created documents, followed by **elicitation interviews**, which is the case study presented in Chapter 8. You can see that quite quickly the costs start to add up. This project could have been made cheaper if required by removing the transcription (with the research team undertaking this themselves) and the two dissemination activities. If the project was an unfunded student project, it might have felt acceptable to remove the incentives for participants. However, if the researchers are being paid to undertake the project and the research is accessing a marginalised population, it is generally accepted as good practice to include incentives in order to reduce the power imbalance between the (paid) researcher and the participant.

Ethical concerns

In general, ethical principles relate to not causing harm, either to participants or to the reputation of research. When undertaking your own research study, you will need to follow your university's or organisation's ethical approval procedure. In some instances, the use of found documents as data means that ethical approval is not required. That is not, however, to mean that there is no potential for participants to be upset or harmed (Vayena et al. 2012; Trevisan and Reilly 2014), or even for there to be no potential negative outcomes to researchers (Grant 2018). Often it is considered acceptable to use data that is available in the public domain for research purposes, but this covert research is not always viewed as appropriate (McKee and Porter 2009), particularly if individuals are not fully **anonymised** (Hlavach and Freivogel 2011). In some instances, it may be impossible to fully

TABLE 2.2 Example of a research budget

Item	Calculations	Costs
Travel to interviews	45p per mile (Cardiff University rate). 30 journeys. Assume an average of 20 mile round journey ($£0.45 × 30 × 20$)	$£540$
Materials for visual data production packs to send to participants	Pens, coloured paper, emotion stickers, scissors, glue, photocopying, additional sandboxing figures	$£150$
Incentives	$£25$ per participant. 30 interviews ($£25 × 30$)	$£750$
Transcription ($£100$ per recorded hour × 30 interviews × 1.5 hours)	$£100$ per recorded hour. 30 interviews. Assume an average of 1.5 hours per interview. ($£100 × 45$)	$£4,500$
Dissemination: conference attendance for two at the British Sociological Association	Conference fee $£400$, hotel for two nights $£120$, travel $£80$ (2 × (400+120+80))	$£1,200$
Dissemination event at Cardiff University	Room hire – in kind Catering $£20$ per guest, 80 guests ($£1,600$) Photocopying and stationary, $£80$	$£1,680$
TOTAL		**$£8,820$**

anonymise data, due to investigating a phenomenon that includes both public documents (such as newspaper reports) and private documents which cover the same event (Williams 2014). Likewise, a blanket policy of **anonymisation** may also be inappropriate (Moore 2012). Due to the breadth of disciplines this volume is designed to appeal to, it is not possible to include a comprehensive guide on all ethical matters, but Hannah Farrimond covers a range of 'hot topics' and ethical dilemmas in an accessible way in her book (Farrimond 2013). I also advise consulting the ethical guidelines of your professional body (or the body which represents the discipline you are studying) and the academic faculty in which you are based, prior to commencing your research. Doing so will ensure you have reflected on what best practice would be in your study.

Alongside this, where we (as researchers) ask participants to create a document, we need to ensure that they are clear how this will be used. Will we ask them to give us the document afterwards, and can they say no? Will we use their words **verbatim** in reports and other dissemination activities? What about using their handwriting in outputs from the study? Overall, I would suggest that if you are asking participants to create documents for your study, you give them as much choice as possible on the consent form, so they can draw the line where they are comfortable. An example of the wording that you might consider including on your consent form (for the participant to review) is shown in Box 2.1; it is usual practice in health research to ask participants to sign their initials next to each statement they agree to. Where ethical issues are particular to the data source or analysis technique throughout the case studies in Chapters 3–8, relevant resources will be highlighted.

BOX 2.1 EXAMPLE OF CONSENT FORM CONTENT FOR A STUDY ASKING PARTICIPANTS TO KEEP A DIARY AND THEN DISCUSS THIS DURING AN INTERVIEW

These statements are mandatory to take part in the research

- I have read the participant information sheet (version number.....; date.......) and had the opportunity to have my questions answered
- I would like to take part in the research
- I know that I can withdraw my consent and stop taking part in the research at any time, without any negative consequences

These statements are optional to take part in the research, please only initial those that you feel comfortable with

The interview

- I agree that you can audio record the interview
- I agree that you can use my exact words in written <u>reports</u> and scientific meetings (as long as these do not identify me or my family)
- I agree that you can use my exact words in <u>teaching</u> (as long as these do not identify me or my family)

Your diary

- I agree that you can keep a copy of my diary
- I agree that you can use my exact words in <u>reports</u> (as long as these do not identify me or my family)
- I agree that you can use my exact words in <u>teaching</u> (as long as these do not identify me or my family)
- I agree that you can use copies of my handwritten words and images in <u>reports</u> (all names of people and places will be removed)
- I agree that you can use copies of my handwritten words and images in <u>teaching</u> (all names of people and places will be removed)

Good data management

How not to lose all of your data (and the will to live)

The most important thing to remember is to ALWAYS BACK UP EVERYTHING. It is so important that I'll say it again:

ALWAYS BACK UP EVERYTHING!

In terms of documents that form your data, this means you should have an original version of the document that does not contain any of your analytical thinking and <u>at least one</u> backup of this original version. A variety of ways exist to do this. Your university or organisation is likely to have a code of conduct for the storage of data that contain personal details about participants. As such, if you are using organisational documents or documents created by individuals, you will need to ensure that you are compliant with your university or organisation's code and any legislation in your country (for instance, in the European Union the General Data Protection Regulation is of importance).

I suggest that upon receiving any hard (paper) documents or portable electronic versions (such as a USB stick), you make an electronic copy as soon as possible, and you are very careful about how you transport and store those documents in the brief period before you are able to return them to your office space. I name each document (see **Document Identification Numbers, DINs** below) and save an electronic copy in a folder that only contains my data for that project. I would save this to my university's networked space, which is backed up each day, and also make a further electronic copy. Depending on the sensitivity of the data (and the ethical approval I have been granted), I take a variety of approaches. For example, in my work using newspaper articles as data, I use a well-known commercial online file storage site, as this enables myself and my co-researchers from other universities to easily share access to online space. For each piece of paper-based data that contained personal details, I would make an **anonymised** copy of the data, by photocopying the original and then colouring in the details that are personal with a black marker pen, and then re-photocopying. When none of the personal details can be seen, I would scan these in to create **anonymised** digital copies, shredding the copy that I have used marker pen on. I then store the original hard copies in a (lockable) cupboard in my office on the university's property, in line with the ethical approval I have been granted (which often says that original documents should be retained for a year or three or even sometimes seven years). Within your ethical approval letter or your department's guidelines, you will find details of how long your original data should be kept following the end of the project, and if it is necessary to maintain hard copies of documents. Should you not require (or have permission to keep) the hard copies, these must be securely destroyed. If hard copies must be maintained and you run out of physical space in your office, your university or organisation will have an archiving policy, although it may require students and staff to pay archiving fees. These should be built into project budgets where applicable.

Document Identification Numbers

In order to create a robust database of documents, you need good file naming conventions. I create a database of documents, with each document having a unique **DIN** and a row on the spreadsheet. For example, if I received ten companies' health and safety policies, I would create a table which would include the organisations' names, pseudonyms or the number I have assigned them, how many documents they provided me with and the number of pages (see Table 2.3). This then means that in my analytical notes, I am easily able to refer to individual documents (and within larger documents the page number) in order to easily find the original data again. I may also create a table for each individual document, noting what is included on each page, if a very detailed approach to analysis is required and I am not using a **CAQDAS** package to facilitate analysis and retrieval.

Version control

In addition to good data management of your documents, using version control for your analysis and writing can help to avoid unnecessary duplication. This is important if one file becomes corrupt, or you delete some content that you later decide was needed. I use a system which was in place when I worked for the NHS. To make a new file, I create a name for my document, so for this document, I called it Chapter 2, and I then save it with a version number, starting at 0a, the file name ends with the date. Each day that you work on the document, you save it with a new version number and date. When I wrote this paragraph, I was working on Chapter 2 v0f 24.07.17, showing that I had five earlier versions of this chapter. When I have a final version, it is called v1 and continues to have the date as part of the file name. So several months later, after going through peer review, this chapter became Chapter 2 v1 15.10.17. You don't need to use my system, but I suggest that you use a system that involves a new name every time you work on some writing.

TABLE 2.3 Example of a sample database, including DINs

DIN	Organisation	Title	Number of pages	Notes
1	School 1	Health and safety at work policy	12	Very little detail
2	School 1	Health and safety report 2014–15	72	Detailed description of incidents and responses
3	Hospitality 1	Healthy lifestyles at work policy	4	Emphasis on individual health behaviours

If you are using **CAQDAS**, that is a computer programme to facilitate your analysis, it is important to use version control and back up these files too. Both **ATLAS.ti** and **NVivo** files can become corrupted, and I have had some worrying experiences when I had not made a recent backup at the point that a file corrupted with both programmes. Hopefully you will not need to repeat my mistakes to learn from them, as I can tell you that I was really stressed on both occasions! Within **ATLAS.ti**, you can 'save as' to make a new version of your analysis file, and I recommend you do this each time you work on your analysis. Alongside this, you can make a 'copy bundle' of all documents and your analysis. This means if your main file becomes corrupt, you can 'unpack' your copy bundle and have a working version of your files again within minutes. When working with **NVivo**, you should also make copies. There is not a way within **NVivo** to 'save as' a new name. The easiest way I have found is to copy and paste within 'file explorer' (when using Windows) and rename the second version. Further guidance can be found in the Help sections of both programmes.

Analysis techniques

It is important that, in advance of analysing your data, you have decided which analysis technique you will be using, and what steps this involves. By making this decision in advance, your research will have scientific **rigour** above studies that do not. This may seem like an obvious statement to make, but there are instances of published research papers reporting using a method that they did not use, or not reporting the analysis techniques they have used at all (Braun and Clarke 2006). In each of the empirical chapters, a unique analysis strategy is showcased, including **Critical Discourse Analysis (CDA)** (Chapter 4), **narrative analysis** (Chapter 8) and **content analysis** (Chapter 6). By understanding the processes followed in the six analysis techniques, I hope that deciding on your analysis strategy will be easier. That said, it is not possible to provide details on all analysis techniques within this book, and you may wish to consult more detailed guidance on qualitative data analysis (see, for example, Flick 2014).

Whichever analysis technique you choose to use in your project, you should consider whether to analyse the data by hand (such as using a highlighter on printed copies) or using a computer in some way. It is possible to use computer programmes that were not specifically designed to facilitate analysis, such as Microsoft Word or Excel, or a specific computer programme designed to facilitate qualitative analysis, known as **CAQDAS**, such as **NVivo** or **ATLAS.ti**. In practice, you may find that you use more than one strategy, for example downloading lists of data extracts that have been given a particular code and analysing them in a more detailed way on paper (or screen). There is no right or wrong answer; whether you code using a computer or printed copies, it is you, the researcher, making decisions regarding whether a data extract fits within one or more codes. These can be codes that you have already created (**deductive** coding) or creating a new code to use on this section of data (**inductive** coding). It is beyond the scope of this book to describe in detail how hand coding and computer-assisted coding work in a real-life example, but snippets will be provided along the way through the worked examples. For more details on how to use **ATLAS.ti**, see Suzanne Friese's (2014) guide, and for **NVivo,** see Bazeley and Jackson (2013). I have also found YouTube videos to be very helpful to learn new functions within **CAQDAS** programmes.

Disseminating your findings

Reporting qualitative research with numbers

Throughout the case studies, you will see that sometimes findings are reported only in terms of themes, but at other times, numbers are used in reporting. The most obvious example of this is in Chapter 5, where there were literally thousands of pieces of data. I have encountered journals where there is a preference for quantification within qualitative research. Quantification can sometimes help **readers** to understand how common a phenomenon is. Overall I would suggest that consideration of how to present findings is reliant upon consideration of (i) the **research question**, (ii) the data source (quantity, type, etc.) and (iii) the analysis method. It is important to think about these things from the outset. When designing your project, before analysis begins, you should have an idea of how you expect to present your results. Will you provide a lengthy description, which contains data extracts and your analytical thoughts that fit alongside them? Will you provide numbers and percentages? Or will you fit somewhere in the middle? Knowing the expected output medium will help you to decide how much to focus on individual pieces of data or extracts of interest as you are analysing the data.

Maximising impact

One of the major UK funders of social science research is the Economic and Social Research Council (ESRC), part of the publicly funded Research Councils UK (RCUK). Increasingly, they focus on how research can impact on other academics and society when deciding whether to allocate funds. They define impact as

> **the demonstrable contribution that excellent research makes to society and the economy**. This occurs in many ways – through creating and sharing new knowledge and innovation; inventing ground breaking new products, companies and jobs; developing new and improving existing public services and policy; enhancing quality of life and health; and many more.
>
> *(Research Councils UK 2017, emphasis original)*

In order to achieve real-life impact, the RCUK have guidance on developing 'Pathways to Impact'. Their central suggestion is that you should largely plan your impact activities in advance of undertaking your study. As such, at the planning stage, you should consider whom you will need to involve to achieve the wider societal aims of your research project and discuss your research with them at the earliest opportunity. Examples of good practice are provided in terms of the researchers' interaction with policy, business, the voluntary sector (third sector, charities) and public engagement.

Discussion with stakeholders can help to shape your research design by identifying possible weaknesses, as well as guidance in relation to data collection, analysis, disseminating the findings and helping to change practice. In order to keep up to date on best practice in relation to impact, I suggest you consult the RCUK website or the website of the primary funder in your country to consider (i) what good practice looks like, and (ii) how people have been able to achieve this. Once you have done so, you should be in a strong position to discern how you can best achieve impact from your research, within the confines of your study's budget, both in terms of time and money.

Conclusion

This chapter has provided an overview of what documents are and has outlined ways in which studies with documents should be designed, signposting to more detailed resources where relevant. Alongside guidance for high-quality research design, suggestions have been provided in terms of backing up and storing data, writing and analysis materials, to reduce duplicated effort in your research. When planning your research project, this chapter should be read in conjunction with Chapter 9, which includes a checklist for good research design practices. The book now moves on to Section I, which critically describes three case studies that focused on research with documents found in isolation from their **authors**. Chapter 3 considers content from the print media in relation to public disorder, Chapter 4 uses official and historical documents to understand the state's treatment of those in poverty, and Chapter 5 focuses on individually created documents that are transmitted via social media. Section II of the book presents three further case studies, focused on documents that are used alongside another form of data.

Notes

1 In an episode of the sitcom *Friends*, one of the characters is reading Stephen King's *The Shining* and finds it frightening, so puts it in the freezer.
2 However, some public sector organisations may be required to share some data on request. In the UK, this is known as a Freedom of Information (FOI) request.

References

Alvesson, M. and Sandberg, J. 2013. *Constructing research questions: doing interesting research.* London: Sage.

Armstrong, D. 1995. The rise of surveillance medicine. *Sociology of Health and Illness:* 17(3), pp. 393–404.

Bambra, C. and Smith, K. 2010. No longer deserving? Sickness benefit reform and the politics of (ill) health. *Critical Public Health*: 20(1), pp. 71–83.

Barlow, C. 2016. Documents as 'risky' sources of data: a reflection on social and emotional positioning – a research note. *International Journal of Social Research Methodology*: 19(3), pp. 377–384.

Bazeley, P. and Jackson, K. 2013. *Qualitative data analysis with NVivo*. London: Sage.

Bell, J. and Waters, S. 2014. *Doing your research project: a guide for first-time researchers*. New York: Open University Press.

Braun, V. and Clarke, V. 2006. Using thematic analysis in psychology. *Qualitative Research in Psychology*: 3(2), pp. 77–101.

Bryman, A. 2012. *Social research methods*. Oxford: Oxford University Press.

Coffey, A. 2009. Analysing documents. In: Flick, U. ed. *The SAGE handbook of qualitative data analysis*. London: Sage, pp. 367–379.

Collins, H. and Evans, R. 2007. *Rethinking expertise*. Chicago, IL: University of Chicago Press.

Eastwood, L. 2014. Negotiating UN policy: activating texts in policy deliberations. In: Smith, D. and Turner, S. M. eds. *Incorporating texts into institutional ethnographies*. Toronto, ON: University of Toronto Press, pp. 64–92.

Farrimond, H. 2013. *Doing ethical research*. London: Palgrave Macmillan.

Foucault, M. 1963. *The birth of the clinic*. London: Routledge.

Friese, S. 2014. *Qualitative data analysis with ATLAS.ti*. London: Blackwell.

Grant, A. 2018. Shock and offence online: the role of emotion in participant absent research. In: Loughran, T. and Mannay, D. eds. *Emotion and the researcher: sites, subjectivities and relationships*. Bingley: Emerald

Green, N. 2008. Formulating and refining a research question. In: Gilbert, N. ed. *Researching social life*. 3rd ed. London: Sage, pp. 43–62.

Hammersley, M. 2007. The issue of quality in qualitative research. *International Journal of Research & Method in Education*: 30(3), pp. 287–305.

Hlavach, L. and Freivogel, W.H. 2011. Ethical implications of anonymous comments posted to online news stories. *Journal of Mass Media Ethics*: 26(1), pp. 21–37.

Hughes, D. and Griffiths, L. 1999. Access to public documents in a study of the NHS internal market: openness vs secrecy in contracting for clinical services. *International Journal of Social Research Methodology*: 2(1), pp. 1–16.

Krauss, M.J. et al. 2015. Hookah-related twitter chatter: a content analysis. *Preventing Chronic Disease*: 12, p. E121.

Latour, B. 2005. *Reassembling the social: an introduction to Actor-Network-Theory*. Oxford: Oxford University Press.

Lipsky, M. 2010. *Street-level bureaucracy: dilemmas of the individual in public services*. New York: Russell Sage Foundation.

Lomax, H. 2015. Seen and heard? Ethics and agency in participatory visual research with children, young people and families. *Families, Relationships and Societies*: 4(3), pp. 493–502.

Mannay, D. 2016. *Visual, narrative and creative research methods: application, reflection and ethics*. Abingdon: Routledge.

Mannay, D. and Morgan, D. 2015. Employing visual methods in exploring family, community and personal relationships. *Families, Relationships and Societies*: 4(3), pp. 481–482.

McKee, H.A. and Porter, J.E. 2009. Playing a good game: ethical issues in researching MMOGs and virtual worlds. *International Journal of Internet Research Ethics*: 2(1), pp. 5–37.

Moore, N. 2012. The politics and ethics of naming: questioning anonymisation in (archival) research. *International Journal of Social Research Methodology*: 15(4), pp. 331–340.

Moore, N. et al. 2016. *The archive project: archival research in the social sciences*. Abingdon: Routledge.

Packard, J. 2008. 'I'm gonna show you what it's really like out here': the power and limitation of participatory visual methods. *Visual Studies*: 23(1), pp. 63–77.

Platt, J. 1981a. Evidence and proof in documentary research: 1 some specific problems of documentary research. *The Sociological Review*: 29(1), pp. 31–52.

Platt, J. 1981b. Evidence and proof in documentary research: 2 some shared problems of documentary research. *The Sociological Review*: 29(1), pp. 53–66.

Prior, L. 2003. *Using documents in social research*. London: Sage.

Punch, K.F. 2016. *Developing effective research proposals*. London: Sage.

Reavey, P. 2011. *Visual methods in psychology: using and interpreting images in qualitative research*. London: Routledge.

Research Councils UK 2017. Excellence with impact. Available at: http://www.rcuk.ac.uk/innovation/impact/ [Accessed: 8 August 2017].

Rose, G. 2001. *Visual methodologies: an introduction to researching with visual materials*. Sage.

Schutt, R.K. 2015. *Investigating the social world: the process and practice of research*. London: Sage.

Scott, J. 1990. *A matter of record: documentary sources in social research*. London: John Wiley & Sons.

Scott, J. 2006. Assessing documentary sources. In: *Documentary research*. London: Sage, pp. 23–42.

Scourfield, J. et al. 2012. Sociological autopsy: an integrated approach to the study of suicide in men. *Social Science & Medicine*: 74(4), pp. 466–473.

Seale, C. 1999. Quality in qualitative research. *Qualitative Inquiry*: 5(4), pp. 465–478.

Sheridan, J. et al. 2011. Timelining: visualizing experience. *Qualitative Research*: 11(5), pp. 552–569.

Smith, D.E. and Turner, S.M. 2014. *Incorporating texts into institutional ethnographies*. Toronto, ON: University of Toronto Press.

Tait, A. 2017. Fish food and fascism: what two viral stories in one morning tell us about fake news. Available at: https://www.newstatesman.com/science-tech/social-media/2017/11/fish-food-and-fascism-what-two-viral-stories-one-morning-tell-us [Accessed: 2 December 2017].

Thomas, W. 1966. *On social organization and social personality: selected papers*. Chicago, IL: University of Chicago Press.

Trevisan, F. and Reilly, P. 2014. Ethical dilemmas in researching sensitive issues online: lessons from the study of British disability dissent networks. *Information Communication & Society*: 17(9), pp. 1131–1146.

Vayena, E. et al. 2012. Ethical issues in health research with novel online sources. *American Journal of Public Health*: 102(12), pp. 2225–2230.

Walliman, N. 2015. *Social research methods: the essentials*. London: Sage.

White, P. 2009. *Developing research questions: a guide for social scientists*. London: Palgrave Macmillan.

Williams, R. 2014. *An investigation into the Defeat Depression campaign*. Cardiff: Cardiff University.

SECTION I

Documents found in isolation from their authors

3

TRADITIONAL MEDIA

Investigating the construction of societal norms

Summary

This chapter focuses on news media coverage of social issues. The media's ability to change public perceptions of the size and seriousness of issues, known as a 'moral panic', is also considered. Two examples are given of times when the media has played a significant role in altering UK public opinion: first, through the Hillsborough disaster, where the media reported lies in line with a police cover-up of a major incident in which 96 people died at a football ground; and second, through the case of Stephen Lawrence, a young Black man who was murdered in a racially motivated attack, where the media campaigned for social change. The main body of the chapter is a detailed case study of how the UK **tabloid press** described participants and victims of the London Riots of 2011. The data sources are the three most read UK newspapers at the time of the incident. Guidance is provided in relation to study setup including **research questions**, sampling and data management. A **thematic analysis** approach was used, and this is described in detail. The findings showed that the media perpetuated a view that rioters were dangerous 'thugs' rather than protesters. Particular challenges of using news media as data are outlined, including the political slant of sources, uncovering hidden **meanings**, ethical concerns and copyright issues. Additional data is provided at the end of the chapter to enable you to practise **thematic analysis**.

Key learning points

- How the media shape our opinion of society, and thus have considerable power
- What a 'moral panic' is, and how one is created
- How to design a research project using news articles
- How to undertake **thematic analysis**

Background: news media, society and research

The print media

Having arisen during periods of industrial growth, the printed **press** can be defined as "a repository of material and imagined relationships" (Nerone and Barnhurst 2003, p. 435). The **press** can be owned privately or by the state, and includes **broadsheet newspapers** and the **tabloid press**. In general, **broadsheets** contain a higher quality of reporting than **tabloids**. In contemporary society, news should be considered international, particularly as the ownership of the **press** may not be held nationally (for example, News Corporation is an international conglomerate of shareholders who run newspapers in many developed countries). Until recently, the public were dependent on news sources for information that they could not gather in other ways (Ball-Rokeach and DeFleur 1976). This has changed with the advent of an interactional Internet, which allows users to create and share content (Wall 2015), and access a wide range of news content online. Overall, the media still wields considerable influence in shaping agendas, including in relation to politics, as we will explore in greater detail below.

News as a data source, quality and bias

One critical point to understand about the media is that it is not producing a neutral reporting of events. Each organisation is a business which will carefully consider whether to cover an incident, and if it is to be covered, what 'spin' (that is, the angle or tone) to convey (Branston and Stafford 2010). In constructing the stories that they choose to tell, and the headlines that represent them, newspapers serve powerful interests, including governments and wealthy corporations or individuals (Jemphrey and Berrington 2000). This behaviour distorts power relations in society. First, the media benefit because people want to know more about the issue so purchase more newspapers (Markovits and Silverstein 1988). Second, politicians may also benefit from a change in public opinion, which can allow a previously unpopular policy to be introduced (Bonn 2010). Alongside matters of editorial style and judgement, Macdonald (2008) states that researchers should consider that newspapers might contain errors, including errors of fact (such as distortion of events), arising for a number of reasons, including **bias** from a source. Errors may be corrected in later issues, but the retraction notices are usually small and placed away from the front pages.

When **journalists** and **editors** come together to 'author' news articles, a range of factors influence the content they create. Accordingly, if we assess news media using Scott's (1990) criteria (see Table 2.1), there are several areas of concern. **Authenticity** may be challenged because it is not possible to understand which **editors** have been involved in shaping the content beyond the stated 'author'. Alongside this, **credibility** is likely to be severely challenged, as **journalists** are not often expected to write sincerely about their experiences and do not have to accurately describe events. The fact that many people are involved in setting the political agenda of newspapers means that it is necessary to consider newspaper ownership and the agendas of senior **editors** in order to understand more than surface **meanings**. This makes undertaking research with news media very different to documents that have been written by individuals. Alongside the text contained in articles, visual images have considerable power and may be used to 'tell' a story that could not be said in words; for example, (negative) racial stereotypes can be typified through images in a way that it is no longer acceptable to say in words (Hall 1997). As such, the viewing of images alongside text is crucial to fully understand intended **meanings**. Considering Scott's (1990) final criteria, we are usually able to obtain a high degree of **representativeness** due to online **archives** of news media sources.

The media creation of moral panics

What a 'good' citizen is considered varies across time and geographical areas and is situated within shifting gender, political and social class frameworks (Hacking 1986). As such, behaviour that was seen as good or acceptable in one period of time or country can be unacceptable in another. For example, rape within marriage was legal in the UK prior to 1991; these days, it is no longer legal, but victim blaming continues in court. The media has a strong role in shaping societal views within this context. One way in which the media can exert subtle power in this area is through the use of language, which may be used to highlight problems, or to perpetuate or extend myths about a particular group, who are viewed in terms of their difference and "otherness" (Hall 1997, p. 225). A less subtle way the media can shape public opinion is through the demonisation of particular social groups, by exaggerating certain problematic issues while minimising or ignoring issues of similar importance (Marsh and Melville 2011). This behaviour makes **readers** believe that the issue is of much larger importance than it really is, and is known as creating a "moral panic" (Cohen 2002, p. 1).

News media, prejudice and misreporting

There are many examples of times where the media has been involved in creating 'moral panics' and perpetuating negative views towards a group of people.

Anti-welfare and anti-immigration sentiment has been common in Western countries over the past two decades, with negative language such as the terms "underclass" and "chav" (Hayward and Yar 2006, p. 9) propagated by the media to describe a disadvantaged 'other'. Within the UK and the USA, negative attention was directed towards single mothers during the 1990s and to the long-term sick and disabled in the following decade, again highlighting negative views directed towards the poor (Bullock et al. 2001). This evolving rhetoric was strongly tied to political sentiment at the time. Likewise, the media underreport certain types of crime. In her analysis of missing and murdered Aboriginal[1] and white women in Canada, Kristen Gilchrist notes that white victims received more than three times the coverage and many more front cover stories than their Indigenous counterparts (Gilchrist 2010).

However, the media may be more explicitly involved in shaping stories through active misreporting of events. One such example is the reporting of the Hillsborough tragedy. On 15 April 1989, 96 people died and hundreds more were injured following a major incident at the Hillsborough football stadium during the Football Association (FA) Cup Semi-Final between Liverpool and Nottingham Forest. Initially the police and media reports blamed fans, who were described as drunk and violent (Scraton 1999). Many years later, following considerable campaigning by the public, the official inquiry into the disaster acknowledged a wide range of police incompetence. In particular, it was noted that the police allowed too many supporters into some areas of the stadium, resulting in mass overcrowding and a crush incident (Hillsborough Independent Panel 2017). Alongside this, the emergency services' response to the crushing incident was inadequate and ineffective.

Media reporting of disasters and major incidents tends to follow set patterns, with a focus on the number of victims, the likely cause and the apportioning of blame (Jemphrey and Berrington 2000). In the aftermath of a major incident, the media are able to play a major role in creating the story through the dissemination of official or contested accounts (Miller 2004). In the case of Hillsborough, the media accepted and extended the police's reported view of the incident, placing the blame for the incident on the supporters. For example, Scraton (2004) provides an excellent overview of the media attention at the time, noting that two days later, the *Sheffield Star* ran a headline suggesting that Liverpool fans had been drunk, were stealing from the bodies of the dead and had urinated on police officers who were trying to resuscitate the dying. Following on from this local coverage, The Sun newspaper, a UK national **tabloid**, published an article with the headline "THE TRUTH" (19 April 1989) which perpetuated the lies already in circulation, resulting in a boycotting of the newspaper in the Merseyside area that has lasting effects today. Such reporting also occurred in **broadsheets** (Jemphrey and Berrington 2000).

Accordingly, the victims, stereotyped as thugs and thieves, were presented as receiving the sort of treatment that they deserved. Such reporting should be seen in the context of pre-existing negative stereotyping by the media directed towards the people of Liverpool prior to this incident, and within the context of "football hooliganism" as a moral panic at that time (Jemphrey and Berrington 2000). This coverage perpetuated negative views of Liverpudlians (as the people of Liverpool are known) for many years (Jemphrey and Berrington 2000). The use of negative stereotyping and spreading of false information is not always the case in news reporting. On occasion, a 'good victim' identity is created and perpetuated by the media regardless of previous stereotyping, as we will see below in the case of Stephen Lawrence.

News media as a (potential) agent of change

Occasionally the media may appear to act against the state in order to attempt to facilitate social change. One instance of this was as part of the response to the failed conviction for the racist murder of Stephen Lawrence, a Black teenager, in 1993. The case involved a wide variety of legal processes, including a failed conviction under normal processes, a private prosecution, a coroner's public inquest and a public inquiry led by Sir William Macpherson (Home Office 1999). The report of the inquiry found that the police's account of the crime "had stopped making sense" (McLaughlin and Murji 1999, p. 374) and produced a "devastating indict-ment" on the Metropolitan Police Force (McLaughlin and Murji 1999, p. 371).

Alongside the legal processes, considerable attention was given to the case in the national media, although little attention was focused on the crime for the first four years (Cottle 2005). This highlights the importance of the failed prosecution and later the public inquiry report, the Macpherson report, in making the case newsworthy (New Statesman 2013). The case of Stephen Lawrence was unusual in that victims of crime portrayed by the media are often younger (Stephen was 18 years old), female and almost exclusively white (Gilchrist 2010). In fact many racially motivated murders, including those at the hands of the state, in the years before and since the case have gone largely unreported (Edwards and Harris 2016). Following the five white suspects' refusal to answer questions at the in-quest in 1997, the Daily Mail ran a front-page story (14.2.1997) described as "the most impactful of my lifetime" (p1) and "brilliant...the best example of aggres-sive **tabloid** journalism to pursue the public interest that I can remember" (p3) (New Statesman 2013). Personally, I can still recall seeing this headline when it was published and thinking it was incredibly brave of the Daily Mail; I was only 15 years old at the time. The Daily Mail accused five suspects, previously found not guilty of murder, with the headline: "MURDERERS: The Mail accuses these men of killing. If we are wrong, let them sue us". It can be argued that this article helped to prompt the public inquiry, although this view is contested (McLaughlin and Murji 1999).

For Cottle (2005, p. 50), the emotive way that the media reported the Stephen Lawrence case was designed to create a feeling of "mounting crisis" within the UK police and legal system. This was in stark contrast to the majority of reporting of ethnicity and crime in the media at the time, which characterised those who were not white, and particularly young Black men, as a dangerous 'other' (Barak 1994). In the lead up to the publication of the Macpherson report, analysis of content from two UK newspapers, including the Daily Mail, found that published articles perpetuated a continuation of the racist status quo. This included anti-immigrant sentiment, suggesting that racism was associated with a minority group of young, working-class white men (not the average citizen) and undermining attempts to bring around widespread change (McLaughlin and Murji 1999).

The continuing importance of the media in the digital age

Analysis of news media content may be considered less important these days, because we are able to consume, create and share 'news' whenever we desire through social media. However, the perceived neutrality of the printed **press**, including **tabloids**, by many **readers** is still important in creating and sustaining moral panics. Furthermore, alongside analysis of mainstream media content, we can consider alternative arenas in which news media contribute towards views of current events. This includes the number of shares of news stories on social media and the interactive comment sections attached to many online news sites. I undertook research on **readers**' comments in relation to breastfeeding in public, which has protected status in law in the UK as part of the Equality Act 2010. At the time of writing, this law was regularly breached, and the media continued to report on this occasionally. In my research into an example of a woman being asked to leave a shop because she was breastfeeding, I analysed comments from the Mail Online (the online version of the Daily Mail). The majority of the 884 comments made by members of the public used negative language to describe women who breastfed in public, suggesting that these mothers were bad parents, lazy and unattractive. Women who breastfed their babies in public were also sometimes labelled as sexual predators, who were exposing their bodies for their own sexual gratification (Grant 2016). Alongside this, I examined public opinion relating to the same case on the social networking platform Twitter through the collection and analysis of 1,210 tweets. These comments were largely neutral or supportive of breastfeeding in public, whilst the Mail Online comments were mostly negative, showing differences between the platforms used to discuss the news (Grant 2015).

London Riots case study

In the first of six empirical case studies, this chapter moves on to describe the process of undertaking a research project using news articles as data. The case study is structured in a chronological fashion, to match the process that you would undertake to run a similar study. First, the background context of the issue under study, the London Riots of 2011, is described. I then move on to explain how I developed a **research question** and a study that was achievable in the time available, through limiting the size of the **sample** I used. Next, I describe the way in which I kept records relating to the articles to be included. I then outline one approach to undertaking **thematic analysis** by explaining the steps I took to perform an analysis of the news articles. The case study ends with a brief discussion of findings and consideration of the particular challenges faced when doing research using news media as data. At the end of the chapter, you have the opportunity to practise the analysis skills by undertaking **thematic analysis** of some additional data.

Context

During the summer of 2011, serious disorder occurred around the UK, although it began and was largely concentrated in London. The rioting escalated from a protest about the death of Mark Duggan, a 29-year-old Black British man who was shot and killed by the police, and the subsequent failure of the police to inform his family of his death (Independent Police Complaints Commission 2012). The House of Commons Home Affairs Select Committee, which investigated the rioting in the aftermath, stated that the geographical spread of the disorder was "unprecedented in the modern era" (House of Commons Home Affairs Committee 2011, p. 3). It also made note of the fact that in addition to damage to property, shops were looted (that is, entry was forced and goods were stolen) and five members of the public were killed. Soon after, politicians began suggesting solutions to prevent similar disorder occurring in the future (The Guardian and London School of Economics and Political Science 2011). Evidence provided to the Home Affairs Select Committee, however, showed that the disorder had been different in character in the different cities involved. For example, three quarters of reported crimes in Nottingham were damage to property, whilst half of offences in Birmingham involved some kind of theft (House of Commons Home Affairs Committee 2011, p. 3). Therefore, not all of the rioters were involved in looting.

Research design

In order to study the disorder around the UK using written sources, many pre-existing documents could be used: newspaper coverage, the report and evidence presented to the Home Affairs Select Committee and politicians' speeches on the matter, to name only a few. As such, formulating a **research question** is essential in defining which documents fit within the study **population** and narrowing this down to a **sample** for study. As Nicola Green (2008) states, **research questions** should be interesting, relevant, feasible, ethical, concise and answerable. Accordingly, we can define an initial question that is broader than we can answer, and then shape this to ensure it matches the six criteria once we have done some scoping of potential data sources.

As I have described above, the media, including news companies, play a large role in creating our understanding of events. The media can suggest that a group of people is problematic, and that something should be done about it, by creating a 'moral panic' (Cohen 2002). As such, I was interested in how the media portrayed those who took part in the riots and their victims. It is important to consider the strengths and limitations of your data source, as always, and some of the limitations are described earlier in this chapter in relation to the media.

Initial research question

How were participants and victims of the London Riots portrayed by UK news media?

Refining your research question and sampling

In order to begin identifying your population, you may choose to use the newspaper indexing site **Nexis**® (to find out if you have access to **Nexis**®, look at your university academic databases webpage or speak to a librarian). Within **Nexis**®, the words you use for your topic will be important in influencing the number of articles that are returned; if you choose something very specific, you may miss some relevant articles, but if you choose something too broad, you may be overwhelmed by the number of articles that you need to review for relevant content. When searching within **Nexis**®, you may choose where your key words appear within the article (from the most specific "in headline" to "anywhere in text"). You must also choose a date range and the sources to be included in your **sample**, for example a single news publication or "UK National Newspapers". You can also choose to exclude articles from websites.

Alternatively, searching individual news sites will help to uncover online versions of articles on your topic. Again, you must choose which publications to search within, the key words to use and a date range during which you will consider articles that are returned. The choices made at each point in determining your population should be considered and documented carefully, as in Table 3.1. It may be that you have a limited amount of time to analyse your data, and

TABLE 3.1 Initial search terms used to identify newspaper articles in relation to the London Riots

Item	Initial thoughts
Search term	London Riot; London disorder
Where should the search term be?	Anywhere in the text
News source	UK National Newspapers
Concept of interest	Participants in riots; Victims of riots
Date range	Short time period around the immediate time of the riots

therefore you may need to look at the population of relevant data and see how many articles are returned. For an undergraduate dissertation, using **thematic analysis**, 100 articles would usually be sufficient data (unless the topic of interest is only peripherally considered in the data).

As you can see from Table 3.1, I have a defined topic of interest (London Riots, i.e. not those that occurred at the same time in other parts of the country) and an idea that I will use a narrow time period to look at how participants and victims were portrayed. What is not yet narrow is where in the text the search term should be, and the news source(s) that I will consider. Although local newspapers would have contained stories on such a major incident, moral panics require a volume of public belief; therefore, I chose to target national newspapers because of their higher circulation numbers.

Within the scope of this project, undertaken solely for this book, I could not possibly consider all news sources and placements of the search terms contained in Table 3.1, because of the large number of results and the limited time available. For example, a search for all UK National Newspapers for 1 January 2011–31 December 2011 uncovered 797 results. To make sure that a large body of articles were not excluded by the term 'riot', I also searched for 'London disorder', which uncovered eight articles, all of which had the term 'riot' in the title. This allowed me to be confident that the search term 'London Riots' was adequate to return all relevant articles.

In order to narrow the search parameters so that I had a **sample** of around 100 articles, I changed the placement of the search term so that it had to be in the headline or leading paragraph. **Nexis**® is able to perform this function through the use of drop-down menus and also allows you to save your search results at each stage. The save search function is valuable in the write-up of research using news media, and can allow you to access the articles that have been uncovered without having to run the searches again. This search returned 470 articles. At this stage, the only remaining way to narrow the scope was to reduce the number of news media sources included. It is important to note that if you are searching news websites by hand, you should keep exemplary records during this stage.

In order to reduce the sources in a way that was meaningful to the identification of moral panics, I returned to the concept of influence, and used the number of **readers** as a proxy for this. It is possible to identify newspaper circulation levels, and I found the results for 2011 (the time under study; you may wish to consider the most up-to-date sources in your research) (The Guardian 2011). At the time, The Sun had a daily newspaper circulation of 2.8 million and the Daily Mail 2 million. However, when we consider that news is now also consumed online, we may wish to consider a combination of online and newspaper circulation, which provides different results (The Guardian 2012). When weekend and online editions were considered, the Daily Mail had 18.5 million **readers** a month, The Sun 17.8 million and the Daily Mirror 12.7 million; The Sun and the Daily Mail were still the most read of the **tabloid press**. A review of the number of articles was conducted within **Nexis**® (Table 3.2). The total

TABLE 3.2 News sources included in final sample

Source	Monthly online/paper readership (April 2012)	Number of articles	Final sample?
Daily Mail, Mail on Sunday	18.5 million	9	Yes
The Sun	17.8 million	48	Yes
Daily Mirror; Sunday Mirror	12.7 million	68	Yes

of the three newspapers with the highest **readership** amounted to around 100 articles, so all three were included. The three data sources were all part of the **tabloid press**.

Final research question

Once you have settled on a population of documents and your **sample**, it may be necessary to return to your **research question**, to ensure that your data can definitely answer the question. Often this means making the question suitably narrow. So my question evolved to become as follows:

How were participants and victims of the London Riots portrayed by the three most popular UK national newspapers during 2011?

Good data management with newspaper articles

As was mentioned in Chapter 2, good data management is essential when working with documents, particularly if you have a large number of sources. Once you have downloaded your documents, it is important to start a database using a row for each source (see Table 3.3 for an example). When creating a new database, I number each document that has been downloaded with a **DIN – Document Identification Number**. In this instance, I have included an abbreviation for the newspapers at the beginning of the **DIN** (such as S for The Sun and DM for Daily Mail), which I find helpful during analysis and writing up.

The first stage in data management is to identify duplicates. This occurs frequently with newspapers that run a second edition of a newspaper or an international version. Where the article has the same title, **author** and word count, I compare the two sources, and if they are identical, I do not consider the duplicate in analysis. In this project, several sources from The Sun (e.g. S44 and S45) had a very similar title but the second article had an extended word count, and therefore both articles were included in the analysis. The only alternative reason for excluding articles was because they were in the Eire (Irish) edition of the paper, and that is outside of the UK (Ulster editions which covered Northern Ireland were included).

TABLE 3.3 Extract from database of documents contained in the sample, showing inclusion and exclusion decisions

DIN	Publication	Number in Nexis®	Title	Duplicate	Exclude for other reason?	Include
S21	The Sun	30	Rob rap for lad,17	No	No	Yes
S22	The Sun	31	Rob rap for lad,17	Yes (of S21)	n/a	No
S23	The Sun	45	Mugging: Teen held	No	No	Yes
S24	The Sun	46	LOOTER, 11, IS BUS LOUT	No	No	Yes
S39	The Sun	52	'LOOTER' WAS ON BAIL FOR MURDER; Gang kill suspect	No	Eire edition	No

TABLE 3.4 Final sample in London Riots case study

Source	Number of articles downloaded from Nexis®	Number of duplicates	Number of Eire/Ireland editions	DINs of final sample	Final sample
Daily Mail, Mail on Sunday	9	0	0	M1–9	9
The Sun	48	5	2	S1–21, S23–34, S36, S38–41, S43–47	41
Daily Mirror; Sunday Mirror	68	41	5	D1, D3, D4, D6, D7, D9, D11, D16, D18, D22, D24, D27, D33, D34, D37, D43, D49, D58, D60–62, D66	22
Total	125	46	7		72

Once I had checked for duplicates, I created a new table that contained my final **sample** to be included in analysis (Table 3.4). Although this may seem like extra work, this type of table can usually be directly transferred to your report, saving you time later on.

Analysis technique: interpretive thematic analysis

What is thematic analysis?

Thematic analysis can be described as a "method for identifying, analysing, and reporting patterns (themes) within data" (Braun and Clarke 2006, p. 6) in order to summarise issues across the data set (Green and Thorogood 2013). It is largely descriptive and does not rely on researchers to dig below surface **meanings** within the data (Ayres 2008). **Thematic analysis** is a very common analysis technique because it is flexible and thus suited to many types of data (Green and Thorogood 2013). For novice researchers, **thematic analysis** may be the easiest approach as it is less challenging and prescriptive than other techniques, and can work with whichever **theoretical perspective** is important in your research, or indeed without a theoretical perspective. An alternative to **thematic analysis** is **framework analysis**, which may be easier for some novice researchers (especially those who are more linear in their thinking), and if qualitative analysis is completely new to you, you may wish to consider reading the section on **framework analysis** within Chapter 7 before uncritically deciding to use **thematic analysis** in your own research.

Thematic analysis may be either **inductive, deductive** or both. **Inductive thematic analysis** allows themes to be generated during the analysis process, in a 'bottom up' way (Braun and Clarke 2006), with the only pre-defined framework being what is in the researcher's head. This is the preferred technique of Aronson (1995). By contrast, a **deductive** analysis may involve themes being pre-specified, to ensure that the analysis can answer the **research questions** within your project. In practice, I often use an approach that is both **deductive** and **inductive**: I start with an idea of what the important themes will be in order to answer my **research question**, but I also allow myself to add additional codes in an **inductive** fashion. In this case study, my **research question** involved (i) victims and (ii) participants, so I knew that my codes would need to relate to these two groups of individuals, creating **deductive** codes for these categories. I then used **inductive** sub-codes relating to 'victims' and 'participants'.

How to do thematic analysis

Several descriptions have been provided regarding *how* to do **thematic analysis**. Within research, there is rarely a clear right or wrong technique, so I would argue that if you have decided that **thematic analysis** is the technique you should use, you may choose whichever type of **thematic analysis** feels best suited to your research. However, you should be able to describe exactly what you have done, with references to methodological literature, and justify why you have decided to make these decisions. One common pitfall in the reporting of **thematic analysis** is to see the analysis as a *passive*, as opposed to an *active*, process, where themes 'emerge' from the data. Braun and Clarke (2006) argue that within

thematic analysis, themes are selected because of the interests of the researcher, and therefore researchers are not simply finding 'the truth' from within the data but are creating a truth based on their pre-existing knowledge and interest. The guidance provided by Braun and Clarke (2006) involves six steps (see Box 3.1), although researchers may not necessarily follow a linear process when undertaking **thematic analysis**, returning to earlier stages as appropriate.

BOX 3.1 PROCEDURE TO UNDERTAKE THEMATIC ANALYSIS (BRAUN AND CLARKE 2006)

1. Familiarisation with the data, through reading data and making notes of any ideas
2. Generating initial codes, by coding 'interesting features' across the entire data set
3. Searching for themes
4. Reviewing themes
5. Defining and naming themes
6. Producing the report

Alongside the structure provided by Braun and Clarke, Green and Thorogood (2013) provide some helpful practical hints. They suggest that if hard copies of data are used during analysis, researchers ensure that there is enough room around the edge of the data to make notes. A more conceptual tip is that the main technique to **thematic analysis** is a system of "scissors and paste"; pieces of data that are assigned to a particular code or theme are either actually or metaphorically 'cut and pasted' to them (Green and Thorogood 2013: 177). These days, many researchers will choose to use a computer in their analysis, either through a **CAQDAS** programme (like **NVivo** or **ATLAS.ti**) or will do their cutting and pasting in a tidier way than using hard copies, such as using a word processing computer programme. Whichever technique you use, ensure you save an original copy of your documents that does not contain your analytical notes or any 'cutting'. This will enable you to return to a 'clean' copy of the data at a later stage.

London Riots case study: data analysis

It is relevant to note that I have introduced the literature on 'moral panics' at the beginning of this chapter. This concept was already framing my thoughts as I analysed the data, and can be contrasted with other literature that may have been relevant, but I was less familiar with. When undertaking thematic analysis, it is important to be aware of, and acknowledge, our pre-existing ideas (Braun and Clarke 2006). In stage 1, all 79 articles were imported into **NVivo** (version 11) for analysis, and each article was read. In stage 2, I created **deductive** codes for 'participant' and 'victim', as my **research question** was specifically about the portrayal of victims and participants in the London riots. I then reread all of the articles and made notes in order to **inductively** generate initial sub-codes. This resulted in ten sub-codes for participants of the riots and seven sub-codes for victims of the riots, which can be seen in Table 3.5.

In stage 3, I reviewed my coding for themes. That is, I looked for similarities between sub-codes to see if they could be joined together. I was able to split the sub-codes into fewer themes in stage 3, and review them for fit with the data, by returning to the data extracts in stage 4. In stage 5, I named the sub-themes and also the smaller themes they contained (sub-sub-themes). In relation to 'participants', these were 'demographics' (age, race/ethnicity, family and famous), the 'crime' ('crime accused of', 'justifications' and 'not to blame for taking part') and 'media representations' ('names given by media' and 'should have known better'). The same process was undertaken for 'victims' of the riots.

Alongside this coding, I kept a notebook for analytical thoughts that came along as I was writing. For instance, in sources D1 and to a lesser extent M49, the article is talking about historical rioting, but portrays the participants of these historical riots sensitively, with valid reasons for their protests. However, content relating to previous riots does not fit within my coding framework unless it is to make a direct comparison to the current riots and rioters (as in M49). This is not explicitly a stage in **thematic analysis**, but it is good practice to keep a note of your thoughts as you are analysing your data.

TABLE 3.5 Inductive codes and deductive sub-codes generated during analysis

Inductive main code	Deductive sub-codes
Participants	Age
	Characteristics
	Crime accused of
	Family
	Famous
	Justification
	Names given by media
	Not to blame for taking part
	Race/ethnicity
	Should have known better
Victims	Effects of riots
	Famous
	Foreign
	Preparing for riots
	Student
	View of victims (newspaper commentary)
	View of offenders (victim commentary)

Findings

Notes on the presentation of findings

Findings are briefly presented below, as per stage 6 of **thematic analysis**, in relation to participants in the riot and those who were victims of the riot. In your own reporting, you are likely to have more space available to expand on the themes generated within your analysis. When presenting a data extract, I use the **DIN** that I created alongside the extract, which is good practice as long as it does not identify a participant. Where the names of individuals were noted, these have been removed to protect anonymity. In some chapters later in the book, I have explicitly decided to present findings quantitatively alongside data extracts. However, this felt inappropriate in this project, as some themes were referred to a lot of times, but almost in passing, whilst other themes were referred to less often, but in considerable detail. You should consider whether it would be appropriate to use any quantification in your own reporting of studies using news media.

Perpetrators of rioting

Demographics featured heavily in the reporting of participants, and one of the most striking elements was that their age was nearly always quoted in years. However, alongside this factual information, terms relating to the age of participants such as 'kid' (S1), 'teenager' (M22), 'youths' (M60) were used in headlines and throughout the articles. The oldest (S30) and youngest (D4) rioters to be charged were also noted. Within the newspaper articles, there was a small quantity of examples that appeared to suggest the individual rioter might not have been fully responsible because of family circumstances or poverty. These were mostly taken from statements of mitigation presented to the court: '(Name of lawyer), defending, said: 'She struggled financially and found herself led into the path of temptation'" (S12).

Articles always included reference to the crime committed, often describing the specific act in detail rather than simply the name of the criminal offence, such as theft. For example, "He was caught red-handed stealing a bin from a Debenhams store in his hometown" (D4). On the other hand, the theme 'should have known better' included those who were viewed as additionally deviant because of their relatively good social circumstances. This included those from rich families, participants who were famous, with one actor referenced in three articles those, and those who were seen as inherently 'good' in some way, such as volunteers, including one young woman who was described in four articles:

> A teenage (volunteer for high profile organisation) charged with hurling bricks at police during the London riots on August 7 has been charged with a second violent disorder offence the following night.
>
> *(M16)*

The language used to describe those involved in rioting often marked out the perpetrators as being a deviant 'other' associated with 'gangs' or gang culture including "feral children with no respect for law and order" (D4), "Brazen thugs" (M43) and "baying mobs of youths" (M58).

Victims of rioting

The media coverage of victims was focused on the victims of high profile attacks, such as arson or violence. One incident, which was covered in detail in several sources, included the story of a shop which was set on fire:

> The owners of the family furniture store were devastated after seeing the charred remains of the building that fell victim to the riots. (name, age), last week told of his devastation at seeing his business go up in smoke.
>
> *(M37)*

Alongside this, residents of a building that had to be evacuated because of arson attacks were described in some articles: "A COUPLE made homeless by this inferno yesterday told how baying mobs ignored their pleas not to torch their block" (M58). However, victims of the riots were not always depicted on an individual level with discussion of community impacts occurring regularly: "A woman cradling her young daughter said: 'I've lived here all my life and (this area)'s always been a bit rough but this is just terrible. It's so sad'" (M60).

Emotive language and ties to other negative events that had affected London was used to describe the potential effects. In relation to a prominent building that was subject to an arson attack, one of the articles stated, "THIS once-elegant listed building had survived Hitler's bombers during the Blitz...In one night (the local population) had seen their vibrant community wrenched from them" (M61).

Discussion

Overall, participants were described demographically and often as young. In addition, emotive language displaying their delinquency and relationship to 'gangs' was used. Victims were considered in relation to the effect of the riots, rather than their demographics, and were generally assumed to be a 'good' hardworking group, in contrast to the rioters. It can be seen that young people were viewed as a problem, and that these articles could have created, or helped to sustain, a moral panic. One policy response to the London Riots was the development of the Troubled Families Programme. The Programme specifically aimed to 'turn around' the lives of families like those involved as offenders in the London Riots. However, there is little evidence that this will work due to embedded social inequalities (Hayden and Jenkins 2014).

Challenges of undertaking research with news articles

In undertaking analysis of media coverage of a high-profile event, there is often more potential data (the **population**) than could possibly fit within a project; as such, sampling decisions need to be made carefully. The use of particular data sources, for example, **tabloids** over **broadsheets**, impacts on the way in which stories are told, and thus sampling decisions impact on findings. For example, **tabloid newspapers** involve telling the story of an incident through a particular format, including short paragraphs, and journalistic speak, which sensationalises content. Researchers may feel that it would be appropriate to move beyond the **thematic analysis** used in this chapter to uncover some of the deeper, hidden meanings, through the use of **discourse analysis** (see Chapter 4 for an example).

By using **Nexis**® to identify data, the textual content of articles is made available without the accompanying images. These images can be used to imply things (in relation to ethnicity and gender, for example) that are not explicitly said in words. It was not possible to include the analysis of images within the space constraints of this chapter, but this does mean that only a partial account has been analysed. Researchers can choose to look up stories online and find accompanying images for their data set, and this approach would have been used if more space was available. In Chapter 5, the value of multi-modal (text and image) analysis is explored, and I recommend that you undertake multi-modal analysis of news media content wherever possible. **Thematic analysis** can also be used to analyse images.

Decisions around the ethical sharing of news articles should also be considered. Whilst the data is freely available in the public domain, in an era of open access publication, it may be ethically prudent to remove any names of individuals or places from data extracts. Furthermore, it may be necessary to seek approval from the publisher ahead of sharing data extracts. At the time of writing, Routledge recommended that copyright approval would be required if more than 50 words were to be shared from a single article, and that permission would always be required to share images.

Exercise: using thematic analysis

The analysis above focused on how participants and victims of the London Riots were described by the three print news sources with the highest circulation. However, other interesting topics were covered within the data, including potential reasons for the riots, which were often suggested as solutions to prevent further unrest in the future. Below four fictitious newspaper articles about the London Riots are available for you to practise analysis.

Instructions

Using the four newspaper articles, undertake a **thematic analysis** to answer the following **research question**:

What potential <u>solutions</u> to prevent further rioting are suggested in the newspaper articles below?

I suggest that you consult Box 3.1 for guidance on how to conduct **thematic analysis**, and that you read Braun and Clarke (2006). You may wish to photocopy the data to facilitate your analysis.

Data

Source 1

Rioters should be put on national service

The London Riots were organised by thuggish gangs intent on stealing trainers and TVs and were nothing to do with the shooting of Mark Duggan.

With the youngest perpetrator aged 11, it is clear that something needs to be done to stop further outbreaks.

Local UKIP councillor (name) stated, "All of those involved in rioting should be sent on national service. They need discipline, and the army would give it to them!"

The closing of local youth centres was blamed by others. Local resident (name) said, "There's nothing around here for young people to do. They spend the evenings hanging around on street corners being bored".

Source 2

Boris has tough decisions ahead

Following the worst riots in over a century, with some 1,600 people arrested across England, an independent think tank has advice for Boris Johnson, Mayor of London.

(Think tank) says that since 2010, the rate of child poverty has increased significantly, with 37% of children living in London in poverty, some 700,000 children.

Chief executive (name) said, "This rioting should be a big wake up call for the government. People are sick and tired of living in complete poverty. Most parents work hard, and yet low wages mean many still have to claim benefits as they are unable to make ends meet. This is unacceptable in a country as rich as the UK and must stop".

Alongside poverty, budget cuts have affected youth services, with many youth work positions axed and youth clubs closed down.

(Name), from children's charity (charity name), stated, "We used to provide services throughout the borough in six locations, but now we are only able to run youth groups in two locations due to budget cuts. Our youth workers play an important part in providing stability and positive role models to young people who grow up in disadvantage".

It is estimated that the cost of the London Riots was around £130 million.

Source 3

> ## Bill for riots expected to reach at least £133 million
>
> As thuggish youths attend court for trial, accused of offences ranging from theft to violence, the expected cost of the damage has been announced as a MINIMUM of £133 million.
>
> The chief of police for (area) suggested that spending cuts were to blame for the riots. Chief Superintendent (name) stated that her force had had to make spending cuts of over 25% over the past five years. This made it impossible to stamp out the riots when they began.
>
> In real terms, this means that there are less bobbies on the beat stopping crimes in the making and making our streets safer.
>
> (Chief Superintendent) said, "With the reduction of officers based in the community, we are unable to build on our strong relationships with local communities".
>
> Have your say – do you think there are enough police in your area?

Source 4

> ## Time in the slammer for teen hooligan
>
> A teenager charged with theft during the London Riots appeared in court yesterday.
>
> The youth, aged 17, from (area), was sentenced to three months in prison for stealing food from a supermarket, including chocolate, sweets and bread.
>
> (Name), who defended the hooligan, said "the teen is the daughter of a known criminal, whom she has been influenced by. She is also living with her mother on a low income and was returning home with the goods to feed her younger siblings, which attested to her good character".
>
> The judge noted that if she was found guilty of similar offences in the future, she would be sentenced more harshly.

Note

1 The terms Black and Indigenous are capitalised in this chapter and throughout, because the way we use language relating to race and ethnicity, including our use of capitalisation, can be a way of reinforcing existing power structures which disadvantage non-white groups. See: https://www.cjr.org/analysis/language_corner_1.php for more details.

References

Aronson, J. 1995. A pragmatic view of thematic analysis. *The Qualitative Report*: 2(1), pp. 1–3.

Ayres, L. 2008. Thematic Coding and Analysis. In: Given, L. (ed) *The SAGE encyclopaedia of qualitative research methods*. London: Sage, pp. 867-868

Ball-Rokeach, S.J. and DeFleur, M.L. 1976. A dependency model of mass-media effects. *Communication Research*: 3(1), pp. 3–21.

Barak, G. 1994. *Media, process, and the social construction of crime: studies in newsmaking criminology*. New York: Garland.

Bonn, S. 2010. *Mass deception: moral panic and the US war on Iraq*. New Brunswick: Rutgers University Press.

Branston, G. and Stafford, R. 2010. *The media student's book*. Abingdon: Routledge.

Braun, V. and Clarke, V. 2006. Using thematic analysis in psychology. *Qualitative Research in Psychology*: 3(2), pp. 77–101.

Bullock, H.E. et al. 2001. Media images of the poor. *Journal of Social Issues*: 57(2), pp. 229–246.

Cohen, S. 2002. *Folk devils and moral panics: the creation of the mods and rockers*. Hove: Psychology Press.

Cottle, S. 2005. Mediatized public crisis and civil society renewal: the racist murder of Stephen Lawrence. *Crime, Media, Culture*: 1(1), pp. 49–71.

Edwards, S.B. and Harris, D. 2016. *Black Lives Matter*. Edina, MN: ABDO Publishing.

Gilchrist, K. 2010. 'Newsworthy' victims? *Feminist Media Studies*: 10(4), pp. 373–390.

Grant, A. 2015. '#discrimination': the online response to a case of a breastfeeding mother being ejected from a UK retail premises. *Journal of Human Lactation*: 32(1), pp. 141–151.

Grant, A. 2016. 'I… don't want to see you flashing your bits around': Exhibitionism, othering and good motherhood in perceptions of public breastfeeding. *Geoforum*: 71(2016), pp. 52–61.

Green, J. and Thorogood, N. 2013. *Qualitative methods for health research*. London: Sage.

Green, N. 2008. Formulating and refining a research question. In: Gilbert, N. ed. *Researching social life*. 3rd ed. London: Sage, pp. 43–62.

Hacking, I. 1986. Self-improvement. In: Hoy, D. C. ed. *Foucault: a critical reader*. Oxford: Basil Blackwell Ltd, pp. 235–240.

Hall, S. 1997. *Representation: cultural representations and signifying practices*. London: Sage.

Hayden, C. and Jenkins, C. 2014. 'Troubled Families' programme in England: 'wicked problems' and policy-based evidence. *Policy Studies*: 35(6), pp. 631–649.

Hayward, K. and Yar, M. 2006. The 'chav' phenomenon: consumption, media and the construction of a new underclass. *Crime, Media, Culture*: 2(1), pp. 9–28.

Hillsborough Independent Panel 2017. Hillsborough Independent Panel. Available at: http://hillsborough.independent.gov.uk/ [Accessed: 21 February 2017].

Home Office 1999. The Stephen Lawrence inquiry. Available at: https://www.gov.uk/government/publications/the-stephen-lawrence-inquiry [Accessed: 3 December 2017].

House of Commons Home Affairs Committee 2011. Policing large scale disorder: lessons from the disturbances of August 2011. Available at: http://www.parliament.uk/business/committees/committees-a-z/commons-select/home-affairs-committee/inquiries/policing-large-scale-disorder/ [Accessed: 3 December 2017].

Independent Police Complaints Commission 2012. Mark Duggan - Metropolitan Police Service. Available at: https://www.ipcc.gov.uk/investigations/mark-duggan-metropolitan-police-service [Accessed: 24 February 2017].

Jemphrey, A. and Berrington, E. 2000. Surviving the media: Hillsborough, Dunblane and the press. *Journalism Studies*: 1(3), pp. 469–483.

Macdonald, K. 2008. Using documents. In: Gilbert, N. ed. *Researching social life*. 3rd ed. London, UK: Sage, pp. 285–303.

Markovits, A.S. and Silverstein, M. 1988. *The politics of scandal: power and process in liberal democracies*. New York, NY: Holmes & Meier.

Marsh, I. and Melville, G. 2011. Moral panics and the British media–a look at some contemporary 'Folk Devils'. *Internet Journal of Criminology*: 1(1), pp. 1–21.

McLaughlin, E. and Murji, K. 1999. After the Stephen Lawrence report. *Critical Social Policy*: 19(3), pp. 371–385.

Miller, D. 2004. *Tell me lies: propaganda and media distortion in the attack on Iraq*. London: Pluto.

Nerone, J. and Barnhurst, K.G. 2003. US newspaper types, the newsroom, and the division of labor, 1750–2000. *Journalism Studies*: 4(4), pp. 435–449.

New Statesman 2013. The Daily Mail has its better angels too. Available at: https://www.newstatesman.com/politics/2013/10/daily-mail-has-its-better-angels-too [Accessed: 3 December 2017].

Scott, J. 1990. *A matter of record: documentary sources in social research*. London: John Wiley & Sons.

Scraton, P. 1999. Policing with contempt: the degrading of truth and denial of justice in the aftermath of the Hillsborough disaster. *Journal of Law and Society*: 26(3), pp. 273–297.

Scraton, P. 2004. Death on the terraces: the contexts and injustices of the 1989 Hillsborough Disaster. *Soccer & Society*: 5(2), pp. 183–200.

The Guardian 2011. ABCs: National daily newspaper circulation July 2011. Available at: https://www.theguardian.com/media/table/2011/aug/12/abcs-national-newspapers [Accessed: 24 February 2017].

The Guardian 2012. Digital and newspaper readerships combined: figures for major UK newspaper and magazine. Available at: https://www.theguardian.com/news/datablog/2012/sep/12/digital-newspaper-readerships-national-survey [Accessed: 24 February 2017].

The Guardian and London School of Economics and Political Science 2011. Reading the riots: investigating England's summer of disorder. Available at: http://eprints.lse.ac.uk/46297/ [Accessed: 3 December 2017].

Wall, M. 2015. Citizen journalism. *Digital Journalism*: 3(6), pp. 797–813.

4

HISTORICAL AND OFFICIAL DOCUMENTS

Moving beyond simple interpretations

Summary

In this chapter, unlike the other case studies in this book, two types of documents – historical and official – are considered together. By examining these together I highlight the differences between sources, which can help to provide alternative understandings of reality. First, I consider historical documents, including those that are text only and those that are graphical or also include images. Examples of where the analysis of historical documents has been useful for contemporary society are briefly outlined. Alongside this, literature on the analysis of **official documents** is described. The main body of the chapter involves an empirical case study of welfare reform. Within the worked example, historical documents on the 1834 Poor Law Amendment Act are analysed alongside transcripts of parliamentary debates relating to the Welfare Reform and Work Bill 2015. The process of refining the **research question** and sampling data to be used is described. The data are analysed using **Critical Discourse Analysis (CDA)**, which involves thematic coding, consideration of power relations and conclusion drawing. Examples are given at each stage. Discourses of note in both data sources are the power relationships in society and the deservingness of claimants. However, it also illuminates the power relationships within and between the different organisations involved. In the historical documents, power was held by those administering benefits on the ground, whilst the **official documents** allowed an insight into the power relationships between political parties in contemporary society. The chapter also considers the unique challenges in undertaking research with official or historical documents. An exercise is provided to allow **readers** to undertake **CDA**.

Key learning points

- How historical documents and **official documents** have been used to understand society
- How to assess quality and **bias** in historical and **official documents**
- How to undertake research projects using multiple sources of data
- How to **sample** data from **archives**
- How to use **CDA**, including consideration of language and power relationships

Background 1: historical documents

When trying to understand the past, it is often not possible to collect data from individuals who were involved in the phenomenon of interest. As such, historians often rely on textual (such as official records, diaries, letters, literature and poetry) and graphical data (including art works and maps) that are available to them, to try to "meaningfully reconstruct" the past (Gottschalk 2006, p. 43). We may also consider multi-modal content, for example propaganda materials often use images alongside words to enhance their **meanings**. Typically historians refer to each piece of data as a 'source', and they can be defined as "relics...or as the testimonies of witnesses to the past" (Howell and Prevenier 2001, p. 17). Historical documents are divided into primary sources, which were **authored** by eyewitnesses to the phenomenon, and secondary sources, from those who were not present at the event they describe (Gottschalk 2006).

The use of historical documents in research

A range of historical research with potential impacts for contemporary society has been undertaken. One area that is particularly useful for understanding changing geographies is the use of historical maps. For example, prior to the use of aerial photography in the 1950s, historical maps had to be relied on to understand changes to land and water bodies over time. For instance, Bromberg and Bertness (2005) considered changes to salt marshes that occurred alongside urbanisation in America. Alongside this, in their research using historical maps, Haase and colleagues consider current environmental issues through historical land use (Haase et al. 2007). They note that by changing the use of land, such as for more intensive farming, water systems are affected. By using modern data analysis techniques, the team was able to understand how the terrain was changing and to make recommendations for sustainable land use. However, the use of modern-day techniques, such as GIS (Geographic Information System), has also been recommended to understand historical land use, showing a level of distrust of historical maps (Gregory and Healey 2007).

Alongside this, in history, **official statistics**, documents and artefacts have shed light on a broad range of topics, including war. **Official documents** have been used to categorise the casualties in the First World War, in relation to disease, injury or death (Mitchell and Smith 1931). By contrast, in Emily Brayshaw's (2018) work on documents and uniforms as the last remaining mementos of a fallen First

World War soldier, comfort, horror, grief and memory are discussed with reference to these artefacts. By considering the overt codes of camaraderie in posters asking men to enlist, she highlights the importance of relationships between military service, patriotism and glamour, as represented through dress. Alongside this, the sex appeal of soldiers (and the promise of sex for would-be soldiers) is described through the lyrics of songs played in music halls. Whilst soldiers were away at war, Brayshaw argues, photographs of them in uniform became "substitute bodies", which were viewed alongside letters to help construct a shared reality between soldiers at war and their families at home. By contrast, when soldiers died during conflict, their returned uniforms and other artefacts could reconstruct conditions during the war for the families at home. Through consideration of smells and mud on documents and uniforms, a shared understanding of the horrific conditions of war was created, which was further distressing to family members.

Quality and bias in historical documents

When undertaking research using historical data sources, detailed guidance can be found within Brundage (2018). Also, there is a range of checklists available to ascertain **bias** and quality. Many of the elements are similar to those found within Scott's (1990) criteria, but where subject-specific guidance is provided, it is best practice to use it. It is important to consider the availability and selection of sources (Gottschalk 2006) as well as who the **author** was (Scott 1990) as these will influence results, as with any form of research. The historical guidance that I find most helpful is from Bill McDowell (2002, pp. 111–112), which is summarised in Box 4.1. It may also be relevant to consider if the document could possibly have been forged, or if social conditions were such that the **author** may reasonably have been expected not to tell the truth within the documents (Gottschalk 2006). Alongside this, Black (2010) notes that historical records may not always be accurate or complete. For example, records on births, marriages and deaths in the UK were routinely incomplete prior to the 1800s.

BOX 4.1 CONSIDERATIONS FOR ASSESSING QUALITY AND BIAS IN HISTORICAL DOCUMENTS (McDOWELL 2002, pp. 113–114)

- Whether the source was intended to be a factual document only, or if it may have been trying to persuade readers
- Who was the intended audience: a small private audience or a broader public?
- Were the documents intended to remain confidential?
- Was the author an expert in this matter?
- Was the document likely to have been written after it purported to have been?

Many historical documents are contained within **archives** and museums. Within **archives**, therefore, a third actor is often involved in creating **meaning** alongside the **author** and the **reader**. This individual, often an **archivist**, librarian or relative, has made an active choice about what should be preserved from the documents available to them, and what should be considered as unworthy of study, or not for the public gaze. Changes in the availability of high-functioning copying or scanning devices may also result in more or less of a set of documents being added to an **archive** (Howell and Prevenier 2001). If documents are displayed in a museum, in the creating of displays, particular extracts may be given prominence, or a historian may be involved in creating a narrative to fit alongside the document. It is our job, as researchers, to remember that the **archive** is not neutral, and to consider how the selection or presentation of sources may have impacted on the data that is available to us.

Alongside official **archives**, a range of private historical documents exists in private collections. The advantage of studying private documents, such as diaries and letters, over **official documents** is their greater attention to everyday mundane activities. These can illuminate how society operated and was experienced by individuals within it. However, it is important to recall that the voices of the least privileged in society may be missing or misrepresented. Women, minority groups (Brundage 2018) and children (Hendrick 2000) were virtually excluded from history until recently. Accordingly, in analysing historical sources, we need to consider religion, socio-economic status, the prominence of (flawed) biological arguments around superiority of racial groups, the environment, science and technology, and power structures (Howell and Prevenier 2001). Conclusions must be drawn carefully and critically. Moreover, viewing historical documents through our own contemporary worldview will highlight that there are static and dynamic elements and **meanings** contained in historical documents (Brundage 2018).

Background 2: contemporary official documents

Official documents are those that carry some contractual or legal standing. They may be both historical and contemporary. When **official documents** are considered in relation to documentary research, there is often a strong emphasis on **official statistics**, which include numbers and percentages (Prior 2003; Macdonald 2008). This may be because such documents were among the earliest public records, or because such statistics are both newsworthy and of interest to politicians. That said, counts of phenomena can be easily manipulated through changing definitions (Best 2001) and can allow for systemic **bias** (Pager 2004). Other types of **official documents** produced by governments include consultation and policy documents. Policy documents have been critically described as a demonstration of state power, which do not include all relevant information and can be written in ways so as to mislead some groups of **readers** (Codd 1988). Accordingly, like **official statistics**, these also need critical consideration.

Finally, **official documents** can be those held by individuals, such as identity cards and passports, deeds to property and wills, or legal documents, such as warrants and indictments.

The use of official documents in research

Despite interest in **official statistics, official documents** are often ideally suited to qualitative research. This can be considered in relation to research on suicide. Examining official records on 184 prison suicides in Finland over a 20-year period, Matti Joukamaa (1997) was able to highlight frequency of suicides overtime based on numerical data, but also found that visits to healthcare professionals frequently occurred prior to a suicide. Suicide has also been studied using a qualitative analysis of 100 case files produced in a UK coroners' court. This research was able to highlight three points during the life course when people are most at risk of suicide, refuting the simplicity of established discourses around who were most at risk of suicide (Shiner et al. 2009). Furthermore, a study of suicide prevention policies has allowed for recommendations to be made as to best practice in suicide prevention for hospitals (Bowers et al. 2000).

It has been suggested that when undertaking analysis of policy documents, researchers should consider the explicit aims of the policy and the outcomes that will be targeted and measured as a result of it (Cheung et al. 2010). In doing so, we may see that the policy problem and policy solution do not match. This has been repeatedly found in relation to attempts to make societies more equal. For example, in Herbert's (1984) research on Affirmative Action, a policy that was, on the face of it, intended to reduce inequalities in employment, systematic racism was identified. Policies created at local levels to make educational institutions more inclusive to Black and minority ethnic groups have also been subjected to critiques that they may position those from non-white backgrounds as outsiders, and thus fail to meet their aims (Iverson 2007).

Quality and bias in official documents

The assessment of quality and **bias** within **official documents** is ideally suited to using Scott's (1990) criteria (see Table 2.1). As with many documents written by more than a single individual, it is hard to measure **authenticity** in **official documents**, as it is not clear who has been involved in creating them. **Credibility** may also be affected, as **authors** write their documents in line with existing norms, targets and sanctions (Grant 2013). With contemporary official records, many are available in the public domain, and therefore we can access **representative samples** of some sources. However, access to other **official documents** is highly regulated. The language used within policy documents can often imply one thing, when it is referring to something else. Likewise in other types of **official documents**, the words used and the **meanings** intended may be based on contemporary norms and values.

Welfare reform case study

In the second case study of this book, historical and **official documents** are brought together in a single research project, focusing on 'poor relief' and its contemporary equivalent: 'welfare reform'. The case study is structured in a chronological fashion, to match the process that you would undertake to do a similar study, using either historical or **official documents**. Before exploring the research, context is provided in relation to the provision of financial aid to those who are unable to find paid work. Following this, a **research question** is provided alongside a rationale for the use of particular sources of historical and **official documents** within the **sample**. In order to consider power relationships within society, a **discourse analysis** approach was utilised, and the steps involved in undertaking **CDA** are described through the case study. Following this, the challenges of undertaking research using this approach are described.

Context

In Chapter 3, I outlined how the media can create a moral panic around a particular group of people. This may have given the impression that the conditions to create a systematic prejudice against a group of people generally arise quickly. In this case study, I show that this is not necessarily the case, and that old prejudices can continue to affect groups of people for decades or even centuries. I focus on people who are living in poverty, although I could easily have focused on other marginalised groups, such as people with disabilities, those of non-white ethnicity and women. For example, those of Black ethnicity continue to be routinely disadvantaged in a range of ways because of their ethnicity, including systematic bias in young Black men's interactions with the criminal justice system (Gelman et al. 2007).

The first event to contextualise this chapter is the historical system of 'poor relief' in the UK (which we would call 'social security' or 'welfare' these days). Although our case study is set in the nineteenth century, poor relief, originating from a series of Acts known as the 'poor laws', and funded by the state was not a new policy, originating in England and Wales in 1388 (Fraser 2009). However, in the early 1800s, there were suggestions that the current poor law was inadequate. Detailed examination on the **official documents** of the poor law at this time highlights that it was not clear who took up the offer of poor relief at this time, or what relief was provided in practice (Oxley 1974). In 1834, the Poor Law Amendment Act was passed to abolish this system of local poor relief. Instead, the Act encouraged the construction of workhouses. A workhouse can be defined as an institution where people lived when they could not afford to live in their own homes, where they received food and shelter in return for working. Reports were written by the local and national poor-law guardians and commissioners, allowing for some historical analysis.

The second event to be covered is modern-day welfare reform in England and Wales. The contemporary **official documents**, which will be used to understand the system of poor relief, arise from the Welfare Reform and Work Bill 2015. In the UK, reforms to social security benefits have been made regularly since the 1940s. In general, during times of Labour governments, benefits (or tax credits) provide a slightly higher standard of living, in recognition of the structural causes of poverty. By contrast, the Conservative governments of Margaret Thatcher and beyond have focused on individualistic causes of poverty, and thus justified cutting benefits, on the grounds that claimants are undeserving. In Chapter 7, however, we see that a simple distinction between the two governments is not always appropriate, with the New Labour governments since 1997 also making some cuts. The 2015 Welfare Reform and Work Bill was specifically introduced to allow a reduction in taxes: "(the Bill will be in) support of the Government's aim to move from a high tax, high welfare and low wage society to a low tax, lower welfare and higher wage society" (Iain Duncan Smith, Secretary of State for Work and Pensions, 20/07/15).

Research design

Broad research question

What **discourses** about those living in poverty are found in relation to the roll-out of the 1834 Poor Law Amendment Act and the 2015 Welfare Reform and Work Bill?

Sample and data collection: historical sources

When considering **official documents** or those stored in an **archive**, it is prudent to consider why these documents were gathered and made available, and what impact this may have on the source of the data in order to consider **validity** and reliability (Macdonald 2008). I had planned to use responses to the Poor Law Amendment Act consultation as data. This was because I had previously used the data whilst teaching, and knew that it showed the divisions between those in favour of the act and those who were not. However, the document had gone missing from the library I had planned to borrow it from. As the research here is undertaken for the purposes of teaching, I did not pay the fee to be able to access the document from another library. However, if this were a funded research study focusing on those consultation responses, then that is what would have been required. Instead, at the point where it became apparent that the source was not available, I was able to modify my **research question**, to ensure the research was still deliverable.

I searched the UK National Archives website (www.nationalarchives.gov.uk/) for 'poor law', and I was able to find a broad range of documents available – some 348 types of documents, ranging from cabinet papers following the First

World War to records relating to poor law schools. From an initial inspection, it was clear that there were too many categories for me to be able to meaningfully explore all of the records in the time available, so I reduced the scope of my search to the 'Poor Law Amendment Act'. This time, 14 sets of documents were available, making selecting a set of documents much easier. Two sets of documents seemed particularly relevant: "workhouses" and "workhouse inmates and staff". Examination of both sources showed that the primary set of documents available online was the 'Poor Law Union Records (1834–1871)'. Further documents were available from the physical **archive**, the National Archive at Kew, including correspondence between poor law commissioners and the poor law board. This would have been interesting to study, but it was beyond the confines of this (unfunded) study to travel to the **archive** in order to examine them.

Accordingly, I searched the 'Poor Law Union Records' on the National Archive portal, which highlighted 575 records available for study online. Three of these were from after 1900, so were excluded, leaving 572 records available for study. It was possible to download a full set of details into a spreadsheet, showing the **sample** to be used within the research. The spreadsheet exported provided a 'citable reference' and a separate ID number for each source (the National Archive's equivalent of a **Document Identification Number (DIN)**), context description, document description, dates and subjects covered. The digital image of the original document needed to be viewed on the National Archives website, or each document downloaded individually. Due to the size of the project, I selected every 10th document to be included, a way of randomly selecting a **probability sample**, creating a **sample** of 57 documents. In order to keep a copy of each of the data sources (which is good practice in case the online **archive** is ever unavailable) the 57 documents were downloaded. I modified the spreadsheet to include a new column for my **DIN** (see Chapter 2), which ranged from 1 to 57, as I felt the smaller numbers would be easier to use during analysis.

Sample and data collection: contemporary official documents

In order to find a contemporary comparison to the poor law documents from the 1800s, I decided to analyse policy documents relating to the Welfare Reform and Work Bill 2015, as this was the most recent Bill at the time of writing. A range of **official documents** can be found in relation to the Welfare Reform and Work Bill 2015 on the UK Parliament website (www. parliament.uk/). These include when the Bill was 'read' in Parliament, transcripts of all debate and every amendment made to the written Bill. I actively chose to focus on documents from before the Bill became an Act in 2016 (that means, before it was transferred to being part of UK law), as this is when decisions about how harsh or lenient the policy should be are discussed by politicians.

In order to answer my **research question**, I excluded content related to narrow legal principles as this would not focus on the discourses used in relation to claimants. This meant that the amendment papers available on the Parliament website were less relevant. Written evidence presented to the committee, which can be found on the Parliament website, was also excluded, as this focused on the views of those outside of government and so was less relevant to understanding the government's views. Instead, I reviewed transcripts of parliamentary debates and committee stage papers. As many of these focused on narrow, technical, points of law, rather than the ethos behind the law, I focused on a single key debate, when the Bill was reintroduced to the House of Commons on 20 July 2015 (see www.theyworkforyou.com/debates/?id=2015-07-20c.1256.0 for a full transcript). Whilst one debate may not seem like a lot of data, it comprises over 37,000 words, which is ample data on which to do **discourse analysis** alongside the historical sources.

Analysis technique: CDA

What is discourse analysis?

Discourse analysis can be described as "the study of social life, understood through analysis of language in its widest sense" (Shaw and Bailey 2009, p. 413). Its difference to other analysis strategies is its consideration of data beyond surface **meanings**. As was noted in Chapter 3, regarding **thematic analysis**, there is also no single definition of **discourse analysis**, which can lead to confusion and frustration among researchers, when the **reader**'s definition of **discourse analysis** is different to the writer's interpretation. Rosalind Gill (2006, p. 216) writes about using **discourse analysis** with documents and suggests that it involves "the spirit of sceptical readings", which I find a very helpful definition to keep in mind. She also provides a worked example of applying **discourse analysis** to a newspaper article, which may provide a second case study for you to consult, if you are using this approach and would like to consult a further worked example.

In this case study, I have chosen to focus on a single type of **discourse analysis** in order to provide methodological clarity. **CDA** can be described as a theoretical framework for analysis of data that is textual, including interview transcripts and documents (Fairclough and Wodak 1997; van Dijk 2001). **CDA** is based on the premise that documents are powerful objects, as they have the power to create new – and reinforce existing – beliefs and ideologies within society. Here we can see overlaps between the way in which moral panics are created (see Chapter 3) and how documents have functions in society (see Chapter 2 and Prior 2003). Accordingly, **CDA** aims to highlight **discourses** within data in order to highlight and describe power relations, and to consider ways in which discourses that are negative for society can be challenged.

How to do CDA

CDA can be used in order to reach beyond surface **meanings**. It involves an initial examination of the data for core themes, the identification of patterns of language and an analysis of how the language used may affect particular groups in society. The first step to take when analysing the data is to consider the themes found within the data, and this can be seen by undertaking some initial coding for ideas that are prominent in the data. Second, we dig deeper and consider the language, hidden **meanings** and 'calls for action'. Overall, this will allow us to draw inferences about what the **authors** thought about the people they were writing about and make more general conclusions about power relations within that society. These steps are summarised in Box 4.2.

BOX 4.2 PROCEDURE TO UNDERTAKE CRITICAL DISCOURSE ANALYSIS

1 Identify the overarching themes from the documents. In order to do this, familiarise yourself with the data and undertake some initial **inductive** coding.
2 Review the data and coding to consider power. In particular, consider words that have associated meanings and if any one individual is asking for an individual or group to change their behaviour in any way.
3 Draw conclusions about the power relations.

Welfare reform case study: data analysis

Consideration of historical data sources prior to analysis

I undertook a period of pre-analysis consideration of the data. In doing so, it became apparent that it was very difficult to read the original (handwritten) text compared to contemporary handwritten documents. This issue has been highlighted as problematic in historical research (Scott 1990). This led to my using the summaries provided by the **archivist** to provide overarching accounts that helped me make sense of the handwritten text. Although these were very helpful in understanding these challenging documents, this will have influenced my perception of events and should be noted as a source of **bias**.

More generally, it could be seen that the documents comprised a log of poor relief given, or a summary of relief provided over a particular period of time. They were **authored** by those administering the poor law, and thus the **authors** were experts in the matter. We can surmise from the **authorship** and intended audience that practices that went against the actual rules or spirit of the poor law may not have been included, both those more lenient and more harsh.

Identifying overarching themes

Both sets of data were **inductively** coded for core themes. The themes and sub-themes identified within historical documents included:

- Pragmatic issues relating to the running of workhouses
- Condition of buildings
- Number of people claiming poor relief
- Finances
- Deservingness of claimants
- Particular groups who were seen as undeserving
- Cost of poor relief
- Ways of ensuring poor relief was not abused (monitoring and sanctions)
- Conditions imposed on those claiming (workfare)

A range of themes was found within the contemporary **official documents**, which were not always similar to those found in the historical documents. This may have been because of the varying natures of the two data sources, as a transcript of a parliamentary debate allowed for a critique of the ruling party to be included. For examples of the themes, definitions and examples of data in the contemporary **official documents**, see Table 4.1.

Consideration of power relations and language

Within the historical documents, it was possible to understand some of the ways in which power operated in the workhouse system. One of the most obvious ways in which power is felt throughout the data set is that a culture of suspicion between local workers, known as poor law guardians, and more senior officials appeared normal. Accounts and reports were, of course, intended to be reviewed by those who were more senior in the organisation, but this routinely resulted in the finding of wrongdoing at a local level. For example, in DIN 4, a possible instance of fraud by the local magistrate was identified, and suspicion appeared to grow because of inadequate record-keeping in another area. Alongside this, in DIN 7, a local board of guardians agreed to supplement low wages, which was not allowed in the national policy; this is considered to be an "abuse" of the system. By contrast, DIN 39 is reasonably banal and provides a small amount of information regarding who paid rent for the workhouse. The fact that this record was made and kept highlights the surveillance culture within the administration of the poor law, where each small change was documented in writing.

Another way in which the unequal power relations can be seen in the data is between the workers and residents, or "inmates" as they were referred to, of the workhouse. There was little evidence of emotive or sympathetic language in content relating to inmates. For example, those accepting poor relief are often referred to as "vagrants" or "inmates" (DIN 3). Others are referred to as "drunk"

TABLE 4.1 Themes in parliamentary debate on Welfare Reform and Work Bill 2015

Theme	Definition	Example
Political sparring	Blaming the other political party for social problems	"I do not have that number [of children affected by welfare cuts]to give the hon. Lady. However, her party is also committed to making large welfare savings. It is very easy to support the theory, but if Labour Members oppose all the large measures that are taken in practice, they are not going anywhere. They have to answer this question. If they are committed to large savings, but they do not support all these measures, which measures would they like to see? That is the challenge" (Nigel Mills, Conservative)
Welfare reform as good	Welfare reform will encourage those who can work to do so	"…work is the best route out of poverty, and being in work should always pay more than being on benefits" (Iain Duncan Smith, Conservative)
Welfare reform as protecting those in need	Those who cannot work will be supported by the state	"while protecting the most vulnerable" (Iain Duncan Smith, Conservative)
Welfare reform as bad	Welfare reform will have negative consequences. Many of these included poverty	"…when he drew up proposals for this Bill, did he look at the levels of child poverty in Britain? Did he look at the levels of homelessness, destitution and rough sleeping in Britain? How does he think this Bill is going to improve that situation? Alternatively, will it make the holes in the welfare state safety net rather bigger, with more people falling through it as a result?" (Jeremy Corbyn, Labour)
Affordability of welfare	Current welfare as unaffordable due to Government debt and borrowing	"We will also continue to bear down on the deficit and debt, achieving a surplus by the end of the Parliament. We are spending £3 billion on debt interest payments alone every month—the figure is £33 billion a year, which is £1,236 per household. Every pound we spend on paying off the debt is a pound we are paying to others such as overseas investment funds, rather than on the necessary public services such as schools and hospitals or on being able to reduce taxation further" (Iain Duncan Smith, Conservative)

(DIN 6). Children are referred to as "mischievous" due to the architecture of one workhouse (DIN 7) and "unruly" in another document (DIN 13). Pregnancy was also often discussed in terms of deservingness, in DIN 50, one of the people requiring poor relief is described: "pauper inmate (first name, surname) of (town), recently delivered an illegitimate child in the workhouse…". Likewise, in DIN 10, a claimant is described as having her poor relief taken away, because she is "pregnant despite being a widow". Her child is later referred to as a "bastard child", a judgemental term for children born outside of marriage used in the 1800s. Mothering and instilling "good character" to children is also described in DIN 13, so that the children's "poor characters... (did not make) them unemployable (and) a permanent burden".

Occasionally, throughout the documents it can be seen that power relations are being questioned or disrupted. In DIN 52, reference is made to previous correspondence, between a local officer and national official, noting that applicants for support are only being given a small amount of support if they are able bodied, and then asked to move to another area to seek work. In this document, however, the national official distanced themselves from this unfair treatment for the poor, and noted that record-keeping had been inadequate in that workhouse. This may be viewed as a suggestion that, should a further complaint be made, the record-keeping of the workhouse could be looked at in more detail in the future.

When presenting findings from **discourse analysis**, written prose can be provided (as above), or a table can be used to provide examples, as shown below in relation to the contemporary documents. In the contemporary **official documents**, we can also detect power relations through the language used. Table 4.2 shows that the words used, tone of delivery and implied **meanings** were displays of power. Alongside this, a range of descriptors was used in relation to potential claimants.

Findings (drawing inferences)

One of the most striking concepts in the historical documents was the way in which organisations that were supposed to support people in need of urgent financial support were run. In the data, it was possible to see distrust and suspicion between local delivery agents and the central organisation, and some instances of local staff ignoring central policy. Likewise, in relation to the contemporary **official documents**, we can see how ongoing challenges between the two major political parties are played out through this important subject. In both sets of documents, concern towards the wellbeing of the individuals who will need to claim poor relief does not appear at the fore.

It can also be seen that concepts of deservingness were present in both sets of data; in the historical documents, this was related to whether people were able to work, and the concepts of having a child outside of marriage was also highlighted as an issue. In the contemporary official document, having a child outside of marriage was, on the face of it, no longer a major topic of concern, although references were made to previous periods in recent history where single parents were demonised. Discourses relating to "responsibilities" to go alongside financial support were regularly included in discussion in the contemporary documents, although these can also be seen within the historical documents, where potential claimants were asked to move to the workhouse to demonstrate their genuine need.

TABLE 4.2 Language and power in parliamentary debate on Welfare Reform and Work
Bill 2015

Displays of power	*Example*
Formal language used	"I am grateful to the hon. Lady for her point of order. If a mistake has been made by the Vote Office, I am quite sure that Mr Speaker will be annoyed on behalf of the House by that mistake (Eleanor Laing, Conservative)
Confident tone of delivery	"It is clear that the Bill will push more children, families and vulnerable people across Scotland and the UK deeper into poverty. Rebranding child poverty plans as "life chances measures", and completely removing any legal obligation to meet those targets, only proves how badly this Government are failing our society on welfare" (Hannah Bardell, Scottish National Party)
Unpleasant or menacing tone	(in response to a question about changing level of benefits from Emily Thornberry) "…as hon. Lady will know if she uses her intelligence—" (Iain Duncan Smith, Conservative)
Using statistics to back up a point	"Child Poverty Action Group figures indicate that 21% of the children in my constituency grow up in poverty. As a result of the benefit freeze, a couple with two children earning £400 per week will be £34.20 worse off each week. Does the Secretary of State agree that the Bill punishes families on low pay?" (Angela Crawley, Scottish National Party)
Descriptors for those who do not claim welfare	"hard-working families" (Iain Duncan Smith, Conservative); "in-work families, who are struggling in low-paid jobs to do their very best for their children" (Helen Goodman, Labour)
Descriptors for those who claim welfare and policy solutions	"people who have health difficulties and who are capable of taking steps into work" (Iain Duncan Smith, Conservative); "troubled families" (Stephen Timms, Labour)
In the best interests of claimants to receive less	"The Bill will help people to achieve their ambitions" (Iain Duncan Smith, Conservative) "We stand for the right to work and the responsibility to work" (Stephen Timms, Labour)
Not in the best interests of claimants to receive less	"…there are some 8,000 people […] with Parkinson's and other progressive diseases who are not going to get better but who, under his proposals, will lose £30 a week. How can he defend that?" (Stephen Timms, Labour)

Discussion

By considering how financial assistance for those in poverty was described
within the context of these historical documents and the contemporary official documents, **CDA** allows us to consider how poverty and societal inequality
were viewed at two points in time. Returning to McDowell's (2002) and Prior's
(2003) concepts surrounding the purposes of documents, we can see that both

sets of documents were clearly created as part of official business. It is also important to note that these findings are based on a small selection of the available documents to understand both the experience of the poor law in the 1830s and modern-day welfare reform, and the use of a larger or alternative data set may have uncovered different discourses.

Challenges in undertaking research with historical and official documents

In undertaking research with historical documents, access and **representativeness** are often a major challenge. This is different in relation to contemporary **official documents**, as many of these are now freely available in the public domain. Within England and Wales, documents that are not available in the public domain may be accessed through a Freedom of Information request (based on the Freedom of Information Act 2000).

When undertaking analysis, each particular type of historical documents will have its own peculiarities and challenges. If you are undertaking research using historical documents, I recommend consulting an edited collection by Miriam Dobson and Benjamin Ziemann (2009), which contains chapters on undertaking analysis of letters, court files, autobiography and speeches among other topics. By contrast, analysis of contemporary **official documents** is rather more straightforward. One area to consider is where pictorial or graphical information is presented alongside text. This was not the case in the documents in this study. However, if graphical information is presented, this should be included in analysis to understand how this changes discourses. An example is provided by Ball (2011) in relation to company accounting reports.

Exercise: using CDA

The analysis above utilised historical and **official documents** to contextualise views and policies relating to benefit payments to those living in poverty across two periods in time. There are, as always, multiple data sources that could have been accessed to consider this topic. Below, fictitious responses to the proposed change to welfare legislation in the Welfare Reform and Work Bill 2015 are provided.

Instructions

Using the three data sources provided below, undertake a **CDA** to answer the following **research question**:

What discourses are presented about poverty and government support to remove people from poverty?

I suggest that you consult Box 4.2 for guidance on how to conduct **CDA**. You will also benefit from reading at least one of Fairclough and Wodak (1997) or van Dijk (2001). You may wish to photocopy the data to facilitate your analysis.

Data

Source 1

Written evidence 63: A long-term sick service user

I am a mother, aged 39, with two children, aged 4 and 7. I attended (name) University and graduated with an honours degree. After this, I worked for my local council. I have suffered from rheumatoid arthritis since the age of 19, causing debilitating pain. In 2006, my health problems became so severe I needed to leave work. Following this, my house was repossessed, and I was homeless for a time until I was placed into bed-and-breakfast accommodation for 4 months with no means to cook food – only a kettle. I was not able to give my children a proper diet, as we were expected to eat all of our meals outside of the B&B. Eventually my local housing association found me a one bedroom flat that I live in with my two children.

I have been reliant on benefits since I had to leave work in 2006, and I have very little in the way of support, financial or otherwise. Last year, for reasons I do not understand, all of my benefits apart from child benefit [a benefit given to the mother or father of all children aged under 16 in the UK] and housing benefit [a benefit to pay the housing costs for those on a low income] were cut off. I found it difficult to speak to officials about this, as the phone line was always busy and I received conflicting advice on what to do when I eventually got through to someone on the phone line. I was fortunate to receive donations of food from my local food bank at this time, and I do not know how I would have fed my children without these.

After my benefits were cut off, I received a letter saying that I no longer qualified for Employment and Support Allowance (ESA) [a benefit in the UK given to people who are long-term sick or disabled]. I do not know why this decision was made, as I had not recently had a medical examination. I spoke to my local Citizens Advice Bureaux, who told me to immediately appeal the decision. In order to appeal, I had to travel to (big city), a two-hour drive away for an assessment. The examination was very superficial, taking far less than five minutes, and not including any examination of my body or discussion of my condition. After this, I received another letter saying that I was not eligible for ESA.

Over the last year, the children and I have had to live on £100 a week child benefit. I am in arrears with water and electricity, so often cannot heat the flat. For food, I am forced to beg and rely on handouts I receive from the food bank, family and neighbours. The Citizens Advice Bureaux are helping me to appeal the appeal decision.

The way I have been treated is nothing short of the government playing with my life. That we are a rich country but mothers have to beg for food for their young children is a disgrace. Your proposed Bill will introduce more hardship and cut funding further. I hope that my story can make you understand that further cuts are not the answer.

Source 2

Written evidence 84: anti-poverty charity

In our remit to support those in poverty, and to act as their advocates, we strongly oppose this bill. We feel that the Bill is aiming to make further cuts to the incomes of some of the poorest in our society.

We wish to remind the government of the structural causes of poverty, which seem to be absent from the thinking around this bill.

In the UK, individuals who are most likely to become homeless are those from poorer backgrounds. It is untrue that homelessness affects the middle (and upper) classes to the same extent, or in the same way. Several groups are at the highest risk for becoming homeless: those who have served their country in the armed forces, care leavers, those who face addiction. Young unemployed mothers are also at risk.

The common factor among these groups is poverty. Cuts to benefits lead to poverty. Poverty leads to homelessness.

The proposed Bill will increase the number of sanctions that those who are on benefits (through no fault of their own) face. Cuts to benefit levels at a time when inflation is at its highest for decades can only possibly lead to more poverty.

Alongside this general poor bashing, we are particularly concerned that the Bill suggests removing the requirement for the UK governments to reduce child poverty. Accordingly, not only are you making life impossible for adults who are in poverty, but you are also condemning their children to a life of worse health and lower educational success. This will in turn affect their likelihood of success in the work place, which would be their path out of poverty.

Source 3

Written evidence 90: A local business owner

I am extremely concerned about your proposed Bill. The vast majority of people that you call scroungers are genuinely seeking work, or the only work available to them is so badly paid that they could not afford to take it.

Over the years, in my role as a small business owner, I have been able to provide support to the staff in my business during times of Income Support [a type of benefit in the UK for people who work] delays and errors. Several of my ex-employees have left work over the past few decades on the grounds of worsening disability. We maintain solid friendships. They have told me that they are not able to see a member of staff in person in the Job Centre to talk about their case, and sometimes they cannot talk to a person on the telephone, but instead they have to go to the library to use a computer (because they do not have enough money to purchase their own) and fill in a complaint form. Computer time is limited in (town) library because there is such heavy demand, and it can be frustrating for those who struggle to use a computer, especially if they are unable to complete the work they need to do to appease the Department for Work and Pensions within their allotted 45 minutes.

I have read reputable evidence (attached) that the sanctions system in the UK is the worst in Europe, and that less than 1% of claims are fraudulent. If the government acknowledges that this is the case, I do not understand why you continue to punish those who have been unfortunate enough to be born into working-class families. Also, there can be no justification for increasing penalties and cutting the incomes of some of the poorest members of our society. This Bill cannot be allowed to pass in good conscience.

References

Ball, M. 2011. Images, language and numbers in company reports: a study of documents that are occasioned by a legal requirement for financial disclosure. *Qualitative Research*: 11(2), pp. 115–139.

Best, J. 2001. *Damned lies and statistics: untangling numbers from the media, politicians, and activists*. Oakland, CA: University of California Press.

Black, I. 2010. Analysing historical and archival sources. In: Clifford, N. et al. eds. *Key Methods in Geography*. London: Sage, pp. 466–484.

Bowers, L. et al. 2000. Suicide and self-harm in inpatient psychiatric units: a national survey of observation policies. *Journal of Advanced Nursing*: 32(2), pp. 437–444.

Brayshaw, E. 2018. Remembering Roland Leighton: uniforms as the materials of memory and mourning in World War I. In: Newby, Z. and Toulson, R. eds. *The materiality of mourning: cross-disciplinary perspectives*. Abingdon: Routledge.

Bromberg, K.D. and Bertness, M.D. 2005. Reconstructing New England salt marsh losses using historical maps. *Estuaries*: 28(6), pp. 823–832.

Brundage, A. 2018. *Going to the sources : a guide to historical research and writing*. London: John Wiley & Sons.

Cheung, K.K. et al. 2010. Health policy analysis: a tool to evaluate in policy documents the alignment between policy statements and intended outcomes. *Australian Health Review*: 34(4), p. 405.

Codd, J.A. 1988. The construction and deconstruction of educational policy documents. *Journal of Education Policy*: 3(3), pp. 235–247.

van Dijk, T.A. 2001. Critical discourse analysis. In: Schiffrin, D. et al. eds. *The handbook of discourse analysis*. Oxford: Blackwell, pp. 352–371.

Dobson, M. and Ziemann, B. 2009. *Reading primary sources: the interpretation of texts from nineteenth- and twentieth-century history*. Abingdon: Routledge.

Fairclough, N. and Wodak, R. 1997. Critical discourse analysis. In: van Dijik, T. A. ed. *Discourses as social interaction*. London: Sage, pp. 258–284.

Fraser, D. 2009. *The evolution of the British welfare state: a history of social policy since the industrial revolution.* London: Palgrave Macmillan.

Gelman, A. et al. 2007. An analysis of the New York city police department's 'Stop-and-Frisk' policy in the context of claims of racial bias. *Journal of the American Statistical Association*: 102(479), pp. 813–823.

Gill, R. 2006. Discourse analysis. In: Scott, J. ed. *Documentary research*. London: Sage, pp. 209–232.

Gottschalk, L. 2006. The historian and the historical documents. In: *Documentary research*. London: Sage, pp. 43–82.

Grant, A. 2013. Welfare reform, increased conditionality and discretion: Jobcentre Plus advisers' experiences of targets and sanctions. *Journal of Poverty and Social Justice*: 21(2), pp. 165–176.

Gregory, I.N. and Healey, R.G. 2007. Historical GIS: structuring, mapping and analysing geographies of the past. *Progress in Human Geography*: 31(5), pp. 638–653.

Haase, D. et al. 2007. Changes to central European landscapes – analysing historical maps to approach current environmental issues, examples from Saxony, Central Germany. *Land Use Policy*: 24(1), pp. 248–263.

Hendrick, H. 2000. The child as a social actor in historical sources: problems of identification and interpretation. In: Monrad Christensen, P. and James, A. eds. *Research with children: perspectives and practices*. London: Falmer Press, p. 272.

Hill, H. 1984. Race and ethnicity in organized labor: the historical sources of resistance to Affirmative Action. *Journal of Intergroup Relations*: 12(4), pp. 5–50.

Howell, M.C. and Prevenier, W. 2001. *From reliable sources: an introduction to historical methods*. Cornell: Cornell University Press.

Iverson, S.V. 2007. Camouflaging power and privilege: a critical race analysis of university diversity policies. *Educational Administration Quarterly*: 43(5), pp. 586–611.

Joukamaa, M. 1997. Prison suicide in Finland, 1969–1992. *Forensic Science International*: 89(3), pp. 167–174.

Macdonald, K. 2008. Using documents. In: Gilbert, N. ed. *Researching social life*. 3rd ed. London: Sage, pp. 285–303.

McDowell, W.H. 2002. *Historical research: a guide*. London: Routledge.

Mitchell, T.J. and Smith, G.M. 1931. *Medical services: casualties and medical statistics of the Great War*. London: HMSO.

Oxley, G.W. 1974. *Poor relief in England and Wales 1601–1834*. London: David & Charles.

Pager, C. 2004. Lies, damned lies, statistics and racial profiling. *The Kansas Journal of Law & Public Policy*: 13, pp. 515–619.

Prior, L. 2003. *Using documents in social research*. London: Sage.

Scott, J. 1990. *A matter of record: documentary sources in social research*. London: John Wiley & Sons.

Shaw, S.E. and Bailey, J. 2009. Discourse analysis: what is it and why is it relevant to family practice? *Family Practice*: 26(5), pp. 413–9.

Shiner, M. et al. 2009. When things fall apart: gender and suicide across the life-course. *Social Science and Medicine*: 69(5), pp. 738–746.

5

DOCUMENTS CREATED
BY INDIVIDUALS

Collection and analysis of multi-modal content

Summary

This chapter focuses on research using individually created documents, such as letters, diaries and their online equivalents. Individually created documents can offer insights into everyday lives that would be hard to obtain using other methods. However, it can be difficult to obtain representative **samples** of documents. The detailed case study within this chapter aimed to understand how a type of smoking was portrayed on social media. Data was collected from Twitter in relation to waterpipe (also known as shisha, hookah and hubble-bubble) smoking. Both tweets (a form of micro**blog**) and accompanying photos were collected and analysed. The process of generating a **research question**, pilot data collection and the actual data collection using Twitter's **Application Programming Interface (API)** is described. The data was analysed using a simple **semiotic analysis**, to understand whether tweets were positive, negative or neutral. This was supplemented with an **inductive thematic analysis** of the content of each tweet to understand the key things people were discussing alongside waterpipe smoking. Furthermore, a **content analysis** was undertaken of a sub-sample of images that were attached via URL to tweets. The findings of the **semiotic analysis** of textual content were validated through analysis of the images, showing a high level of similarity. The chapter will also explore the particular challenges of using individually created documents as data and, in particular, examines ethical issues. Additional data is provided to enable readers to practise **semiotic analysis** of tweets.

Key learning points

- How letters, diaries and social media have been used to understand everyday life
- How to design a research project using everyday individually created documents
- How to analyse multi-modal documents, that is, documents that contain both text and images
- How to use multiple analysis strategies within a project
- What ethical issues should be considered in the analysis of individually created documents

Background: individually created documents, understanding meaning and research

Individually created documents are those written by a single person without being edited by anybody else. There may or may not be an expectation that the document will be read by somebody other than the writer. Historians have used individually created documents as a staple source of data for hundreds of years. However, they have often been neglected by qualitative social scientists in favour of interviews and observations. This is unfortunate, as individually created documents can provide insight into phenomena that it would not be possible to explore through other qualitative methods. Until relatively recently, individually created documents would have been written on paper, but in today's society, electronic media, such as emails, **blogs** and social media content, should also be considered. Below, I consider the literature on individually created documents in relation to offline or paper documents, and online, electronic documents. Unlike in other chapters, matters of quality and **bias** are dealt with for each type of data (letters, diaries, social media), as considerable variation occurs between sources.

Offline documents, research, quality and bias

Within anthropology and history, there is a tradition of using autobiographical accounts and other individually created documents as data. In this section, I critically describe the use of letters, diaries and other offline documents in social research.

Letters, research, quality and bias

Letters can help us return to earlier points in history. For example, in *Dear Mark Twain* (Ramussen 2013), the **reader** is transported to the nineteenth century, gaining an understanding of the way that those who wrote to Mark Twain, a novelist, experienced his work and also their everyday lives, including the aspirations of would-be novelists. If you are interested in research using letters, the original letters to Twain are available in a six volume series, providing researchers and historians with valuable insights into daily life the Victorian era. As well as societal norms, letters may also shed light on relationships between the **author** and intended **reader**. For example, in Roper's research on letters from soldiers to their families during the First World War, insights are gathered into the relationships between the men and their families, but also into gender roles during this period in time (Roper 2006).

Analysis of letters need not be restricted to historical periods. Letters are written for a variety of purposes, including in order to attempt to influence policy through letters to the **editor** of newspapers (Smith et al. 2005). In health services research, letters written to medical doctors prior to an appointment have been analysed to understand patients' experiences of pain (Perrot et al. 2017). In less serious matters, analysis of consumer interaction of various types continues, including a study of fan mail sent to radio programmes (Katz 2012). Like the letters to Mark Twain, much of the content is illustrative of the **author**'s wider life and does not exclusively, or sometimes at all, focus on the link to the radio show.

The use of letters as a way of expressing feelings on topics can also be used as a researcher-elicited method, and **elicitation interviews** will be covered in more detail in Chapter 8. One example, which provided a rich understanding of the interaction between private family life and organised religion, was where researchers asked religious gay men and their religious families and friends to write letters to religious leaders as part of an **action research** study (Etengoff 2017). In doing so, Etengoff notes that they were able to understand activities and interactions between the families in the study and religious practices.

Alongside these individually created letters, it is relevant to note that letters are not always individually created. For example, most **readers** of this book will have received a letter from a company that provides services such as electricity or water to us. Such letters are still useful to analyse in order to understand how corporations communicate with the public. In one study into letters from German utility companies, it was found that companies sought to hide price increases from consumers (Pick and Zielke 2015). Moreover, education services often send letters to parents regarding their children. A focus group study was undertaken with parents who were **readers** of letters sent to them about their children's weight. It found that the letters were not always understood and could negatively affect parents' self-esteem (Moyer et al. 2014).

Diaries, research, quality and bias

Diaries and other autobiographical texts that have made it into the public arena can also shed an interesting light on social life. However, we must consider that those which become available for analysis, and even more so those that become edited for publication, are rarely a representative **sample**. One excellent collection, analysed and disseminated by Alexander Masters, is based on a series of 148 diaries, spanning 50 years, found by chance in a skip[1] (Masters 2016). Within the text, Masters includes extracts of original data whilst weaving a narrative of the **author's** life. Of interest is the way that Masters' understanding of the **author's** views and opinions changes over the years, showing that even with such a detailed data source from one individual, understanding **meaning** is never straightforward. Other diaries that have provided insightful context into periods of historical social life include *Anne Frank: The Diary of a Young Girl* (Frank and Pressler 2011). The diary was based on the experiences of a Dutch young woman in hiding during Nazi occupation of the Netherlands. In a very different realm, a text based on the diaries of Martha Ballard, a seventeenth-century midwife, has been sympathetically narrated during translation to paperback (Ulrich 1991). Finally, Andy Alaszewski has undertaken research on suffering in people who have experienced a stroke through their diaries (Alaszewski 2006a), giving voice to a group of people who may literally find it challenging to be heard.

Whilst traditional pen and paper diaries may be a favourite with historians and social researchers, they have been subjected to criticism; that entries may be infrequent or irregularly spaced and written sometime after key events have occurred, allowing time for a memory lapse. Questions of the **authenticity** of the **author** are often raised when diaries have been edited prior to publication by the original **author** or another individual has edited text (Melnick 1997). That is not to say, however, that diaries are inherently presenting events and feelings as experienced by the **author**: those who are writing with the expectation that their writing may have an audience other than themselves may distort events (Scott 1990). A preferred self may also be reported, regardless of if the **author** believes the material will be viewed by others (Goffman 1959). If you are intending to use diaries in your own research, I suggest that you read Andy Alaszewski's guide (Alaszewski 2006b), which provides a detailed account of the research process.

Diaries, like letters, may be kept at the request of a researcher on a particular topic (Thomson and Holland 2005). This document **elicitation** approach is covered in more detail in Chapter 8. One example of a study into researcher-directed diaries comes from Christine Milligan and colleagues' studies into communal gardening as an activity to promote health and wellbeing in older people. In one study, participants were asked to complete diaries over a relatively long period of time and showed good compliance (Milligan et al. 2005). The diaries highlighted a sense of achievement from gardening but also the physical challenges in undertaking gardening for older people (Milligan et al. 2004). The researchers noted that a reasonably high rate of support was provided to participants to enable completion of research diaries, showing that if you use diaries as a data collection method, consideration should be given to providing adequate support to participants. Likewise, it may be of most benefit to make diaries available both in hard copy and online; for example, in Jones and Wooley's (2015) study into experiences of public transport, daily emails were sent by the researchers to the participants. Online diaries may also benefit from links to other forms of technology, such as providing biofeedback where assessments are being made of health or wellbeing (Bolger et al. 2003).

Other individually created offline documents

Often we think of offline documents as exclusively containing formal items like diaries and letters; however, other less formal documents may also provide an interesting view into the life of the **author** and intended **reader**. One interesting use of everyday notes is from Jason Wilde, an artist who gathers everyday materials and uses them in installations. In *Vera & John*, Wilde (2017) shows the mundane details of family life. The documents are brief notes written on the back of envelopes by Vera (Wilde's mother), mostly to John (Wilde's father). Vera provides instructions to John, mostly regarding what will be served for dinner, but in doing so, provides an insight into both domestic and leisure activities within Vera and John's marriage. In an interview, Wilde noted that his mother was not aware that he was collecting these documents, and therefore her expectation of who the audience would be would likely have only included immediate family members (Rhodes 2017). Within his **archive**, Wilde presents the documents but does not provide a commentary for each document or a summary of what these documents tell us. **Readers** may wish to view the **archive** themselves (www.jasonwilde.com) to consider what the notes tell us about the relationship between Vera and John. Another interesting example of informal individually created documents is the use of Post-it® notes, which are frequently used to record reminders, but also to provide feedback in seminars and events. Research has been undertaken into their use as feedback at an American museum, in order to create a collective memory of events (Maurantonio 2015).

Online documents, research, quality and bias

When we think of 'documentary analysis', we often tend to think of hard copies, however online documents are providing a new and rich source of data for social scientists. This section starts with a discussion of the range of sources available, before focusing on social media and the Mass Observation Archive, which can be seen as a precursor to social media in the twenty-first century.

The breadth of online sources

In recent decades, we increasingly spend time at a computer, tablet or smart phone. Originally the Internet was created for the average user to consume information, but we are now able to create and share content that we have created via **blogs** and posts on social media and forums. At the time of writing, social media was the most popular way of the average person sharing online content, with Facebook having the most registered users (Statista 2017). Newer social media platforms emerge frequently, and this provides a broad spectrum of opportunities for individuals who wish to document their lives online. This expansion of freely available online content provides rich opportunities for researchers to access large volumes of data, including on sensitive topics that can be hard to study using traditional qualitative methods. This research, known as 'data mining', has been encouraged by funders, such as the UK Research Councils (Economic and Social Research Council 2013). In considering **meaning**, it is important to understand that what we are viewing is very much influenced by the **authors'** consideration of their likely audience, which will impact on presentations of the self (Scott 1990; Christopherson 2007; Hogan 2010; Dicks 2012). Moreover, there are ethical implications in using online content, including the use of data from closed groups, whether consent should be taken, maintaining participant anonymity and safe dissemination (Mann and Stewart 2000; Markham and Buchanan 2012; Woodman et al. 2016).

Social media and forums: research, quality and bias

Social media provides valuable opportunities to understand a range of phenomena. Within my own research, I have used online data to understand the way in which a protest regarding mothers' rights to breastfeed in public (as protected by law in the UK and many other countries) was covered in two online sources: Twitter and online news comments (Grant 2015; Grant 2016). Other social researchers focusing on matters relating to equality have also used individually created data from online sources to describe contemporary society. In her article on disgust directed towards working-class white parents, Imogen Tyler used Urban Dictionary as data (Tyler 2008). Alongside this, Kate Boyer's work on parenting includes a range of sources within one study, including comments from an online parenting forum (Mumsnet) alongside interviews and survey responses (Boyer 2012). Other applications which have utilised social media have included understanding of violence and disorder, including the London Riots of 2011, described in more detail in Chapter 3, (Bennett 2012), terrorist attacks (Burnap et al. 2014), and racism within football (Cleland 2014). Furthermore, George Jennings has used analysis of Facebook and YouTube videos to understand the application of traditional martial arts philosophy in the modern day (Jennings 2016).

As the case study within this chapter uses data from social media, Scott's (1990) criteria will be considered more fully than for other individually created documents. If you are using an alternative data source, I recommend you critically consider it in relation to the criteria in Table 2.1. In considering Scott's (1990) four criteria, we can see that the considerations with social media are different to many other sources. First, thinking of **authenticity**, whilst we know that the data is an original document, we may not always be able to ascertain who the **author** was, and it is challenging to identify demographic characteristics from social media posters (Sloan et al. 2013). Second, in relation to **credibility**, it is not possible to know whether posters are reporting an accurate narrative or they are sincere; for example, sarcasm may be particularly difficult to understand in short posts. Third, focusing on **representativeness**, we may not always be able to access all data, due to privacy settings and deleted posts, and in relation to some platforms, researchers may not be able to access all of the data on particular topics (in relation to Twitter, see for example: González-Bailón et al. 2014). Finally, there are obvious limitations in relation to **meaning**; abbreviations and **emojis** may be hard to accurately interpret without knowledge of a person's writing style, and where posts are brief it may be hard to understand the full context.

Public archives, research, quality and bias

Public **archives** of everyday experiences provide a valuable source of data for researchers on a broad range of topics. The most well known of these is the Mass Observation Archive, hosted at the University of Sussex, which contains detailed accounts of everyday social life in Britain collected during the 1930s–1950s and again since 1981 (The Mass Observation Archive 2017). Members of the public are asked to detail their experiences in the form of a questionnaire, with several different topics each year. These are publically available, as long as users abide by the modest restrictions imposed by the **archive**. In recent years, the topics for data collection have been diverse, including the British referendum regarding European Union membership, poverty, dementia and working families' lives. Whilst writers may be constrained by the Mass Observation methodology (Hurdley 2014) and the data are not from a representative **sample** of the British public (Sheridan 1993), the insights into British life are of considerable interest. Academic writing linked to the project has been diverse, including writing on working-class female sexuality in the 1930s (Gurney 1997), on social class identities in the period after the Second World War (Savage 2007) and a 21-chapter book on leisure in the 1930s, ranging from holidays to daily routines and sex (Cross 1990).

Shisha and social media case study

In this empirical case study, the process of undertaking a research project using data from Twitter is described in a step-by-step fashion. First, I provide background information on waterpipe (shisha) smoking. I then describe the development of a **research question** and the data collection methods, resulting in a **sample** of almost 10,000 tweets. The data was analysed using semiotic, thematic and **content analysis**, and the use of multiple analysis strategies is discussed. Details on how to do **semiotic analysis** are provided. I then provide examples of how the analysis was undertaken, highlighting relevant data extracts alongside findings. Finally, particular challenges of using social media as data is described. At the end of the chapter, I provide additional data so that you can practise **semiotic analysis**.

Context

Waterpipes (also commonly known as shisha, hookah, hubble-bubble and a range of other names) are an object through which to smoke tobacco, where the smoke passes through water (or some other liquid) prior to inhalation through a hose. They are often attractive looking pieces of apparatus, and in recent years the rate of young people smoking waterpipes has increased considerably (Primack et al. 2013). Those who smoke waterpipes believe that they are less harmful than cigarettes (Akl et al. 2013). This is not accurate, as users experience similarly raised rates of lung cancer and other respiratory diseases (Waziry et al. 2016). Furthermore, in contrast to cigarette smokers, who often express a desire to quit smoking in the future, waterpipe smoking is generally portrayed positively in interview and questionnaire studies (Hammal et al. 2008; Sharma et al. 2014). This is worrying for health, as positive views of waterpipe smoking are associated with continued use (Barnett et al. 2013).

Research design

As the use of social media has increased, I felt that it would be interesting to see how waterpipe smoking was portrayed on social media. Users often post content about their activities with a positive, idealistic view of themselves and their activities (Manago et al. 2008). That said, there are variations by platform and social group, hinting that Twitter may result in a more nuanced self-presentation (Frederick and Clavio 2015). Due to a lack of access to posts on Facebook and its large user base, Twitter was chosen as the most suitable platform for data collection. The full findings of this research project are published in the journal *Public Health* (Grant and O'Mahoney 2016). The research aim, piloting and data collection are described below.

Initial Research aim

To understand how waterpipe tobacco smoking is portrayed on Twitter.

Refining the research question and piloting

In order to understand the global phenomenon in question, we sought a large and diverse **sample** of tweets. The term 'waterpipe' is used academically, but a large range of names are used to describe waterpipe smoking apparatus and behaviour internationally. For this reason, I spoke with colleagues in public health organisations in order to select eight keywords to be searched for on Twitter:

- 'Hookah'
- 'Shisha'
- 'Sheesha'
- 'Nargile'

- 'Narghile'
- 'Waterpipe'
- 'Hubblebubble'
- 'Arghila'

Pilot data collection suggested that at least 1,000 tweets would be collected per day using these keywords. As data was already restricted to a 1% **sample** of all tweets by the **API**, I felt that it would be desirable to collect all available data within a period of time, so as not to further dilute our **sample** in relation to the population of all tweets. In order to ensure that we had sufficient time to conduct a thorough analysis of the data, I restricted data collection to a 1-week period, estimating that we would collect between 7,000 and 10,000 tweets. I felt that this volume would allow us to understand a broad range of experiences. If a more narrow issue is under study, as in my study of breastfeeding in public, where around 1,000 tweets were considered (Grant 2015), a smaller amount of tweets would enable the main themes to arise (O'Reilly and Parker 2013). Analysis of 10,000 tweets is beyond the scope of most undergraduate projects if a detailed qualitative analysis is to be undertaken, and a **sample** of around 1,000–2,000 tweets feels suitable to me, although the amount of time taken will vary depending on the analysis strategy adopted.

The final research aim was:

To understand how waterpipe tobacco smoking was portrayed on Twitter using **semiotic** and **thematic analysis** of text and **content analysis** of a **sample** of associated images during a 1-week period.

Data collection

There are a range of platforms available which allow tweets to be collected directly from Twitter using the **API**; some allow the user to collect data directly, whilst others require a payment of a fee and deliver a database to you at the end of the data collection period. Often researchers are able to access a 1% **sample** of all tweets relating to their keywords, although there is evidence that the **sample** obtained using API may be slightly unrepresentative of all tweets (González-Bailón et al. 2014). At the time of the research, the best available platform was the Twitter Archiving Google Spreadsheet (TAGS) v5.1 (Hawksey 2014); this has subsequently been updated to version 6 and is likely to be further updated. Subsequently, the Collaborative Online Social Media Observatory (COSMOS) platform at Cardiff University has been made available to all academic users for data collection, although at the time of writing, it was not recommended for those using Windows. The analysis of social media is a fast growing area of academic work, and thus **readers** who are considering the analysis of social media and other online sources in their own data should consult colleagues working in the area and the Association of Internet Researchers (www.aoir.org) for guidance on the best data collection techniques.

Data management

In total, using the TAGS v5.1 data collection method, 9,671 tweets were collected. These were provided in a series of eight spreadsheets relating to each of the search terms. They were downloaded and converted into Microsoft Excel documents. Over half of all tweets contained the keyword 'hookah' (58%, $n = 5648$) and a further 31% contained 'shisha', accounting for almost 90% of data collected. With hindsight, we uncovered duplicate data during analysis, where people had used two of our keywords; it would have been beneficial to combine all data into one spreadsheet and then to sort by Twitter username in order to remove duplicates prior to analysis. If you do this, records should be kept of the number of tweets collected, the number of duplicates removed, and the final number included in analysis. We identified 4,439 unique tweets.

Analysis techniques: semiotic, thematic and content analysis

As always, it is important to determine your analysis technique prior to beginning your research. In this case study, I chose to use a range of techniques, as is fitting with a broad **research question** which aims to understand an under-researched phenomenon. Table 5.1 shows the justification for using multiple types of analysis. Below, I describe ascribing a type of **author** and **semiotic analysis**, and make reference to other chapters where thematic and **content analyses** are used. All textual data were imported into **NVivo** 10 for analysis. Images were subsequently searched for individually and imported into the same **NVivo** analysis file using the **Document Identification Number** to link them to the tweet. Embedded in the analysis is the presentation of some of the findings at each stage; these contain quantification in some places, due to the large volume of data included (see p. 30 for more details on including quantification in your own findings). Additional findings can be found in Grant and O'Mahoney (2016).

TABLE 5.1 Analysis techniques used in waterpipe case study and justification for use

Analysis technique	Justification
Semiotic analysis of text for sentiment	To classify tweets as *positive or negative* because of the potential impacts of health and smoking behaviour associated with this
Thematic analysis of text	To understand *what* people describe in their tweets about smoking waterpipes
Content analysis of images	To understand *what* people display in photographs related to waterpipe smoking and *how* they portray waterpipe smoking
Comparison of sentiment in a sample of images and texts	To assess *semiotic consistency in texts and images*

Determining likely author

Within our analysis, prior to considering the content, we sought to determine the likely '**author**' of tweets wherever possible into one of a range of inductively developed categories: 'individual waterpipe user', 'business', 'local blogger', 'health agency' or 'media'. A sign that identified individual users was the reporting of experiences of smoking a waterpipe, whilst business accounts encouraged **readers** to visit their premises or buy their products.

What is semiotic analysis?

Semiotic analysis at its most basic can be defined as the study of signs and sign systems, which help the **reader** to create **meaning** from the data under study (Eco 1976). A sign could be a particular word or a combination of words, and, using shared understandings between the **author** and **reader**, this creates **meaning**. As such, **semiotic analysis** is culturally specific, which should be considered during analysis (Mick et al. 2004). Therefore, in research using **semiotic analysis**, we need to think like the intended audience.

How to do semiotic analysis

There are many branches of semiotic study, and it is beyond the scope of this chapter to provide a detailed overview. **Readers** with an interest in this area would benefit from consulting David Marcel's (1994) excellent introductory text. The approach that I undertook to **semiotic analysis** in this instance is outlined in Box 5.1. It built on an approach to the **semiotic analysis** of social media in other studies (see, for example, Burnap et al. 2015). The aim for this element of the analysis was to use semiotic signs in the data to code each piece of data as positive, negative or neutral (i.e. they have no sentiment). As our data were taken from the online arena, 'signs' that implied that the tweet was positive or negative could also include the use of **emojis**, as at the time of data collection they were a relatively popular way of reporting sentiment in online text.

BOX 5.1 PROCEDURE TO UNDERTAKE SEMIOTIC ANALYSIS OF TWITTER DATA

1 Read through the data set, searching for keywords, visual elements and concepts and whether these are positive, negative or neutral
2 Identify positive and negative aspects within each individual data extract (where present)
3 Decide and record the sentiment in the individual data extract as 'positive', 'negative', 'positive and negative' or 'neutral' (no sentiment)
4 Consider the semiotics within the data set as a whole

Semiotic analysis of shisha and social media data

It should be noted that at the time of writing, Twitter prohibited the sharing of content without opt-in consent from the **author** of the tweet. As such, we consulted guidance from the Association of Internet Researchers (Markham and Buchanan 2012) about how to ethically work with the data we had collected. Where data is reproduced in our reporting, it has been minimally altered to preserve anonymity whilst retaining both narrative and semiotic tones in all instances. The way that we altered tweets was by changing a single word for another word that was very similar, correcting spelling errors, or replacing places and **emojis** with a written description of what was contained.

To illustrate the stages used in analysis, some data extracts are presented below with the positive words or concepts highlighted in bold, as in stage 2 of the analysis procedure (see Box 5.1). Positive semiotics included those related to relaxation, having fun and positive relationships with others:

- **Chillin'** coz tomorrow is my **day off**. #shisha (url removed) (smoke emoji)
- Feel **exotic** with one of our **#premium #luxury** #hookah (name of restaurant) #(city) (url removed)
- ending the day with 4 coals and a pack of sheesha alone in your room? that's the **nice** #hookah life **I enjoy :)**

By contrast, negative words and signs were less common in the data set but included concepts relating to health risks or addiction from waterpipe smoking:

- **ALARMING** increase in waterpipe #smoking among teens and young adults. However, #hookah is **NOT a safe alternative** (url removed)
- #ecig **#bored** #makeup #hookah #hookapen (url removed)

In stage 3 of the analysis (Box 5.1), for the majority of tweets, looking at these semiotic words and concepts enabled the selection of either 'positive' or 'negative' as the semiotic code. However, we were not able to give 38% of the data a positive or negative classification. This required further exploration beyond the basic **semiotic analysis** we had planned. On further exploration of the data, we divided these into three further categories.

First were those that lacked positive *or* negative sentiment, but allowed an idea of an activity or narrative to be understood. We referred to these as 'narrative, no sentiment'. In the examples below, the narrative has been highlighted:

- **Sheesha stands alone waiting someone to pick it up!** #(country) #(city) #hookah #sheesha (url removed)
- Let's put in perspective how small my **new #hookah pipe** is (url removed)

Second were those that lacked sentiment and did not describe an activity. We named this code as 'no narrative, no sentiment'. Many of the tweets in this category were mostly made up of hashtags, for example:

- #hookah #tattoos #poly #tribal (url removed)
- #Hookah

The final additional category was for tweets that were 'unclassifiable' in terms of sentiment, because they were not written in English and did not contain **emojis**.

In order to consider sentiment across the whole dataset, stage 4 of our planned semiotic analysis (see Box 5.1), we considered semiotics alongside likely author. As we had previously coded tweets for their likely **author**, we were able to use the 'Matrix Coding Query' option within **NVivo** to look at trends in sentiment between groups (see Table 5.2). Here, we noted that 91% of tweets we had identified as likely to belong to an individual contained positive semiotics, which was much higher than the overall figure of 59%.

Thematic analysis of text

Alongside our analysis of sentiment, we analysed the text of the tweets thematically to allow a greater understanding of the content of the data compared to a basic **semiotic analysis** alone. Details of how to undertake **thematic analysis** can be found in Chapter 3. Themes were developed **inductively**, without reference to any pre-identified ideas or areas of interest (Braun and Clarke 2006).

TABLE 5.2 Semiotic analysis of tweets by likely author of tweet

Semiotic analysis		Likely author						
Semiotic code	Semiotic sub-code	Individual user (n = 1,489)	Business (n = 551)	Unable to determine author (n = 2,330)	Geographical blogger (n = 30)	Health agency (n = 27)	Media (n = 7)	Total (n = 4,439)
Positive	–	91%	83%	33%	73%	4%	14%	59%
Negative	–	1%	0	3%	0	59%	71%	3%
Positive and negative	–	2%	1%	1%	0	0	0	1%
Neutral	Narrative, no sentiment	4%	13%	16%	13%	37%	14%	12%
	No narrative, no sentiment	1%	1%	16%	13%	0	0	9%
Unable to detect sentiment	Non-English	0	1%	31%	0	0	0	17%
	Unclassifiable	0	0	0	0	0	0	0

NB: percentages may not total 100, due to rounding; quantities that amounted to less than 0.5% are recorded as 0.

TABLE 5.3 Thematic analysis of tweets: themes and definitions

Theme	Definition
Emotion	Whether it was a good or bad experience – for example, if it was fun, relaxed (positive) or associated with addiction or loneliness (negative)
Location	(1) The broader geographical sense (name of country, city, etc.) (2) The more local geographical sense (inside or outside, public or private space, nature of space, e.g. shisha bar)
Consumed alongside	Alongside waterpipe smoking, was any other consumption mentioned? Including alcohol, food, non-alcoholic drinks, e-cigarettes and energy drinks
Activities	Alongside waterpipe smoking, was any other activity mentioned? Activities included watching TV, listening to music and having a party
Relationships	Who the person said they were with (friends, partner, family, alone)

We identified five broad themes that were present in tweets, which can be summarised as emotions, locations, food and drink, other activities and relationships with others. An extract from our analytical memos highlights the definitions we used (see Table 5.3), which developed iteratively over time. These main themes were accompanied by sub-themes that also had defined boundaries.

When analysis had been completed, it could be seen that the emotional experience of waterpipe smoking was described most often within people's tweets. That is, in 1,255 tweets (28%) the **author** described how they felt about waterpipe smoking:

- Our situation **#BFFs #goodtimes** #redwine #hookah #blues **#laughter** (url removed)

Following this, in over 1,000 tweets, the person's location was described:

- Living the DREAM :) **#(city) #bungalow** #hookah **#beach** #actor #bartender #fun… (url removed)

Other less commonly described aspects of waterpipe smoking included what the person was consuming alongside waterpipe smoking ($n = 788$) or if some other activity, such as a football match, was occurring at the same time ($n = 414$):

- After a (very large) **Persian dinner** nothing is better than #hookah and **(non-alcoholic beverage)** #lastnight #latertweet (url removed)
- **Watching the game** #Shisha #hookah **#worldcup2014** @(name)

Finally, the theme that was included the least was who else was present or involved at the time ($n = 374$):

- **My family**…is (awesome), yo. Love **these guys**… #hookah a **family** that smokes together stays together ;) (url removed)

Content analysis of images

The final stage of our analysis was the **content analysis** of photographs from a sub-sample of tweets with website addresses which led to photographs. This sits alongside the **semiotic** and **thematic analysis** to gain as full an understanding as possible from the data available. Details of how to undertake **content analysis** can be found in Chapter 6. We chose to select a **purposive sample**, with a focus on data that contained the keyword 'hookah', due to the fact that this was the most commonly used term for waterpipe smoking in our analysis. As we would be unable to consider all tweets within the hookah data set due to time constraints, we focused on the first 3,000 tweets in the data set, which was just over half of the 5,648 which had been collected. If you are adopting this approach in your own research, you may wish to choose a **random** or **stratified sample** here. It is difficult to suggest an adequate number of images to include in analysis, as there is no 'gold standard'; however, it is important to justify which images you have chosen to include, as this will affect your findings.

433 tweets were identified as being unique and containing a URL. Of these, 136 cases were excluded, mostly because the data was unavailable to us ($n = 54$), or the URL did not lead to a photograph ($n = 73$). Accordingly, 299 photographs were imported into **NVivo** and subjected to **inductive** and **deductive content analysis** (Weber 2006). **Deductive** themes were the place where the photograph was taken (inside/outside, in a nightclub, etc.), and the presence or absence of others, or a waterpipe (or part of a waterpipe). An **inductive** theme was the presence of smoke (including smoke rings) or sexualised posing. Due to the previously stated ethical restrictions on data use from Twitter, it is not possible to share images from the project.

Integrating a range of analysis strategies

By using a range of strategies, we explored the data more fully than could have been achieved using one strategy alone (see Table 5.1). To bring together the multiple strands of research, we considered if the semiotic and thematic content of the tweet appeared to match with the photograph in terms of the experience of waterpipe smoking. Overall, only 5 of the 299 tweets did not appear to fit with the written semiotic account of waterpipe smoking implied by our reading of the tweets, implying a high degree of overlap between our interpretation of the written semiotic and pictorial content in the hookah sub-sample.

Discussion

One of the reasons for doing this research was that when people think waterpipe smoking is safe or positive, they are more likely to start smoking a waterpipe and are less likely to want to quit (Akl et al. 2013; Barnett et al. 2013). As such, it was important to explore how waterpipe smoking is portrayed on social media. Our **semiotic analysis** highlighted that waterpipe smoking was generally perceived in a positive way and that this was even more common for tweets written by individuals reporting their experiences of waterpipe smoking. This may be because of a tendency to over-report positive experiences on social media (Goffman 1959), but may still have a negative impact on health (Barnett et al. 2013). Overall, the use of multiple data analysis strategies was beneficial to gain a wider understanding of the data, as was required by the broad nature of the **research question**. If you have less time available, a narrower **research question** would allow for the use of a single analysis strategy.

Challenges of undertaking research using individually created documents

In planning your research, it is necessary to consider access issues. I used a platform to collect data using Twitters' **API**, which is not always straightforward, and may result in some lost or inaccessible data. Within my data collection, I had brief periods (7 minutes in a 1-week period) with loss of connection to Twitter in which our data collection tool did not pick up tweets. In another study, a student collected over 100,000 tweets using another platform but was only able to access a proportion of them. For this reason, I recommend a pilot data collection period using your chosen data collection platform.

In understanding the utility of publically available data, we must always be aware of restrictions on online content. For example, some forums require that instead of 'mining' their site for pre-existing content, researchers should post and ask for participants' views and experiences, whilst others explicitly forbid such activity. Likewise, as described above, Twitter's code of conduct states that content must not be replicated without opt-in consent from each individual **author**. It is not possible to describe all restrictions in online data collection and sharing here, but it is recommended that prior to research, you read the most recent version of the Association of Internet Researchers' statement of ethical practice (see www.aoir.org/ethics/) as well as your own professional body's statement of ethical practice and that you consult the individual data source. If you are using hard copy documents, such as letters or diaries, you should also consider the ethical implications, including recognisability of handwriting and anonymity and whether the **author** intended for the documents to be used in research.

As can be seen through the illustrated example, the use of a single analysis strategy with a complex data set can fail to identify everything that can be learned from those documents. This may be particularly likely when analysing multi-modal documents. An alternative approach to a complex data set may be to utilise **discourse analysis** (see Chapter 4 and the excellent example in McCracken (2006)), although in this instance, the brevity of tweets, highlighted by the lack of semiotic content in many, would have made this inappropriate.

Exercise: using semiotic analysis

The analysis above, in part, focused on the portrayal of waterpipe smoking as positive, negative or lacking sentiment. Below, 20 fictitious tweets about water-pipe smoking are available for you to practise using **semiotic analysis**.

Instructions

Using the tweets below, undertake a **semiotic analysis** to answer the following **research question**:

How many of the tweets below report 'positive', 'negative' or 'no sentiment'?

I suggest that you consult Box 5.1 for guidance on how to conduct a **semiotic analysis** of tweets. You should code the text with 'positive', 'negative', 'positive and negative' and 'no sentiment'. You may wish to photocopy the data to facilitate your analysis.

Data

Source 1

Children smoke #cigarettes, legends smoke #hookah ☺

Source 2

(brand of tobacco) #shisha now available from (website). Great new flavours in store now!

Source 3

#carbon #monoxide is DEADLY and INVISIBLE; you can't smell or see it. In #hookah bars there are often dangerously high levels of carbon monoxide.

Source 4

Come use our #hookah at (name) Bar. Enjoy the experience with your friends. #city

Source 5

20% off EVERYTHING at (website). You know you need a new pipe! #hookah #shisha

Source 6

So stressed – #hookah will fix it #stress #addict #EveryDayHookah

Source 7

Great night out with the girls – dinner #hookah #cocktails #dancing

Source 8

I'm sure I've got a pain in my lung. 2 much #shisha for me #QuittingRightNow

Source 9

#hookah #New York #Brooklyn #NYC

Source 10

After dinner at my Auntie's all the old people started smoking #hookah – urgh! #NoThanks

Source 11

Friday night at (name of club). Book your booths and the first #hookah is on the house #VIP #Luxury #LivingTheDream #Friday

Source 12

Chilling with the boy #pizza #hookah #LifeGoals #boyfriend #BestBoyfriendEver

Source 13

#Turkey #Holiday #HubbleBubble pipe everywhere. Love the #apple flavour, gonna need some when I get home, need a bigger suitcase!

Source 14

Enjoy the best shisha in town #(name of bar) #shisha #cocktails #ladysnight

Source 15

Happy birthday @(name of person)!!! Tonight we have #cake #shisha #cocktails

Source 16

Still in my PJs at 2 in the afternoon. Heavy night last night #beer and #shisha

Source 17

So one hour of shisha is like 100 cigarettes? WTF! My poor lungs #shisha #hookah

Source 18

WooHoo! It's Friday, I've finished work and I'm on my way to meet @(name), @(name) and @(name) for a weekend of fun #pool #poolparty #hookah

Source 19

Watching the game with @(name). Come on @(sports team)! pizza on the way and #hookah for later #mates for life

Source 20

My favourite #hookah flavour while I play my favourite #PS4 game, Friday night alone

Note

1 A skip is a large open-topped metal container, designed to accommodate waste from building sites.

References

Akl, E. et al. 2013. Motives, beliefs and attitudes towards waterpipe tobacco smoking: a systematic review. *Harm Reduction Journal*: 10(1), p. 12.

Alaszewski, A. 2006a. Diaries as a source of suffering narratives: a critical commentary. *Health, Risk & Society*: 8(1), pp. 43–58.

Alaszewski, A. 2006b. *Using diaries for social research*. London: Sage.

Barnett, T.E. et al. 2013. The predictive utility of attitudes toward hookah tobacco smoking. *American Journal of Health Behavior*: 37(4), pp. 433–439.

Bennett, L. 2012. Transformations through Twitter: the England riots, television viewership and negotiations of power through media convergence. *Journal of Audience and Reception Studies*: 9(2), pp. 511–525.

Bolger, N. et al. 2003. Diary methods: capturing life as it is lived. *Annual Review of Psychology*: 54, pp. 579–616.

Boyer, K. 2012. Affect, corporeality and the limits of belonging: breastfeeding in public in the contemporary UK. *Health & Place*: 18(3), pp. 552–560.

Braun, V. and Clarke, V. 2006. Using thematic analysis in psychology. *Qualitative Research in Psychology*: 3(2), pp. 77–101.

Burnap, P. et al. 2014. Tweeting the terror: modelling the social media reaction to the Woolwich terrorist attack. *Social Network Analysis and Mining*: 4(1), pp. 1–14.

Burnap, P. et al. 2015. Detecting tension in online communities with computational Twitter analysis. *Technological Forecasting and Social Change*: 95, pp. 96–108.

Christopherson, K.M. 2007. The positive and negative implications of anonymity in Internet social interactions: 'On the internet, nobody knows you're a dog'. *Computers in Human Behavior*: 23(6), pp. 3038–3056.

Cleland, J. 2014. Racism, football fans, and online message boards. *Journal of Sport and Social Issues*: 38(5), pp. 415–431.

Cross, G. 1990. *Worktowners at Blackpool: mass-observation and popular leisure in the 1930s.* Abingdon: Routledge.

Dicks, B. 2012. *Digital qualitative research methods: ethics, archiving and representation in qualitative research.* London: Sage.

Eco, U. 1976. *A theory of semiotics.* Bloomington, IN: Indiana University Press.

Economic and Social Research Council 2013. Big data investment: capital funding. Available at: www.esrc.ac.uk/news-and-events/announcements/25683/Big_Data_Investment_Capital_funding_.aspx [Accessed: 1 December 2015].

Etengoff, C. 2017. Petitioning for social change: letters to religious leaders from gay men and their family allies. *Journal of Homosexuality*: 64(2), pp. 166–194.

Frank, O.H. and Pressler, M. 2011. *Anne Frank: the diary of a young girl: the definitive edition.* London: Penguin.

Frederick, E.L. and Clavio, G. 2015. Blurred lines: an examination of high school football recruits' self-presentation on Twitter. *International Journal of Sport Communication*: 8(3), pp. 330–344.

Goffman, E. 1959. *The Presentation of Self in Everyday Life.* New York: Doubleday.

González-Bailón, S. et al. 2014. Assessing the bias in samples of large online networks. *Social Networks*: 38, pp. 16–27.

Grant, A. 2015. '#discrimination': the online response to a case of a breastfeeding mother being ejected from a UK retail premises. *Journal of Human Lactation*: 32(1), pp. 141–151.

Grant, A. 2016. 'I… don't want to see you flashing your bits around': exhibitionism, othering and good motherhood in perceptions of public breastfeeding. *Geoforum*: 71(May 2016), pp. 52–61.

Grant, A. and O'Mahoney, H. 2016. The portrayal of waterpipe (shisha, hookah, nargile) smoking on Twitter: a qualitative exploration. *Public Health*: 140, pp. 128–135.

Gurney, P. 1997. 'Intersex' and 'Dirty Girls': mass-observation and working-class sexuality in England in the 1930s. *Journal of the History of Sexuality*: 8(2), pp. 256–290.

Hammal, F. et al. 2008. A pleasure among friends: how narghile (waterpipe) smoking differs from cigarette smoking in Syria. *Tobacco Control*: 17, p. e3.

Hawksey, M. 2014. Twitter Archiving Google Spreadsheet TAGS v5. Available at: http://mashe.hawksey.info/2013/02/twitter-archive-tagsv5/ [Accessed: 12 April 2015].

Hogan, B. 2010. The presentation of self in the age of social media: distinguishing performances and exhibitions online. *Bulletin of Science, Technology & Society*: 30(6), pp. 377–386.

Hurdley, R. 2014. Synthetic sociology and the 'long workshop': how Mass Observation ruined meta- methodology. *Sociological Research Online*: 19(3), pp. 1–26.

Jennings, G. 2016. Ancient wisdom, modern warriors: the (re)invention of a Mesoamerican warrior tradition in Xilam. *Martial Arts Studies*: (2), pp. 59–70.

Jones, A. and Woolley, J. 2015. The email-diary: a promising research tool for the 21st century? *Qualitative Research*: 15(6), pp. 705–721.

Katz, E. 2012. 'The happiness game': a content analysis of radio fan mail. *International Journal of Communication*: 6(1), pp. 1297–1445.

Manago, A.M. et al. 2008. Self-presentation and gender on MySpace. *Journal of Applied Developmental Psychology*: 29(6), pp. 446–458.

Mann, C. and Stewart, F. 2000. *Internet communication and qualitative research*. London: Sage.

Marcel, D. 1994. *Messages and meanings: an introduction to semiotics*. Toronto: Canadian Scholars' Press.

Markham, A. and Buchanan, E. 2012. Ethical decision-making and internet research: recommendations from the AoIR Ethics Working Committee (version 2.0). Available at: http://aoir.org/reports/ethics2.pdf [Accessed: 3 December 2017].

Masters, A. 2016. *A life discarded: 148 diaries found in the trash*. London: Macmillan.

Maurantonio, N. 2015. Material rhetoric, public memory, and the Post-It Note. *Southern Communication Journal*: 80(2), pp. 83–101.

McCracken, E. 2006. The codes of overt advertisements. In: Scott, J. ed. *Documentary research*. London: Sage, pp. 213–248.

Melnick, R. 1997. *The stolen legacy of Anne Frank*. London: Yale University.

Mick, D. et al. 2004. Pursuing the meaning of meaning in the commercial world: an international review of marketing and consumer research founded on semiotics. *Semiotica*: 152(1/4), pp. 1–74.

Milligan, C. et al. 2004. 'Cultivating health': therapeutic landscapes and older people in northern England. *Social Science & Medicine*: 58(9), pp. 1781–1793.

Milligan, C. et al. 2005. Digging deep: using diary techniques to explore the place of health and well-being amongst older people. *Social Science & Medicine*: 61(9), pp. 1882–1892.

Moyer, L.J. et al. 2014. The Massachusetts BMI letter: a qualitative study of responses from parents of obese children. *Patient Education and Counselling*: 94(2), pp. 210–7.

O'Reilly, M. and Parker, N. 2013. 'Unsatisfactory saturation': a critical exploration of the notion of saturated sample sizes in qualitative research. *Qualitative Research*: 13(2), pp. 190–197.

Perrot, S. et al. 2017. Pain patients' letters: the visit before the visit - a qualitative analysis of letters from patients referred to a tertiary pain center. *European Journal of Pain*: 21(6), pp. 1020–1030.

Pick, D. and Zielke, S. 2015. How electricity providers communicate price increases – a qualitative analysis of notification letters. *Energy Policy*: 86, pp. 303–314.

Primack, B.A. et al. 2013. Waterpipe smoking among US university students. *Nicotine & Tobacco Research*: 15(1), pp. 29–35.

Ramussen, R. 2013. *Dear Mark Twain: letters from his readers*. London: University of California Press.

Rhodes, G. 2017. Our Life Story Scribbled on the Back of an Envelope. Available at: https://www.theguardian.com/lifeandstyle/2017/jan/28/scribbled-notes-scribbled-back-envelope-messages-mother-father [Accessed: 5 February 2017].

Roper, M. 2006. Maternal relations: moral manliness and emotional survival in letters home during the First World War. In: Scott, J. ed. *Documentary research*. London: Sage, pp. 159–180.

Savage, M. 2007. Changing social class identities in post-war Britain: perspectives from Mass-Observation. *Sociological Research Online*: 12(3), p. 6.

Scott, J. 1990. *A matter of record: documentary sources in social research*. London: John Wiley & Sons.

Sharma, E. et al. 2014. Understanding psychosocial aspects of waterpipe smoking among college students. *American Journal of Health Behavior*: 38(3), pp. 440–447.

Sheridan, D. 1993. Writing to the archive: mass-observation as autobiography. *Sociology*: 27(1), pp. 27–40.

Sloan, L. et al. 2013. Knowing the tweeters: deriving sociologically relevant demographics from Twitter. *Sociological Research Online*: 18(3), p. 7.

Smith, K.C. et al. 2005. Australian letters to the editor on tobacco: triggers, rhetoric, and claims of legitimate voice. *Qualitative Health Research*: 15(9), pp. 1180–1198.

Statista 2017. Number of monthly active Facebook users worldwide 2008–2016. Available at: https://www.statista.com/statistics/264810/number-of-monthly-active-facebook-users-worldwide/ [Accessed: 5 February 2017].

The Mass Observation Archive 2017. The Mass Observation Archive. Available at: http://www.massobs.org.uk/ [Accessed: 6 February 2017].

Thomson, R. and Holland, J. 2005. 'Thanks for the memory': memory books as a methodological resource in biographical research. *Qualitative Research*: 5(2), pp. 201–219.

Tyler, I. 2008. 'Chav Mum Chav Scum'. *Feminist Media Studies*: 8(1), pp. 17–34.

Ulrich, L.T. 1991. *A midwife's tale: the life of Martha Ballard, based on her diary, 1785–1812.* New York: Vintage Books.

Waziry, R. et al. 2016. The effects of waterpipe tobacco smoking on health outcomes: an updated systematic review and meta-analysis. *International Journal of Epidemiology*: 46(1), pp. 32–43.

Weber, R.P. 2006. Techniques of content analysis. In: Scott, J. ed. *Documentary research.* London: Sage

Wilde, J. 2017. Vera & John. Available at: http://jasonwilde.com/v-j-cft/images-8 [Accessed: 4 March 2017].

Woodman, C. et al. 2016. The preferences and perspectives of family caregivers towards place of care for their relatives at the end-of-life: a systematic review and thematic synthesis of the qualitative evidence. *BMJ Supportive & Palliative Care*: 6(4), pp. 418–429.

SECTION II

Documents as an addition to existing qualitative research methods

6

TRIANGULATION OF FINDINGS FROM PRIMARY RESEARCH

Things we might not have otherwise been able to establish

Summary

This chapter is the first of three chapters that examine the use of documents as data alongside, or embedded with, other qualitative research strategies. First, the literature on **triangulation** – that is, using multiple methods to understand a phenomenon – is considered, with an emphasis on how to triangulate in research using documents as data. I also consider how triangulation fits with epistemological concerns and **validity**. As the case study research later in the chapter is advertising materials, freedom of thought (also known as autonomy) is discussed in relation to advertising and the choices we make. The main body of the chapter is a case study of a **content analysis** of advertising materials. The data was from infant formula funded parenting clubs in the UK. The research project aimed to assess compliance with a set of marketing standards that formula companies had agreed to follow. Details are provided for how to undertake content analysis of qualitative data. In doing so, I highlight the importance of developing and piloting a coding framework, although within the case study example, the coding framework that was used was based on the pre-existing code of conduct. A clear, step-by-step guide to undertaking the research is provided. This includes choosing segments of data, which are the unit of analysis, the process of indexing coding without using **CAQDAS** software and conclusion drawing. Additional data is provided to enable **readers** to attempt **content analysis** using the predefined coding framework.

Key learning points

- What **triangulation** is, and how it can help gain a wider and deeper understanding of social life
- How advertising impacts on our thoughts and purchasing behaviour
- How we study advertising materials
- When to consider undertaking a second study to triangulate novel findings from your research
- What **content analysis** is, and how you can use it in your research
- How to report research using advertising materials without breaching copyright laws

Background 1: triangulation

In Section I of this book, research with documents involved documents as the only source of data. In Section II, documents are used alongside other forms of qualitative inquiry. Throughout these chapters, the added value of using more than one form of data will be discussed. This is also known as **triangulation**.

What is triangulation?

The term **triangulation** originates from surveying and involves the concept of measuring space and angles from multiple places in order to make the overall measurement of the space more precise. When describing **triangulation** within research, Flick (2004, p. 178) defines it as "observation of the research issue from [at least] two points". However, an alternative definition is provided by Yin: "In research, the principle [of **triangulation**] pertains to the goal of seeking at least three ways of verifying or corroborating a particular event, description, or fact being reported by a study" (2013, p. 81). Thus, there is not one clear definition of what it means to triangulate. In social science research, the 'points' can be multiple sources of data, **theories** or researchers (Denzin 1989). Most often, however, **triangulation** includes multiple data sources being used to answer **research questions** (Rothbauer 2008).

Triangulation, social constructionism and validity

The stated purpose of **triangulation** when it was introduced in the 1950s and 1960s was to increase the **validity** of findings (that is, the likelihood that they were representative of the phenomenon) (Rothbauer 2008). Some researchers still subscribe to this view (see, for example, Yin 2013). However, **triangulation** has been criticised by some who view it as overly **positivistic**. For those who adopt a **social constructionist** approach to their research, **triangulation** is used to increase understanding through producing new insights, not to confirm the existence of a single 'true' reality. This is because of three factors: contextual variations in behaviour, an inability to ever truly understand behaviour (Flick 2004), and variations in the data that particular research methods can capture (Ritchie et al. 2003). Instead, we may view **triangulation** as beneficial for research in that it enables multiple perspectives to be brought together as a "means of widening or deepening understanding of a subject through the combination of multiple readings", and this can increase our confidence in our conclusions (Ritchie et al. 2003, p. 275). We may also consider the need for multiple researchers, in terms of researcher experience (Lincoln and Denzin 2003) as well as positionality, such as gender, ethnicity, age and similarity to the participants (Wagle and Cantaffa 2008). To conclude, in utilising multiple methods, **theories** or researchers, we may learn something new about the topic under study.

Triangulation and self-reported behaviours

The way in which we see ourselves and our behaviour can be very different to what is observed by more objective means. For example, one statistic that is regularly quoted is that almost everybody believes that they are a better-than-average driver (McCormick et al. 1986). However, when we ask people to recall the amount and type of driving they do, even when using diaries, the self-reported data varies considerably when compared to in-car recording devices (Blancharda et al. 2010). This is known as illusory superiority and is a type of cognitive **bias** that makes us think we perform better than others on a range of tasks. The topics that are included in such self-assessments are not limited to practical skills, but also include relationship satisfaction (Buunk 2001), popularity among peers (Ezra and John Tjost 2001) and engagement with healthy behaviours (Hoorens and Harris 1998).

One other way in which we tend to overstate our abilities is in relation to being freely able to make choices – that is, our ability to be autonomous. In relation to food, people report that they eat unhealthy food because it tastes better than healthy foods (Gough and Conner 2006). However, we know that a broad range of factors influence unhealthy dietary choice, including the foods parents ate around us (Birch and Fisher 2000), and how much exposure you have to shops selling unhealthy meals (Burgoine et al. 2014). Alongside this, a lack of access to healthy foods, through living in a 'food desert,'[1] can severely impact your ability to buy healthy foods regardless of desire (Walker et al. 2010). As such, it is important to understand that we all make choices about what we do that are influenced by factors inside ourselves, but also by factors external to us, including the resources available to us and the social world around us (For more details, see the COM-B model within Michie et al. 2011, 2014). Therefore, when using data that contains peoples' views and opinions on a topic which may be subject to illusory superiority, it can be beneficial to triangulate with an alternative data source.

Background 2: advertising, behaviour and research

In Chapter 3, we discussed how the media can affect our perceptions. Another way in which our views are shaped is through advertising. Again, we consistently underestimate how much influence advertising has on us. In the following section, the ways in which advertisers create 'need' and encourage brand awareness and loyalty are described. I then consider research into tobacco industry advertising, before considering the way in which marketing principles can be used to meet governments' aims.

How advertisers create 'need'

At its most basic level, advertising can be viewed as a tool of a **capitalist** economy used to create "desire for things for which (potential buyers) have no real need" (Jhally 1990, p. 2). Businesses advertise their products in order to increase brand awareness, which in turn leads to consideration of purchasing the product, some individual purchases and some long-term preferences for purchasing that product (Sullivan and Boches 2016). This may involve targeting those who may be predisposed towards your product through a variety of strategies, including raising awareness, sustaining interest, building on fear and guilt or using fantasy and escape (see Brierley 2002 for more details). Narratives throughout advertising, such as a series of adverts using the same characters, play to our brains' desire to hear a complete story, and thus increase the advertisements' appeal (Sullivan and Boches 2016). Sex (or the promise of it) and the use of female and, more recently, male bodies are also commonly used to attract attention, through focusing on particular areas of the body or through provocative body positioning (McCracken 2006; Berger 2015).

Many products are aimed at a particular market, such as teenage women or mothers, using advertising to establish their value as a "hot" good (Berger 2015) through advertising in particular places and spaces (Jhally 1990). This is known as "segmenting" (Brierley 2002). However, while some products are aimed at a wide market, the advertisements used to sell these products will vary across markets, to generate maximum appeal across a broad spectrum of possible buyers (Berger 2015). It has been argued that to do this, advertisers, like ethnographers, need to understand a group, issue or need better than their competitors and convince their potential buyers of this (Kemper 2003). Advertisers know they have met their aim of understanding their target market when potential buyers choose to share adverts for products they view as desirable, and social media can facilitate this sharing. A more critical, **Marxist**, analysis, however, points out that advertising is not about providing information about a product, but about fetishising it as a desirable commodity (Jhally 1990).

One way in which advertising has changed considerably since the late 1990s is through the ability to reach customers online in a variety of ways (Burgoyne et al. 2010). This includes advertising on web pages, mobile phone applications, which are designed to help the consumer, and emailed advertisements. Advertising may be targeted at consumers through the use of tracking and cookies, which allow advertisements for products to follow a consumer from one website to another in response to their search history. If you are irritated with the amount of advertising you see, see Chapter 12 of McStay (2016) for ways you can limit your exposure. Some fundamental ways in which advertising has changed in recent years, however, are in response to the interactional nature of social media, which allows consumers to 'answer back', and by the use of advertising blocking extensions within Internet browsers (McStay 2016).

The use of advertising documents in research

One area in which considerable research attention has been directed is marketing by the tobacco industry. Research using 1,200 tobacco industry documents by Bates and Rowell (1998) provides a provocative account of the tobacco industry's private acknowledgement that smoking was dangerous to their customers' health (see Doll et al. 2004 for more information), alongside their marketing material which denied these potential harms. The stated rationale for this was to recruit adolescents to replace smokers who had died or quit. Examples of data extracts are provided in Box 6.1. If you are interested in doing some archival research, the documents which Bates and Rowell (1998) examined, and other documents, are available in the Industry Documents Library.

BOX 6.1 SELECTED DATA EXTRACTS FROM ANALYSIS OF TOBACCO INDUSTRY DOCUMENTS BY BATES AND ROWELL (1998)

Private acknowledgement of the harms from smoking

"We don't smoke that s***. We just sell it. We just reserve the right to smoke for the young, the poor, the black and the stupid" (Cited in First Tuesday, ITV 1992, in Bates and Rowell 1998).

Public denial of harms from smoking

"The view that smoking causes specific diseases remains an opinion or a judgement, and not an established scientific fact" (Tobacco Institute of Hong Kong 1989, in Bates and Rowell 1998).

Finding replacement smokers

"...a cigarette for the beginner is a symbolic act. I am no longer my mother's child, I'm tough, I am an adventurer, I'm not square ... As the force from the psychological symbolism subsides, the pharmacological effect takes over to sustain the habit" (Philip Morris, 1969, in Bates and Rowell, 1998).

Alongside analysis of historical tobacco advertising documents, research on more recent tobacco industry documents shows the ways in which the industry has continued to attempt to market their products. This has included lobbying to slow the introduction of changes to the size and shape of packaging (Kotnowski and Hammond 2013) and regulation of new products (Carpenter et al. 2009; Peeters and Gilmore 2013). Readers who are interested in exploring this area in more depth can access the excellent Tobacco Tactics website (http://tobaccotactics. org/), hosted by the University of Bath.

Public services and advertising

In recent years, there has been recognition within UK public services that some elements of advertising can help to achieve the government's aims. One way in which this has been realised is through the Behavioural Insights Team, also known as 'the nudge unit', which is partly owned by the UK government. Research and field experiments have been undertaken by the Team to identify how to improve the behaviour of the public in various ways beneficial to the state, including repayment of unpaid fines (Haynes et al. 2013) and organ donation (The Behavioural Insights Team 2013). A second marketing tactic has been building 'brands' around healthy behaviours in order to facilitate healthier choices (Evans and Hastings 2008). This has included a mass media campaign, including TV adverts, to encourage young people not to smoke in the USA, which reduced youth smoking (Farrelly et al. 2009). A second example was a campaign to encourage 9- to 13-year-olds to engage in daily play, including a range of advertising materials in their home, school and community. It was found to be acceptable to young people as it created a 'buzz' and peer-to-peer discussion of the brand's message (Huhman et al. 2008).

Quality and bias in advertising materials

In considering advertising materials as data for research, it is important to assess quality and **bias**. To do so, I am applying Scott's (1990) criteria to assess documentary sources (see Table 2.1). In terms of **authenticity**, it may be difficult to access copies of advertising materials, particularly if you are undertaking a historical analysis; this also affects **representativeness**. Alongside this, as with news articles, there is often more than one **author**, and it may be challenging to find the main person involved in constructing a campaign. In terms of **credibility**, advertising materials would nearly always have a low score: **authors** are not being sincere or describing an accurate narrative. (Pause for a moment and think about the advertising of sanitary towels and tampons, where models are often shown undertaking sporty activities in white clothing whilst blue liquid is poured onto a product.) Finally, **meanings** may be both overt and covert, and therefore it is important to study imagery alongside words.

The marketing of infant formula case study

Within this worked example, the process of using advertising materials in a re-search study is outlined. As with the previous chapters, a chronological approach through the research project is presented. First, the study context, relating to infant feeding decisions and health information, is described. Following this, a brief overview of the original interview study is provided. I then outline the research problem to be considered in this secondary study. Alongside refining the **research question**, I describe the **population** of advertising materials available and the way in which a **sample** was selected. As a pre-existing marketing code for formula companies existed, this was used as a framework to undertake **content analysis**, and the steps involved in **content analysis** are described through this research project. Finally, the challenges of using advertising mate-rials as data are described, and some additional data is provided so that you can practise undertaking **content analysis** of advertising materials.

Context

Breastfeeding is recommended by the World Health Organization (WHO) as the only food needed for babies for the first 6 months of life; thereafter breastfeeding should be continued, alongside the introduction of complementary foods, for at least two years (World Health Organization 2017). Breast milk can be fed to babies directly from the breast or expressed and provided in a bottle, although expressing adds a significant amount of extra work for mothers (Stearns 2010). Rates of breastfeeding in many Western countries are very low, with only 1% of women in the UK providing breast milk exclusively for the first six months of life (Health & Social Care Information Centre 2012). As we know from the literature above, advertising can change people's views and purchasing habits. To combat the power of infant formula advertising, the WHO developed and formally agreed upon a "Code of Marketing of Breast-Milk Substitutes" in 1981. The Code provides clear guidance on the ways in which infant formula can be advertised (World Health Organization 1981). However, breaches of the Code have been regularly reported ever since its introduction (see, for example, Marino and Bolnick 1992; Taylor 1998; Waterston and Tumwine 2003; Forsyth 2012).

The link between providing formula to mothers and a reduction in breast-feeding has been well established through the use of experimental methods (Dougherty and Kramer 1983). Qualitative studies with pregnant women and mothers have also found that infant formula marketing may have a detrimental impact on breastfeeding; this is in terms of whether mothers ever breastfeed as well as how long they breastfeed for. Whilst advertising formula for infants aged older than 6 months (Follow-on Milk) is allowed under the WHO Code, many mothers do not understand the difference and believe that infant formula may have benefits for infants not found in breast milk (Berry et al. 2010; Parry et al. 2013). Research with mothers, grandparents and health professionals show that messages contained in marketing are believed and uncritically accepted by many of those who may provide information to new mothers (Berry et al. 2011). Furthermore, advertising has been found to generate an expectation that breastfeeding will not be possible, reducing women's confidence in their ability to breastfeed (Parry et al. 2013).

Study 1: The finding that needed triangulating

In 2013, whilst working for the National Health Service (NHS), I undertook a study examining the information needs of pregnant women and new parents in order to update the information that would be provided to pregnant women throughout Wales. Pregnant women and women who had recently had babies were invited to take part in focus groups in their communities. The topics to be discussed were the information that they had received and their information needs that were and were not met. One issue that came up in several of the focus groups was that women had signed up for 'parenting clubs', including those funded by infant formula brands, in order to access free gifts and money-off vouchers. Some participants reported that they had then been inundated with emails from the parenting clubs, with some receiving marketing materials regularly by post. This study was undertaken to meet a service need and was not published.

Immediately prior to beginning that project, I had completed a review of community support for breastfeeding (Grant et al. 2013), which was the first time I had undertaken research on infant feeding. Whilst undertaking this work, I had undertaken regular searches of the Internet for information relating to breastfeeding. I too had regularly received targeted advertising on Facebook directing me to join parenting clubs sponsored by infant formula companies. It is possible that these adverts were as a result of tracking and cookies related to my Internet search history (McStay 2016) and that the women who were searching for information on breastfeeding in the focus group research were also subjected to these advertisements. I began to explore literature on breaches of the WHO's Code and was shocked to see that there had been so many breaches. I also found that elements of bad practice had been identified within parenting clubs (see, for example, Baby Milk Action 2016, which works to highlight breaches of the WHO Code), but these had not yet been systematically considered. Although it was not possible for me to directly compare the data from the NHS project, I felt that this issue was worthy of further exploration.

Study 2: Research design

Outline research Question

It was relatively straightforward to design this **research question**, as there was a clearly worded Code that infant formula companies should have been adhering to, making a **content analysis** of adherence to the Code a natural choice. The previous study that had inspired this work clearly identified parenting clubs as an issue, so this naturally became the focus of the question:

Do infant feeding corporations breach the International Code of Marketing of Breast-Milk Substitutes in advertising sent directly to members of their parenting clubs?

Population and defining a sample

At the time of data collection, January 2014, there were four infant formula companies in the UK who had parenting clubs, Aptamil, Cow & Gate, Hipp Organic and SMA. All four were subscribed to as though an infant had just been born. Upon further consideration, it was decided to analyse materials from the first 6 months only, as the Code differentiated between infant formula that is used before and after babies are 6 months of age.[2]

Data collection

Data, in the form of direct-to-consumer advertising, was sent by the infant formula parenting clubs to our proxy 'mother'. Marketing materials were sent in two ways: through the post and by email. The packages sent in the post were often colourful or attractive, containing an obvious 'gift'. By comparison, the flurry of emails felt as though they may be more likely to be ignored. For this reason, the hard copy marketing materials were selected as the data to be included in the analysis. Table 6.1 shows the data received over a period of the first 6 months of membership. Data was carefully archived, with each item contained within the packages photographed, and each page of text scanned electronically.

Final research question

Do infant feeding corporations breach the International Code of Marketing of Breast-Milk Substitutes in advertising sent by post to members of their parenting clubs during the period of birth to six months?

TABLE 6.1 Data in infant formula marketing case study

Item	Weeks postnatal	Company
1	1	Cow & Gate
2	2	Aptamil
3	3	HiPP Organic
4	16	Cow & Gate
5	16	Aptamil
6	19	HiPP Organic
7	26	Cow & Gate

Analysis technique: content analysis

The primary strategy within **content analysis** is to define a framework and implement it systematically across all data. Below, **content analysis** is described in more detail, including the processes required, showing how it is particularly well suited to a research project such as this one.

What is content analysis?

Content analysis involves developing a coding framework to answer the **research questions** and ascribing elements of the data to the codes (Goffman 1986; Krippendorff 2013). As such, it is a "method for systematically describing the meaning of qualitative data" (Schreier 2014, p. 170). In order to ensure high levels of **validity**, this method prescribes that all elements of the data relating to the coding framework are considered in detail, often using **line-by-line coding** (Julien 2008). This, Schreier (2014) argues, ensures that conclusions are based on the data, not on the researchers' assumptions. Both text and images may be subjected to **content analysis**. When undertaking **content analysis** of images (see Chapter 5 for an example), the presence of objects and conscious and unconscious messages within images should be considered (Julien 2008, p. 120).

Whilst quantitative **content analysis** is entirely **deductive**, considering only the data that contributes to the framework and excluding all other data from the analysis, qualitative **content analysis** may involve cycles of adding new codes to the framework to ensure best fit with the data (Schreier 2014). In order to ensure the **research question** is answered, it is of vital importance to ensure the coding framework can answer the **research question**. Often double coding at least a percentage of the data is required within **content analysis**. The purpose of this is to prove that the items in the coding framework are so unambiguous as to be replicable by another researcher (Schreier 2014). However, from a **social constructionist** perspective, I would contest this as we are all influenced by our pre-existing knowledge, views and beliefs, and so it is common for two qualitative researchers to identify varying themes from data. **Content analysis** can be seen as particularly well suited to analysis of "goal-oriented" research, like the analysis of advertising materials, where the researcher is trying to establish **meaning** (George 2006, p. 135).

How to do content analysis

As with many of the types of analysis encountered in Section I of this book, there is no one accepted definition of **content analysis** or qualitative **content analysis** (Schreier 2014). For example, a more quantitative approach to **content analysis** may involve computerised searching for keywords in documents, and using this as the starting point for establishing data extracts to be considered (Weber 2006). In this instance, I chose to use Schreier's (2014, p. 173) procedure, which is broken into core concepts in Box 6.2.

BOX 6.2 PROCEDURE TO UNDERTAKE CONTENT ANALYSIS (SCHREIER 2014)

1 Develop a coding framework
2 Generate definitions for each code within the coding framework
3 Segment the material into units for coding
4 Undertake a pilot phase of data analysis
5 Refine the coding framework
6 Undertake the analysis proper (do not add any further new codes)
7 Consider latent and symbolic meanings within data
8 Double coding

Unlike with **thematic analysis**, it is important to get the coding framework finalised during the piloting phase and to not add any additional codes. As such, it is recommended that a variety of sources of data be used to develop the initial coding framework to account for the variation you may expect throughout your dataset. Codes and sub-codes within the coding structure are then generated. Where particular wording is used within the data, this should be used as the name for a code, rather than using a word with a similar **meaning** (Julien 2008). Alongside this, a name for the code and a description of what should be included should be developed. If more than one researcher will be coding the data, an 'indicator' data extract may be included to highlight the sorts of data to be assigned to a code, but it is important to not make this too narrow. Following this, a pilot phase of coding should occur on data that was not involved in developing the coding framework. The framework can then be refined to add new codes or collapse codes which are overly prescriptive and rarely used. In presenting the findings, Schreier notes that the coding framework can be presented itself to highlight areas of importance within the data.

Marketing of infant formula: data analysis

Developing a coding framework and generating definitions

In this research project, a type of **content analysis** that falls between quantitative and Schreier's (2014) qualitative approaches was used. In order to answer the **research question**, it was necessary to compare the qualitative data to a pre-existing list of regulations contained within the WHO Code for marketing breast milk substitutes and to not generate the codes myself. The **deductive** coding framework, including the article number within the WHO Code and the definition of the code, is included in Table 6.2. If you need to create your own **content analysis** coding framework, I recommend that you review Schrier's chapter in full. From a period of familiarisation with the marketing materials under study, I was able to generate indicators of data which would be likely to

TABLE 6.2 Coding framework in infant formula case study

Article	Definition
4.2 (a)	(clear information on) the benefits and superiority of breastfeeding
4.2 (b)	(clear information on) maternal nutrition, and the preparation for and maintenance of breastfeeding
4.2 (c)	(clear information on) the negative effect on breastfeeding of introducing partial bottle-feeding
4.2 (d)	(clear information on) the difficulty of reversing the decision not to breastfeed
4.2 (e)	(clear information on) where needed, the proper use of infant formula, whether manufactured industrially or home-prepared
4.2	(when materials contain information on infant formula they should include information on…) social implications of (infant formula) use
4.2	(when materials contain information on infant formula they should include information on…) financial implications of (infant formula) use
4.2	(when materials contain information on infant formula they should include information on…) the health hazards of inappropriate foods or feeding methods; and, in particular, the health hazards of unnecessary or improper use of infant formula and other breast milk substitutes
4.2	Such materials should not use any pictures or text which may idealise the use of breast milk substitutes
5.2	Manufacturers and distributors should not provide, directly or indirectly, to pregnant women, mothers or members of their families, samples of products within the scope of this Code
5.4	Manufacturers and distributors should not distribute to pregnant women or mothers or infants and young children any gifts of articles or utensils which may promote the use of breast milk substitutes or bottle-feeding
5.5	Marketing personnel, in their business capacity, should not seek direct or indirect contact of any kind with pregnant women or with mothers of infants and young children

breach the Code. For example, an "important notice" was often displayed within the documents, which stated the superiority of breastfeeding (4.2.a) and the negative effect on breastfeeding of introducing partial formula feeding (4.2.c). This would, on the face of it, allow me to say that this element had been met. However, the text was usually small and not prominent, and other information within the documents may have subverted the words in the important notice.

Segmenting the material into units for analysis

As Table 6.1 showed, the data was already partly segmented. Within the data set, seven packages were received in the post from three infant formula companies (three from Cow & Gate, and two each from Aptamil and Hipp Organic). Within each package, there were multiple documents to consider (see Table 6.3). For example, in data item 1, there was an envelope, soft toy and two separate booklets.

TABLE 6.3 Description of data extracts in infant formula case study

Item	Company	Document ID No.	Brief description of contents	Total pages (A5)
1	Cow & Gate	1.1	Red plastic envelope	20
		1.2	Soft toy	
		1.3	4-Page* letter	
		1.4	16-Page booklet	
2	Aptamil	2.1	Clear plastic envelope (displaying welcome letter)	4
		2.2	Soft toy	
		2.3	4-Page letter	
3	HiPP Organic	3.1	Green plastic envelope	24
		3.2	1-Page A4 letter	
		3.3	4-Page guide to breastfeeding	
		3.4	4-Page formula feeding guide	
		3.5	Recipe book	
		3.6	Stickers for nursery sheet 1	
		3.7	Stickers for nursery sheet 2	
		3.8	Good night sleep guide	
		3.9	2-Page flyer for products	
4	Cow & Gate	4.1	Envelope (noting money-off coupons inside)	56
		4.2	Weaning guide: 56 A5 pages	
5	Aptamil	5.1	6 A5 pages envelope and booklet in one	6
6	HiPP Organic	6.1	Envelope (green plastic bag)	24
		6.2	Plastic spoon	
		6.3	baby rice sample	
		6.4	Full product list by age (including for 4+ months)	
		6.5	Advert for 'kinder Hotels' (no mention of feeding)	
		6.6	Weaning guide	
		6.7	4-Page letter, including money-off coupons for products (not infant milk)	
7	Cow & Gate	7.1	Envelope – large thin clear plastic bag (torn on arrival) 76 A5 pages	76
		7.2	2-Page letter	
		7.3	Magazine (74 pages)	

*   for ease of comparison, smaller and larger sheets of paper have been converted into A5 size units unless otherwise specified.

As so much information was provided in each package of direct marketing material, it became clear that it would not be appropriate to consider the entire package as one segment. As such, I decided that **line-by-line coding** should be undertaken, including consideration of images and the way in which images and text worked together to create **meaning** (Ball 2011). However, in terms of whether content had breached the WHO Code, it felt as though all possible breaches and elements of meeting the Code should be considered together to form a conclusion.

Undertaking the analysis proper

In this project, I decided to code the data by hand – that is, without the use of a **CAQDAS** programme. It felt important to me to see and touch the data and to imagine how a mother receiving this may have felt. In order to do so, I had a printed list of codes, the original data and coloured photocopies of the data (on A3, to allow wide margins for coding stripes and notes). I then coded by hand onto these copies of the data. Extracts, both text and images, that may have breached the WHO guidance were then typed as quotes (or images described) into a spreadsheet (see Table 6.4 for an extract of the blank template). Details on how to consider the way **meaning** is created by colours, images and text within marketing materials are provided within Berger (2015) and Ball (2011), but are not repeated here. These lessons were, however, at the forefront of my mind in considering the documents. The spreadsheet was considerably wider than a standard A4 page, making it difficult to display within the confines of this book. An extract from the table relating to idealising infant formula (part of Section 4.2 of the Code) can be seen in Table 6.5. Within the table, you can see the process of considering the imagery and text within the documents in order to describe

TABLE 6.4 Extract from infant formula marketing analysis table (blank)

Document ID No.	4.2a Benefits and superiority of breastfeeding	4.2b Maternal nutrition, preparation and maintenance for breastfeeding	4.2c Negative effect on breastfeeding of partial bottle-feeding	4.2d Difficulty of reversing decision not to breastfeeding	4.2e Proper use of infant formula, whether manufactured industrially or home-prepared
1.1					
1.2					
1.3					
1.4					
2.1					
2.2					
2.3					
3.1					
3.2					
3.3					
3.4					
3.5					
3.6					
3.7					
3.8					
3.9					

TABLE 6.5 Extract from table which summarised coding in the infant formula marketing case study

Document ID No.	*4.2 Should not contain pictures/text which idealise formula*	*Conclusion*
1.1	'feed their PERSONALITIES' slogan used on envelope	May idealise
1.2	Stuffed cow toy (with logo) looks friendly and welcoming, gives impression that infant formula is good	Idealise formula
1.3	Lots of pictures of happy pregnant women and mums with babies including some pictures of very young babies. No imagery of feeding	May idealise
1.4	Not about feeding, but pictures of happy babies which may be associated with positive views of formula	May idealise
2.1	Mother and baby look very bonded and happy	May idealise
2.2	Mother and baby on front page look very happy and connected. Page 2 they don't look connected	May idealise
2.3	Cute polar bear toy with logo	Idealise formula
3.1	'Packed with organic goodness...' 'the original organic baby food co.' Hipp logo uses four hearts	May idealise
3.2	Images on page 3, which are drawn and show breastfeeding, show it looking odd – women with enormous very low hanging breasts. Do not look how most women would want to look	May idealise
3.3	3 x Cheerful stickers for nursery – colourful Hipp logo in the top corner	May idealise
3.4	Pictures of fruit and veg all look very healthy – may imply their formula is healthy. Probably a stretch to suggest idealising formula	Do not idealise
3.5	Two pictures of babies being bottle-fed – pages 1 and 3. Baby on page 3 is holding bottle themselves, but does look young because of big blue eyes	Idealise formula

material that may have been idealising infant formula (one of the codes). The final column of the table contains my concluding thoughts about whether the individual documents did or did not idealise infant formula. The use of hand coding and an indexing system to retrieve codes requires a very high degree of organisational skills, and the use of a **CAQDAS** programme, such as **NVivo** or **ATLAS.ti**, may be easier to manage for those who are newer to qualitative analysis.

Second coding

In 2016–17, Hannah Williams independently analysed the data, using **NVivo** 11 as part of her undergraduate dissertation. This enabled double coding of the full data set to be completed.

Triangulation between data sources

The second study corroborated the findings from the first study. That is, when parents sign up as members of infant formula parenting clubs, they are sent marketing materials by email (not discussed in this chapter) and post. Some of the marketing materials sent by post contained gifts and/or money-off vouchers, breaching the WHO Code. In light of what is already known about parents' experiences of receiving advertising materials related to infant formula, this is concerning (Berry et al. 2011; Parry et al. 2013).

Discussion

Through conducting a systematic **content analysis**, it was possible to identify many areas within documents that *may* have breached the WHO Code. Due to copyright reasons, it is not possible to display data extracts in this book. Overall, as can be seen in Table 6.5, it was often difficult to say if particular elements of advertising material had *definitely* breached the WHO Code, due to the use of symbolism and covert **meanings**. For example, the inclusion of an "important notice" about the superiority of breastfeeding on many of the sub-documents met article 4.2a and 4.2c (see Table 6.2 for full **meanings**) in **theory**, but this text was often considerably smaller than text which may have undermined breastfeeding. That said, in some areas breaches of the WHO Code were clear-cut; for example, in relation to article 5.4, gifts were provided by two companies (data sources 1, 2, 3 and 6), and this explicitly breached the WHO Code. Due to the challenges of making a clear-cut distinction between whether the data sources breached the WHO Code, I have chosen not to present the findings quantitatively. Alongside the completion of this research, calls have been made in the UK for parenting clubs to be banned as part of the Feeding Products for Babies & Children (Advertising & Promotion) Bill 2016. Unfortunately, due to insufficient time available in Parliament, this Bill will not make it into UK law in the near future.

Challenges of undertaking research using advertising materials

When undertaking an analysis of marketing materials, access to the documents is often reasonably straightforward. However, the right to publish extracts of the data is reliant upon the copyright holder allowing this to occur (McCracken 2006). Should you wish to publish extracts of data alongside your findings, you should contact the organisation that owns the copyright several months in advance of your intended publication deadline. For student projects, which will not be reproduced in the public domain, it may be acceptable to use extracts of data in your reporting. You should check this with your supervisor or your university's research and development team.

Within this study, a **content analysis** approach was used to highlight breaches of a global guideline. However, this did not fully consider the purpose of the documents, as they were devices for corporations to communicate with potential customers (Prior 2003; Flick 2009), and thus were not created to neutrally facilitate infant feeding, nor for analysis by a researcher. In order to detect the subtleties within the text, a **discourse analysis** approach may have added a further layer of analytical complexity. For example, it would have been interesting to consider the way in which women were positioned through an analysis of women's bodies, roles and stated competence within these roles (McCracken 2006).

Exercise: using content analysis

The analysis above focused on the way in which infant formula funded parenting clubs breached the WHO Code. Had I chosen data from charities or health organisations that promote breastfeeding, it is likely that very different findings would have occurred. Below, I present two pieces of fictional information on feeding babies that are similar to information given to new mums, but shorter, for you to analyse. Alongside this, one page from NHS Health Scotland's *Off to a Good Start* (2016) provides original data.

Instructions

Using the data provided, undertake a **content analysis** to answer the following **research question**:

Does the information meet the standards in the 1981 WHO International Code of Marketing of Breast-Milk Substitutes?

I suggest that you undertake a **content analysis** following the stages in Box 6.2. You should analyse the data against the coding framework in Table 6.2, which is based on the WHO Code. Here, your task is to highlight elements of **good** practice and **bad** practice. You may wish to photocopy the data to facilitate your analysis. If you would like to access additional data sources to expand your analysis, NHS Health Scotland's *Off to a Good Start* (2016) provides an additional 72 pages that you could include.

Data

Source 1

How to safely prepare a bottle of formula for your baby

Infant formula powder is not sterile and can contain bacteria. To reduce the risk of tummy bugs and other infections, it is really important to make up baby formula safely.

To keep your baby safe you should:
- Wash your hands before cleaning bottles and making up formula

- Clean and sterilise bottles and teats
- Leave bottles and teats to drip dry
- Boil tap water and leave it to cool until it's at 70°C (for 1 litre of water, this is around 30 minutes)
- Pour the water into a sterilised bottle
- Use the scoop in the formula package to add the correct amount of powder and level this off
- Shake the bottle to mix the powder in
- Cool the bottle under cold running water
- Test the temperature of the milk by shaking a few drops of milk onto the inside of your wrist – it should not feel hot.
- Discard the remaining formula if the baby does not finish the bottle

You should not prepare bottles in advance if at all possible, as prepared feeds allow bacteria to grow.

If you are planning to breastfeed your baby totally or to feed a mixture of breast milk and formula, it is important to note that introducing formula can make it difficult to carry on breastfeeding. If you are finding breastfeeding difficult, you can get advice from the National Breastfeeding Helpline, your midwife or health visitor.

Source 2

A mothers' story

Thinking back about my first week of being a new mum, it was a daunting time. When I was pregnant, I knew that I wanted to try breastfeeding, but I was a bit worried about getting it right. I had a really lovely midwife who told me that everything would be OK and to trust my body.

I gave birth in hospital to a little girl called Anna, and the midwife told me that it was important to put her on my chest (skin-to-skin, she called it) just after birth. We did this, and after a while Anna tried to get to my nipple, and the midwife helped me to get her to attach [latch on].

After this, Anna was feeding a lot, and I was really tired. My mum suggested that I should give the baby a bottle of formula as she was hungry so often, but the midwife told us that feeding this often was normal, because the baby's tummy is so small, and that as her tummy grew, the gaps between feeds would get longer.

That night, I was looking at the NHS Choices website, and found out that if I gave her a bottle of formula now, it would make it harder for me to keep on breastfeeding, as I would make less milk. It also said it was really important to make up bottles of formula carefully, using the right temperature of water and keeping everything really clean, or Anna could get a tummy bug. Because I want to breastfeed as long as I can to give her my immunity, and I don't really want to have to sterilise everything, and formula is so expensive, I felt able to say no to mum each time she said it.

When I got home from the hospital, two days after Anna was born, I felt as though I had got used to breastfeeding and just needed to sleep when she was sleeping. It was OK for the first day, but then all of my family wanted to visit, and I found it difficult to take Anna away from them when I could see she was starting to get hungry, which meant it was harder to feed her, as she was a bit grumpy when I was trying to get her to latch on.

The next day I felt quite sore. My midwife wasn't due to visit, so I found my local breastfeeding support group on Facebook and one of the peer supporters said she could check if I took Anna to the breastfeeding group which was on that day. I went along and the peer supporter watched Anna feed. She showed me how to wait until Anna's mouth was open wide and then to move her to my breast. It was immediately less painful.

Anna is now 2 weeks old, I'm getting used to being so tired, and the breastfeeding is going well. I'm pleased I stuck it out when it was so tiring and recommend the information on the NHS website to new mums.

Source 3

Extract from *Off to a Good Start* (2016), reproduced with kind permission from Off to a Good Start: all you need to know about breastfeeding © NHS Health Scotland 2016.

Notes

1 A food desert is a geographical space, often in a low-income area, where it is difficult to access nutritious food, either because it is absent or prohibitively expensive.
2 Although follow-on milk can be used once babies are over six months old, there is no need to stop using first infant formula.

References

Baby Milk Action 2016. *UK monitoring 2016*. Available at: http://www.babymilkaction. org/wp-content/uploads/2016/08/monitoringuk070916.pdf [Accessed: 22 February 2017].

Ball, M. 2011. Images, language and numbers in company reports: a study of documents that are occasioned by a legal requirement for financial disclosure. *Qualitative Research*: 11(2), pp. 115–139.

Bates, C. and Rowell, A. 1998. *The truth about the tobacco industry in its own words*. Action on Smoking and Health: London, UK.

Berger, A. A. 2015. *Ads, fads, and consumer culture: advertising's impact on American character and society*. Lanham, MD: Rowman & Littlefield Publishers.

Berry, N.J. et al. 2010. It's all formula to me: women's understandings of toddler milk ads. *Breastfeeding Review*: 18(1), pp. 21–30.

Berry, N.J. et al. 2011. Relax, you're soaking in it: sources of information about infant formula. *Breastfeeding Review*: 19(1), pp. 9–18.

Birch, L.L. and Fisher, J.O. 2000. Mothers' child-feeding practices influence daughters' eating and weight. *The American Journal of Clinical Nutrition*: 71(5), pp. 1054–61.

Blancharda, R. et al. 2010. Correspondence between self-reported and objective measures of driving exposure and patterns in older drivers. *Accident Analysis & Prevention*: 42(2), pp. 523–529.

Brierley, S. 2002. *The advertising handbook*. London: Routledge.

Burgoine, T. et al. 2014. Associations between exposure to takeaway food outlets, takeaway food consumption, and body weight in Cambridgeshire, UK: population based, cross sectional study. *BMJ*: 348, p. 1464.

Burgoyne, P. et al. 2010. *Digital advertising: past, present and future*. London: Creative Social.

Buunk, B.P. 2001. Perceived superiority of one's own relationship and perceived prevalence of happy and unhappy relationships. *British Journal of Social Psychology*: 40(4), pp. 565–574.

Carpenter, C.M. et al. 2009. Developing smokeless tobacco products for smokers: an examination of tobacco industry documents. *Tobacco Control*: 18(1), pp. 54–59.

Denzin, N.K. 1989. *The research act: a theoretical introduction to sociological methods*. Upper Saddle River, NJ: Prentice Hall.

Doll, R. et al. 2004. Mortality in relation to smoking: 50 years' observations on male British doctors. *British Medical Journal*: 328(7455), p. 1519.

Dougherty, Y.B.C. and Kramer, M. 1983. Do infant formula samples shorten the duration of breast-feeding? *The Lancet*: 321(8334), pp. 1148–1151.

Evans, W.D. and Hastings, G. 2008. *Public health branding: applying marketing for social change*. Oxford: Oxford University Press.

Ezra, B.W. and John Tjost, Z. 2001. What makes you think you're so popular? Self-evaluation maintenance and the subjective side of the 'Friendship Paradox'. *Social Psychology Quarterly*: 64(3), pp. 207–223.

Farrelly, M.C. et al. 2009. The influence of the national truth® campaign on smoking initiation. *American Journal of Preventive Medicine*: 36(5), pp. 379–384.

Flick, U. 2004. Triangulation in qualitative research. In: Flick, U. et al. eds. *A companion to qualitative research*. London: Sage, pp. 178–183.

Flick, U. 2009. *An introduction to qualitative research*. London: Sage.

Forsyth, S. 2012. Three decades of the WHO code and marketing of infant formulas. *Current Opinion in Clinical Nutrition and Metabolic Care*: 15(3), pp. 273–277.

George, A.L. 2006. Quantitative and qualitative approaches to content analysis. In: Scott, J. ed. *Documentary research*. London: Sage, pp. 119–134.

Julien, H. 2008. Content analysis. In: Given, L. (ed) *The SAGE encyclopaedia of qualitative research methods*. London: Sage, pp 120–121.

Goffman, E. 1986. *Frame analysis: an essay on the organization of experience*. Lebanon, NH: Northeastern University Press.

Gough, B. and Conner, M. 2006. Barriers to healthy eating amongst men: a qualitative analysis. *Social Science & Medicine*: 62(2), pp. 387–395.

Grant, A. et al. 2013. *A qualitative evaluation of breastfeeding support groups and peer supporters in Wales*. Cardiff: Public Health Wales.

Haynes, L.C. et al. 2013. Collection of delinquent fines: an adaptive randomized trial to assess the effectiveness of alternative text messages. *Journal of Policy Analysis and Management*: 32(4), pp. 718–730.

Health & Social Care Information Centre 2012. Infant feeding survey - UK, 2010. Available at: http://www.hscic.gov.uk/catalogue/PUB08694 [Accessed: 7 October 2017].

Hoorens, V. and Harris, P. 1998. Distortions in reports of health behaviors: the time span effect and illusory supefuority. *Psychology & Health*: 13(3), pp. 451–466.

Huhman, M. et al. 2008. Branding play for children: VERB (TM) it's what you do. In: Evans, W. D. and Hastings, G. eds. *Public health branding*. Oxford: Oxford University Press, pp. 109–125.

Jhally, S. 1990. *The codes of advertising: fetishism and the political economy of meaning in the consumer society*. London: Routledge.

Kemper, S. 2003. How advertising makes its object. In: Malefyt, T. D. deWaal. and Moeran, B. eds. *Advertising cultures*. Oxford: BERG, p. 220.

Kotnowski, K. and Hammond, D. 2013. The impact of cigarette pack shape, size and opening: evidence from tobacco company documents. *Addiction*: 108(9), pp. 1658–1668.

Krippendorff, K. 2013. *Content analysis: an introduction to its methodology*. London: Sage.

Lincoln, Y. and Denzin, N. 2003. *Turning points in qualitative research: tying knots in a handkerchief*. Walnut Creek, CA: AltaMira Press.

Marino, R. V and Bolnick, S. 1992. Consumer marketing of infant formula. *Clinical Pediatrics*: 31(8), p. 512.

McCormick, I. et al. 1986. Comparative perceptions of driver ability—A confirmation and expansion. *Accident Analysis & Prevention*: 18(3), pp. 205–208.

McCracken, E. 2006. The codes of overt advertisements. In: Scott, J. ed. *Documentary research*. London: Sage, pp. 213–248.

McStay, A. 2016. *Digital advertising*. London: Palgrave Macmillan.

Michie, S. et al. 2011. The behaviour change wheel: a new method for characterising and designing behaviour change interventions. *Implementation Science*: 6(1), p. 42.

Michie, S. et al. 2014. *The behaviour change wheel: a guide to designing interventions*. Sutton: Silverback Publishing.

Parry, K. et al. 2013. Understanding women's interpretations of infant formula advertising. *Birth-Issues in Perinatal Care*: 40(2), pp. 115–124.

Peeters, S. and Gilmore, A.B. 2013. Transnational tobacco company interests in smoke-less tobacco in Europe: analysis of internal industry documents and contemporary industry materials. *Plos Medicine*: 10(9), p. e1001506.

Prior, L. 2003. *Using documents in social research*. London: Sage.

Ritchie, J. et al. 2003. Carrying out qualitative analysis. In: Ritchie, J. et al. eds. *Qualitative research practice: A guide for social science students and researchers*. London: Sage, pp. 219–262.

Ritchie, J. et al. 2003. *Qualitative research practice: a guide for social science students and researchers*. London: Sage.

Rothbauer, P.M. Triangulation. In Given, L. 2008. *The SAGE encyclopaedia of qualitative research methods*. London: Sage, pp. 892–894.

Schreier, M. 2014. Qualitative content analysis. In: Flick, U. ed. *The SAGE handbook of qualitative data analysis*. London: Sage, pp. 170–183.

Scott, J. 1990. *A matter of record: documentary sources in social research*. London: John Wiley & Sons.

Stearns, C.A. 2010. The breast pump. In: Shaw, R. and Bartlett, A. eds. *Giving breastmilk: body ethics and contemporary breastfeeding practices*. Bradford: Demeter Press.

Sullivan, L. and Boches, E. 2016. *Hey, whipple, squeeze this: the classic guide to creating great ads*. Hoboken, NJ: John Wiley & Sons.

Taylor, A. 1998. Violations of the international code of marketing of breast milk substitutes: prevalence in four countries. *British Medical Journal*: 316(7138), pp. 1117–1122.

The Behavioural Insights Team 2013. Applying behavioural insights to organ donation. Available at: http://www.behaviouralinsights.co.uk/publications/applying-behavioural-insights-to-organ-donation/ [Accessed: 27 September 2017].

Wagle, T. and Cantaffa, D.T. 2008. Working our hyphens exploring identity relations in qualitative research. *Qualitative Inquiry*: 14(1), pp. 135–159.

Walker, R. et al. 2010. Disparities and access to healthy food in the United States: a review of food deserts literature. *Health & Place*: 16(5), pp. 876–884.

Waterston, T. and Tumwine, J. 2003. Monitoring the marketing of infant formula feeds - manufacturers of breast milk substitutes violate the WHO code - again. *British Medical Journal*: 326(7381), pp. 113–114.

Weber, R.P. 2006. Techniques of content analysis. In: Scott, J. ed. *Documentary research*. London: Sage.

World Health Organization 1981. *International Code of Marketing of Breast-Milk Substitutes*. Geneva, Switzerland: World Health Organization.

World Health Organization 2017. Breastfeeding. Available at: http://www.who.int/topics/breastfeeding/en/ [Accessed: 7 February 2017].

Yin, R.K. 2013. *Case study research: design and methods*. London: Sage.

7

DOCUMENTS IN ETHNOGRAPHIC RESEARCH

Things we might not have been able to observe

Summary

The focus of this chapter is on the use of documents as a data source within ethnographic studies. **Ethnography** is a method without a single definition but involves using a broad range of data, including observations, interviews and documentary analysis, in order to understand a phenomenon, society or group. It has been argued that the use of documents is essential to understand any literate society and is particularly important to understand organisations. Examples are provided of ethnographic studies which have benefited from the use of documents. Following this, a detailed case study is presented of an ethnographic study of UK welfare reform. Within this research, I used observations in UK Jobcentre Plus (welfare) offices, interviews with claimants and staff, and analysis of case files. A detailed description is provided of how the documents were sampled, prepared for analysis and analysed using **framework analysis**. I describe the way in which inconsistencies between data sources were handled; they were attributed to data production methods and changes in the presentation of self to multiple audiences. The particular challenges of using documents within **ethnography** generally and within **ethnographies** of an organisation are described. This includes gaining access to documents, the order in which data is collected and the impact this has on the researchers' understanding of the group under study, and the need for high levels of **reflexivity**.

Key learning points

- What **ethnography** is, and how documents are used in ethnographic research
- How to undertake **framework analysis**
- How to analyse multiple sources of data together and account for variation between sources
- How to overcome challenges in accessing documents from your ethnographic research site

Background: using documents within ethnographic enquiry

Ethnographic forms of data collection

Ethnographic research originated from early forms of anthropology, where foreign cultures were studied by researchers such as Zora Neale Hurston (www.zoranealehurston.com), Margaret Mead (see, for example, 1935) and Bronisław Malinowski (e.g. 2004). **Ethnography** can be defined in a plethora of ways, with no single accepted definition (Stewart 1998). Overall, the definitions describe **ethnography** either as research which aims to understand a particular group or culture (Fetterman 2008), or as "primarily...a particular set of methods" (Hammersley and Atkinson 1995, p. 1). The core methods to which Hammersley and Atkinson refer are those of participation, including observation, interviewing and "collecting whatever data are available" (1995, p. 1) to answer **research questions**. Stewart (1998) goes on to state that, having collected such data, the crucial element of ethnographic enquiry is that it brings together disparate observations to form a holistic understanding of the society under study. Such a form of inquiry values the researcher's openness to new ideas and concepts in 'the field' (that is, the place where data collection occurs) rather than attempting to answer narrow **research questions**.

Quality and bias when using documents in ethnographic research

As a result of the very open nature of **ethnography**, and the emphasis on understanding behaviours, ethnographic research is ideally suited to the inclusion of documents. In doing so, documents can shed light on areas of interest in ways that might not be accessed through interviews or observations alone (Hammersley and Atkinson 1995; Atkinson and Coffey 2010). Documents can also serve to act as a way of challenging the authority of the ethnographer, by using direct extracts from written materials as data, instead of the researcher's interpretation of events (Clifford 2003). Accordingly, it has been suggested that when studying "literate societies, written documents are one of the most valuable and timesaving forms of data collection" if they are used effectively (Fetterman 1998, p. 58).

As well as considering documents created by 'insiders' – that is, those who are being studied – researchers should also consider those written by 'outsiders', which may have relevance to the group under study (Stewart 1998). In doing so, the documents may give voice to marginalised or silenced groups, enable you to understand concepts or the use of particular language, and gain insight into those who are similar to your **population** but different in some way (Hammersley and Atkinson 1995). Although we may often think of documents as written records, Sarah Pink (2013) suggests that we as researchers should consider a broader range of items including photographs, videos and audio recordings, with photographs obviously falling into the document category. Pink (2013) highlights that this can include those produced by research participants, as well as those created by the researcher, but she notes that we cannot know their **meanings** as an 'insider' without the use of an **elicitation interview** (the use of **elicitation interviews** is discussed in Chapter 8).

As was mentioned in Chapter 2, documents hold particular relevance to those investigating organisations, where the keeping of text-based records is often common, may structure many aspects of work and often illuminate power relations (Harper 1998; Smith 2005; Smith and Turner 2014). One area that is of particular interest to ethnographers is the way in which documents help to shape interaction between individuals (Prior 2003; Smith 2005), including the way in which each document is distributed and which potential recipients are excluded (Coffey 2009). Alongside this, to understand organisations, ethnographers should pay attention to the way in which documents are constructed, such as the language used and any negotiation around what should or should not be included (Eastwood 2014). Ethnographers may also pay attention to the use of technology in the creation of organisational records and the impact this has on what is written and when (Rankin and Campbell 2014). The use of documents alongside observations may also allow researchers to understand the differences between the official purpose of the organisation and any secondary purposes, including social control functions in public sector organisations (Serber 1981). In the following section, examples are provided which show the value that documents have had within ethnographic studies from two different perspectives: those that use documentary data as the main data source, and those where documentary data is more of a secondary source.

Strengthening findings from ethnographic research studies

Documents at the core

Hammersley and Atkinson (1995) highlight that several classic **ethnographies** have benefited from a strong inclusion of documentary data, such as *The Polish Peasant in Europe and America* (Thomas et al. 1996) and *The Unadjusted Girl* (Thomas 2015). Alongside these, other more recent **ethnographies** have focused heavily on documentary evidence. Dorothy Smith and Susan Marie Turner's (2014) excellent edited collection *Incorporating Texts Into Institutional Ethnographies* is a must read, including exploration of topics as diverse as UN policymaking, nursing and policing through accounts of documents and other ethnographic data.

Among my favourite examples of this type of research is Richard Harper's *Inside the IMF* (1998). In this thorough analysis of the IMF (International Monetary Fund), Harper describes the organisation through documents, their contents and how they are used, through a 'document career' within the organisation (p. 263). In doing so, the **ethnography** focuses on how internal power relations are influenced by documents, including: how documents give structure to meetings and other occasions in the work place, how documents are given voice by members of staff and the way in which documents are read by consumers of the information. Accordingly, the way in which documents are an active part of human/technology networks within an organisation is described at length, and this text is worth reading if you are struggling to understand how documents fit into your own **ethnography** of organisational life.

Documents on the periphery

Many examples exist of the benefits of using documents as data in ethnographic studies that rely heavily on observation or interviews. These often include policy documents. For example, in Gabbay and le May's (2004) ethnographic study in primary care doctors' surgeries, data sources involved observation, interviews and analysis of core documents including guidelines and practice protocols. Comparison of practice and protocols was made and supplemented by questioning physicians as to why they had acted in a particular way. Overall, the **authors** suggested that this approach produced a rounded account of the ways in which guidelines were used in practice and the reasons for adherence or lack of adherence. Furthermore, in Hornberger and Johnson's (2007) study into the implementation of bilingual language policy, they utilised policy documents and other written artefacts, which were largely focused on the policy landscape, in their analysis.

Alternatively, in spaces which rely more heavily on oral accounts, documents can still help to understand the group or phenomenon under study. For example, in *Bouncers,* an **ethnography** of violence in the night-time economy, Dick Hobbs and colleagues undertook covert work as 'bouncers', a type of security guard, but also considered a wide range of documents alongside observation and interview data. The documents included policy documents from central and local government; a guide for magistrates (who sentence those who have committed minor violence in England and Wales); reports from policing authorities; research from the alcohol industry and associated professional bodies; and content from the professional journal for regeneration and town centre management (Hobbs et al. 2003). Thus, the researchers were still able to identify and utilise written content in relation to 'insiders' and 'outsiders' in this space, which at first glance appears understandable through observation alone.

Observation, triangulation and social constructionism

The reliance on the individual ethnographer (although team **ethnography** does exist – see, for example, Creese et al. 2008) can result in **bias** in data collection. Stewart (1998, p. 28) notes, "no one type of data, and no one particular informant, is error-free". Accordingly, there have been calls for ethnographers, and qualitative researchers in general, to be **reflexive** about their role as an actual person with a physical body and presence in **the field**, and the possible **biases** in data collection resulting from this (Coffey 1999). Alongside this, the use of multiple sources of data, known as **triangulation**, is viewed as good practice (Mason 2002), as the researcher seeks out, or is at least receptive to, data that goes against the previously identified trend. This may lead to a higher level of confidence in the **validity** of ethnographic research findings, and thus the research is more likely to shape policy (Hammersley 1992).

As social researchers, we are often encouraged to consider our data within its social context, as part of interpretivist or **social constructionist** paradigms. Such an approach acknowledges the limitations of **positivist** approaches and moves towards considering the potential for there to be multiple truths in any situation. This debate holds true for ethnographic research, where a rejection of **positivism** is encouraged (Hammersley 1992). Accordingly, the use of an interpretivist **epistemology** ensures that the different realities in which the data was constructed are considered during analysis. When using multiple sources of data, the researcher should not expect a similarity in findings, and if this does occur, it may be because the analysis was not critical enough (Meetoo and Temple 2003).

The underuse of documents in ethnographic research

At the time of writing, documents had been underused in ethnographic research (Atkinson and Coffey 2010). Thus, ethnographers – and by extension ethnographic field notes – may routinely pay considerable attention to what is said, to whom and in what circumstances, as well as what activities are undertaken, but what is written is often excluded and is rarely considered in detail. It has been suggested that this may be as a result of **ethnography** emerging from anthropology or marginalised cultures, which strongly relied on the oral transmission of stories due to a lack of written records (Hammersley and Atkinson 1995). These days, however, many ethnographers work within literate societies, and thus excluding documents from such studies ensures only a partial account of the group under study can be given. Another possible explanation is the "mundanity" of documents in our lives, leading to their relative invisibility (Harper 1998, p. 13).

Through the use of an illustrative example, I will show one way in which documents can be analysed alongside other ethnographic data. Through the case study, I will reinforce that the use of in-depth analysis of everyday documents results in accounts of social life which are more rounded than they might have been if documents were not considered. The example involves the study of UK welfare reform for the long-term sick and disabled, which is based on my ESRC (Economic and Social Research Council) funded doctoral studies (Grant 2011a, 2011b, 2012, 2013a, 2013b, Grant 2017).

Constructions of health and welfare case study

In the second of three case study chapters to focus on **triangulation** involving documents as data, this chapter moves on to examine a case study where patient case files were used alongside other ethnographic data. The case study is divided into five key areas. First is a description of the social context in which the research was undertaken, highlighting negative attention directed towards benefit claimants. Following this is a discussion of the **research question**, research design and data collection. The bulk of the example focuses on the way in which documents were prepared for analysis and subjected to **framework analysis** (Ritchie and Spencer 2002). I describe the stages in this easy-to-follow analysis approach, with particular emphasis on inputting data into matrices in order to draw conclusions which answer **research questions**.

Context

Over the past 30 years, significant negative attention has been focused on those claiming welfare benefits on the basis of ill health in the UK and the USA. Moralistic judgements around the long-term sick are created and perpetuated by politicians (Crisp 2008) and the media (Briant et al. 2013). However, these perceptions are widely accepted in society (Taylor-Gooby 2013), including by benefit claimants themselves (Dunn 2010), who often describe an undesirable other who does not deserve assistance from the state (Cohen 2002) (see Chapter 3 for more information on Cohen's work and the concept of 'othering').

At the time of the research, the Welfare Reform Act 2007 was being rolled out across the UK. The reported ethos behind this was that the long-term sick were capable of returning to work with support, but analysis of policy documents highlighted moralistic undertones regarding the rights and responsibilities of citizens were also at the fore (Bambra and Smith 2010). The 2007 Act introduced a range of changes for people who had been claiming, or were new claimants of, long-term sickness benefits, with a wide range of new conditions imposed on claimants where previously few had existed. The changes were widely viewed as punitive and stigmatising, and analysis of policy documents highlighted that the 'support' offered very little that was not previously available (Grant 2011b). The one new type of support offered was the introduction of the Condition Management Programme (CMP). The CMP was delivered through a range of external organisations (including the UK's National Health Service, or NHS), which used health professionals, including occupational therapists and physiotherapists, to promote self-management of long-term physical and mental health conditions. At the time the Act was rolled out, there had been some government-commissioned research into the pilot phase, but it was felt that an in-depth exploration including a range of stakeholders would add to the evidence base.

Research design

Overarching research aim

To understand the views and experiences of a wide range of stakeholders who had direct experience of the Welfare Reform Act 2007, either as a claimant or delivering the policy.

Figure 7.1 shows that a range of qualitative data was collected within the context of an ethnographic case study designed to understand the lived experiences of the Welfare Reform Act 2007. These included transcripts of 42

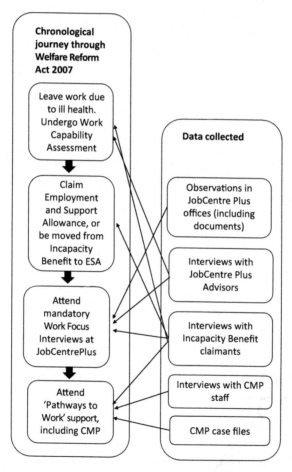

FIGURE 7.1 Claimant journey through Welfare Reform Act and data collected at each stage.

semi-structured interviews. Interviews were undertaken with benefit claimants recruited from the CMP (n = 10), benefit claimants recruited from community organisations not associated with the benefits process (n = 11), Jobcentre Plus (welfare) advisors (n = 8) and clinical staff who worked directly with claimants at the CMP (n = 13). Data also contained field notes, including from observing 14 Work Focused Interviews (the process by which individuals could be referred to the CMP) within one Jobcentre Plus office, as well as case files from the ten CMP participants who were recruited via their interaction with the CMP. Permission was given to observe CMP treatment sessions, but as many participants had moderate to severe mental health conditions and were only able to access limited support from the Programme, it was felt that this would not be ethical. The research thus combined interview, observational and documentary methods of data collection.

To date, the data have been used to answer questions on benefit claimants' experience of Work Focused Interviews (Grant 2011a), barriers to work for benefit claimants (Grant 2012), Jobcentre Plus advisors' experience of targets (Grant 2013b) and occupational therapists' use of discretion within the CMP (Grant 2013a). Ethical approval for the study was obtained through the National Research Ethics Service (NRES) as patients and staff of the CMP fit within their jurisdiction.

Research question

Although ethnographic research involves the use of broad **research questions**, for the purposes of this chapter, the specific question to be answered using the ethnographic data is:

Why did the Incapacity Benefit claimants who took part in interviews and provided access to their CMP case files leave work?

Population and defining a sample

Within the original research, it was desirable to have a wide range of experiences of the Welfare Reform Act 2007. For that reason, CMP staff were asked to introduce the study to those they were treating. Ten participants of the CMP were interviewed. All of these participants consented to my accessing their CMP patient files. Thus whilst the **sampling** of participants had an element of **bias** and was not likely to be representative of the whole **population**, documents, in the form of case files, were available for the entire **sample** of those interviewed.

Data collection

The majority of participants (nine out of ten) were interviewed by telephone between July 2008 and January 2009. All interviews were audio recorded and transcribed verbatim. I did not have access to the participants' patient files ahead of the interview. A semi-structured topic guide was used to ask a broad range of questions, including in relation to participants' journeys from work to Incapacity Benefit (see Box 7.1). Following the interviews, I showed signed consent forms to the CMP staff, who photocopied the case files and gave the copies to me.

BOX 7.1 OVERVIEW OF SEMI-STRUCTURED TOPIC GUIDE

- Health conditions and leaving work
- Experiences of claiming benefits, including Work Focused Interviews
- Experiences of CMP
- Potential to return to work in the future

Preparation of organisational documents

In order to enhance the **credibility** of ethnographic methods, researchers should carefully document all decisions (Hammersley and Atkinson 1995). When I received the case files, they were a collection of loose A4 sheets, with each individual case file in a separate A4 envelope. The sheets of paper did not have any page numbers. The first step I took was to number each sheet and to make a note of the total number of pages in each file. I then set about **anonymising** the case files, by using a thick black marker pen to cover over sections which included personal or identifiable details. These pages were then photocopied again to completely obliterate traces of personal details. As a condition of my ethical approval, the original documents were retained for a period of 3 years, but these were never used again. After this period, they were shredded. As with other documents, it may be helpful to prepare an index or database with each individual sheet or section of the data having a unique **Document ID Number (DIN)**, an extract of which is shown in Table 7.1.

TABLE 7.1 Extract from CMP document database

Participant (number of pages)	DIN (first initial and page number)	Title
Joanne (49)	J1–4	Referral from Jobcentre Plus
	J5–8	Jobcentre Plus evaluation form
	J9–11	Initial assessment form
	J12–15	'Messy' handwritten notes from initial assessment
	J16–25	Clinical notes (written by multiple people)

Analysis technique: framework analysis

What is framework analysis?

Framework analysis has been described by several **authors** since the 1990s but originates from Jane Ritchie and Liz Spencer. Ritchie and Spencer (2002) noted that this method is particularly well-suited to applied qualitative research across a broad range of contexts. Within **framework analysis**, the questions which the data need to answer should usually be known in advance, allowing for the **deductive** construction of core high-level codes, but **theories** and themes can emerge from the data, allowing for **inductive** codes to be formed when necessary. In doing so, **framework analysis** is suited to team working. The main difference between **framework analysis** and **thematic analysis** is the additional step of taking extracts of data from particular codes and displaying them together in a matrix. Due to this, theorising from the data is based on all available data extracts relating to that theme. This thorough approach to analysis has benefits in that it is harder to ignore data which do not follow a trend when it is displayed in matrices. However, it may take longer to undertake analysis using this method. Alongside this, the research is still an active process and researchers must assign codes and develop **meanings** from them, meaning that it is not possible to

---

BOX 7.2 PROCEDURE TO UNDERTAKE FRAMEWORK ANALYSIS (RITCHIE AND SPENCER 2002)

1. Familiarisation with the data; ideally with the entire body of data to be analysed, but if this is not possible, a broad range of sources should be considered. During this stage, the researcher should keep notes of interesting themes arising.
2. Identifying a thematic framework, through reviewing notes of interesting themes in the data, including those that were central to the research questions (**deductive**) and those which are arising directly from the data (**inductive**). This framework should be piloted with a small number of data sources and refined.
3. Indexing: All data is systematically coded using the thematic framework; sections of data may have more than one code applied to them.
4. Charting: Tables are created with headings and sub-headings from the coding framework, and a list of each data source forming the rows, to allow each individual piece of data to be viewed as a whole. This can be as brief or as detailed as is helpful to you. If you are working in a team, it may be the most helpful for this to be more detailed.
5. Mapping and interpretation of the data set as a whole in order to answer the predefined research question.

eliminate all forms of researcher **bias** (Spencer et al. 2014). Researchers who are new to qualitative analysis may find the clear structure involved in **framework analysis** helpful.

How to do framework analysis

There are several guides provided by researchers as to how to undertake **framework analysis**. Variations between these guides were minimal at the time of writing, and the common factor is that data is viewed in matrices. The original **framework analysis**, as conceptualised by Ritchie and Spencer (2002), comprises five processes, which are interconnected (see Box 7.2). A second version of the framework method recently published by Gale et al. (2013) describes the stages slightly differently, but the core concepts remain the same, with the addition of **verbatim** transcription of audio recording of interviews being essential prior to researchers familiarising themselves with the data.

Constructions of health and welfare: data analysis

Stages 1–3: Familiarisation, identifying a thematic framework and indexing

In this example, the analysis strategy outlined by Ritchie and Spencer (2002) is used. I will not describe Stages 1–3 of the analysis process, as the process of coding qualitative data is briefly covered elsewhere in this book (see Chapters 3 and 5) and in detail in a range of sources (see, for example, Saldaña 2013; Miles et al. 2014). If you are new to using **framework analysis**, I suggest reading Ritchie and Spencer's analysis chapter in full prior to beginning your own research.

Stage 4: Charting

As noted earlier, the unique element in **framework analysis** is Stage 4, making sense of the data by creating a matrix of data extracts from your codes. In Stage 4, Ritchie and Spencer suggest that this charting is of a summary of data extracts. In this project, however, I added what could be seen as an additional stage between Stages 3 and 4 where all quotes for themes were displayed in a matrix prior to this step, as in Miles and Huberman's three-step approach to data analysis (1994) which is updated in Miles, Huberman and Sadana (2014). The reason for this was feeling overwhelmed by the quantity of data (this was one sub-element of a much larger PhD) and wanting to ensure that I was not unduly influenced by the more extreme or interesting examples in my data. It may be that if you have a large volume of data, or if you are new to analysing qualitative data, this would be a helpful additional process for you to engage with.

In order to complete this extra stage, I created a series of spreadsheets where all coded data extracts from each participant interview in relation to one theme, such as 'reasons for leaving work', could be viewed together, with a separate row beneath the participant's interview for the participant's case file (see Table 7.2). In addition, I sub-divided the main codes into sub-codes, which were based on my reading and rereading the data as part of the familiarisation and indexing stages. The reason for using spreadsheets in order to produce the matrix was that the cells (the boxes into which data is input) are not limited by page size, so it was possible to create a very large matrix. Due to the large volume of text in the original analysis file, a blank extract from the document is reproduced in Table 7.2. To complete Stage 4, I summarised the information in a new table (Table 7.3), as per Spencer and Ritchie's 'charting' guidance, which allowed all of the main themes within the data set to be viewed together easily at a glance for each of the participants.

The way in which I adapted this method to make it suitable for multiple data sources contributing to a single participant was to use colour. I used three colours – one for information from the interview transcript only (highlighted in grey), one for information from the case file (highlighted in bold) and a third for information contained in both sources (black). Again, this table was a very large spreadsheet, and it is not possible to show the entire table here. The first column of the table is

TABLE 7.2 Extract from spreadsheet of interview quotations and document extracts in relation to 'reasons for leaving work' (blank)

	Main theme: *Reasons for leaving work*		
Sub-theme -> **Data source**	*Health*	*Employment*	*Personal circumstances*
Joanne interview			
Joanne case file			
Emma interview			
Emma case file			

TABLE 7.3 Extract from spreadsheet of summarised major research themes (blank)

Participant	*Reasons for leaving work*	*Experience of claiming benefits*	*Experience of CMP*
Joanne			
Emma			
Chris			
Dai			
Rachel			
Paul			
Jacob			
Sarah			
Catherine			
Rebecca			

TABLE 7.4 Duration of Incapacity Benefit claim and extract from summary spreadsheet of framework analysis – combining interview and documentary data

Participant	Time on Incapacity Benefit	Reasons for leaving work
Joanne	4 Years	Physical and mental health. Long-term bad back – reported was asked to leave work as 'unsafe'. Several bereavements led to depression
Emma	11 Months	Physical. Bad back, diabetes
Chris	19 Months	Physical condition, including ongoing need for trips to hospital several times a week. Employer tried to accommodate with light duties, but Chris was unable to work many hours due to severity of health condition and treatment required
Dai	1–2 Years	Physical – related to an accident at work. Employer was unable to find 'light duties', **pursuing a legal claim against employer**
Rachel	4 Years	Extreme anxiety and depression. Difficult incident at work and very poorly child
Paul	18 Months	Physical. Minor accident at work led to severe health complications. **Physically very weak**. At the end of sick pay moved on to Incapacity Benefit, but still has a contract to return to job when well
Jacob	15 Months	Extreme anxiety. Self-employed
Sarah	8 Months	Physical. Bad back from an accident at work. At the end of sick pay moved on to Incapacity Benefit, but still has a contract to return to job when well
Catherine	2 Years	Depression. Challenging job and very poorly child. **Long periods of sick leave at work over many years for depression**
Rebecca	2 Years	Physical. Bad back. Remained in work for some time with employer adaptations

Source: interview only; **case file only**; both

reproduced in Table 7.4. It can be seen that in terms of the major details, there was little variation between interview and document content, although more variation was notable for other themes and variations in the more subtle content were identified and will be discussed in more detail later.

Mapping and interpretation

The data set was incredibly rich and covered a very wide range of themes. In order to answer our **research question**, it was necessary to focus on the participants' reasons for leaving work, including their physical and mental health. It can be seen that seven of the participants had a physical health condition, three had a mental health condition and one had both a physical and mental health condition. The participants definitely described that they were unwell. However, several of the participants highlighted barriers to their working that were related to the type of work they were able to find and the lack of support for disabled employees in their workplace. The reasons that participants left work, therefore, were a complex interaction between their health, current or most recent job, and their employment prospects (related to qualifications, local labour markets and health conditions). Alongside this, in the group of participants who were recruited away from the CMP, two of the women reported that pregnancy was instrumental in their decision to begin claiming Incapacity Benefit; one participant had learning disabilities and had never been able to find suitable employment. The majority of the participants described a change in their self-identity when leaving work, due to the large part that work had previously played in their lives. As such, following the mapping and interpretation phase, this theme was renamed 'ill health, leaving work and identity'.

Variation by data sources

As we are particularly interested in the potential for new insights to be uncovered through the use of multiple methods, variations in findings between data sources are considered as a normal part of ethnographic inquiry (Meetoo and Temple 2003). It was possible to identify some participants within the data set who had a very high degree of overlap between interview content and case file analysis. This included Rachel, who had experienced extremely traumatic events and recounted much of the detail of these in her interview. By contrast, some of the participants constructed different accounts in their interviews with me compared to the detail contained in their CMP files. The most extreme of these was within Catherine's account.

Catherine had held a relatively senior position within her organisation, with many managerial responsibilities. She reported in her interview that her teenage child had been diagnosed with cancer several years ago, and that this had led to her suffering with anxiety and depression. In her interview account, Catherine stated that her child was "better" and had "moved on with his life" by going to university. She told me that she felt very bad that she was not able to move on when he had done so. In hearing this account, I believed that her son's cancer had gone into remission, and I bought into her hopes for him to successfully pass his degree. Upon reading Catherine's case file, I was shocked to discover that her child's cancer was still likely to be 'terminal'. Catherine's alternative positioning of her son within the interview discourse may have been due to the context of the interview encounter: I was a stranger conducting a telephone interview. Within Catherine's CMP file, it was noted that she found it difficult to discuss her son's illness with friends and acquaintances, as she found it painful to talk about how unwell he was. As such, the different reality presented within the interview encounter was also likely to be symptomatic of Catherine's anxiety and my status as a stranger. It was also interesting to note that Catherine had suffered from depression and anxiety for many years, and her current depression was described more as a relapse than as a discrete event linked to her son's ill health. It was not possible to map a likely reason for this disconnect between the interview and case file data, so it may have been due to the societal stigma towards benefit claimants and mental health patients at the time of the interview, as described in the 'context' section of this chapter.

A second example of the presentation of an alternative reality during the interview context can be found, in relation to physical capacity, from Paul. Paul had snapped his Achilles tendon, and a complication of this was a serious lung condition, resulting in his staying in hospital for over a month. Paul worked in construction, and described the 'heavy' nature of his role and his expectations regarding masculinity (that he should not cry) when he snapped his tendon at work. In his interview, Paul described his plans to go back to work and referred to returning to work frequently in his account of his planned future. However, within his CMP file it was reported that the likelihood of this was very low because of the potential of dust aggravating his ongoing lung condition. Within this instance, the telling of an alternative, likely future, highlights Paul's ideas of what work is (heavy, industrial, masculine) and his inability at the time of the interview to believe that his future self would vary so dramatically from his pre-accident future. Moreover, the comparison between the strong relationship that Paul developed with his occupational therapist over the period of several months ("the lady who I'm seeing, she's great…") and his one-off interview with me, an apparently capable, young woman, would have likely resulted in a different presentation of self within the context of Paul's traditional masculine identity.

Challenges of using documents within ethnographic research

Designing and conducting an ethnographic research study, regardless of whether it includes documents is, in my opinion, one of the most challenging forms of qualitative inquiry. Being able to go into **'the field'** and to know "what to look for, how to organize (your) thoughts and reflections and how to structure (your) ethnographic work" is an enormous challenge (Atkinson 2015, p. 9). Insights into how to conduct rigorous ethnographic work are provided in a range of accessible texts (Hammersley 1992; Hammersley and Atkinson 1995; Stewart 1998; Atkinson et al. 2001; Atkinson 2015; 2017), with further insight into visual **ethnography** provided by Pink (2013).

In the case study, some tenacity was required in order to gain ethical approval to view the documents, as has been well documented by other researchers (Hughes and Griffiths 1999; Scourfield et al. 2012; Barlow 2016). A colleague at the university had been provided with some of these CMP case files for separate research he was undertaking and assured me that I should collect them if possible as they were a very rich source of data. However, because I had not had the approval to examine a file in detail, I was unable to write what I expected to find on my application for NHS ethics. When my application was reviewed, I stated with confidence that I knew the files would be interesting, but that I could not say in detail what they contained or how and why they might be of relevance. A second point worthy of note was that I was unable to access the files until after the participants had been interviewed, even if they had previously orally consented to their files being shared. As barriers to accessing documents in the field are not uncommon, this should be considered when designing studies, for example, by leaving sufficient time in project plans. Alongside this, in rare cases, permission to use documents in research may be revoked (Serber 1981), highlighting the need to keep detailed field notes from the outset if copying documents is not allowed.

The order in which researchers are exposed to participants, interview data and documents is also of importance. As noted earlier, I interviewed the participants prior to viewing the documents. This allowed me to build up a picture of the participant from their interview, prior to being influenced by the content of the case files. In undertaking my initial analysis (Grant 2011b), I was not as **reflexive** as I would now have liked. As such, I have subsequently reanalysed the data, using the framework approach which has allowed me to construct a picture of the participants from the interview alone, the documents alone and finally a combined view of the participants. I would highly recommend that researchers keep detailed field notes as they are undergoing processes of analysis when they combine several sets of data, in order to aid **reflexivity** (Coffey 1999).

Exercise: using framework analysis

The earlier analysis compared interview transcripts with patient case files from the CMP for the ten participants in my doctoral research where both sets of data were available. In order for you to practise using **framework analysis**, a fictitious set of data is provided that could have come from the CMP.

Instructions

Using the four pieces of data, use **framework analysis** to describe:

The patient's health condition
The treatment plan
The patient's interaction with the treatment plan
Barriers and facilitators to undertaking treatment

I suggest that you consult Box 7.2 for guidance on how to undertake **framework analysis**. More practically, you may find it helpful to create a spreadsheet with the four topics as columns and the four data sources as rows. Some extra information is provided to help you understand the language used by medical professionals. You may wish to photocopy the data to facilitate your analysis.

Data

Common shorthand in medical notes

pt = patient
(L)/(R) = left/right
pain +/pain ++ = increased pain/seriously increased pain
4/52 = 4 weeks

Source 1

Extract from case notes for patient 12

Initial assessment: 7/1/16

Pt presents with significant pain in (L) ankle for 4 yrs. She reports pain ++ when walking for 4/52. She has avoided walking and is taking ibuprofen 400 mg $\times$ 4 daily. On assessment, she has weakness and laxity over anterior talo-fibular and calcaneo-fibular ligaments and additional range of movement. Unable to perform heel-rise test satisfactorily, heel dips also of low standard. Deep tissue massage undertaken. Pt provided with ankle exercise handout No. 4 and requested to undertake ten reps at least four × day. Asked to phone if struggling with exercises. If advice is needed, recommend a gentle touch, as patient is emotionally fragile.

(Signature), Physio

21/1/16

Pt returned to the clinic. Reported poor compliance with exercises. Stated that she had found them difficult. Repeated she should call if needed support. Concerned about dependence on service, so spent session supporting pt to do exercises and self-massage. Returning to clinic in 4/52. Strongly reiterated patient should phone if unable to do exercises.

(Signature), Physio

Source 2

Ankle exercise handout 4

1 Heel raises
   Stand on one leg (your **bad** leg).
   Rise up onto tiptoes, hold for a second and slowly lower to the ground.
   Repeat ten times.
   Hold on to the back of a chair to help you balance if needed.
2 Heel dips
   Stand on one leg (your **bad** leg).
   Bend your knee and slowly lower yourself towards the ground to a maximum of a 90-degree angle. Push back up so that you are standing with a straight leg.
   Repeat ten times.
   Hold on to the back of a chair to help you balance if needed.

Source 3

Extract from interview transcript – patient 12, 17.2.16

Q: How did you find the assessment?
A: It was horrible! The physio, and I know she has to do it, she really, really hurt when she was pressing on my ankle. In another way, it was good, because I've been waiting so long. So it was good to see her and to be told that there was nothing seriously wrong. She told me that I could carry on taking the tablets I've been taking, but I needed to make sure I took them with food, which I didn't know before. So that was good – she really knew her stuff.

Q: And I think she gave you some exercises to do?
A: Yes, they're horrible too! I'm supposed to stand on one leg, like a flamingo, and then bend down. So it's like doing a squat, but only on one leg. I couldn't do them when I was with her. I felt really embarrassed, because she was showing me as though it was nothing. I tried doing it, but using both legs so just doing a squat but it was so painful. I felt really sick and light-headed, so I needed to sit down.

Q: How did the physio react?
A: I think she found me ridiculous. I think she felt quite annoyed with me that I couldn't do it. She told me to take my time, but she kept on looking at her watch, and the waiting room was full when I arrived. There were loads of other patients that needed to see her.

Q: So were you able to do your exercises at home?
A: I kind of did them. I gave it a good go. Instead of standing like a flamingo, I tried doing it with two legs and holding onto the worktop in the kitchen so it didn't feel as hard. It still really hurt, and I thought I was probably doing more harm than good. So I did it for a few days, and my ankle was feeling more sore than ever, and I spoke to my husband and he told me that I should stop if it was making me hurt more.

Source 4

Extract from field notes from intervention session 2 (19.2.16)

Today I've been shadowing (name of physio). The consultation room is a small, windowless cupboard that could really do with a coat of paint. The desk is old and battered, but the examination couch for patients is very modern (it moves up and down with a remote control). All day she repeats the same pattern. Collects the new file from the patient notes trolley, walks to the waiting room and calls a name. The patients mostly have injuries with their legs (Tuesday seems to be the day for leg injuries), but as she only has ten minutes per patient she hurries them back to her room.

2.50 pm

The physio is running late, and she has commented to me that she must leave on time today and has another three patients to see before 3.30. It is time for the follow-up session with (name of patient 12). I wait in the consulting room while she collects the patient.

PHYSIO: So how have things been?
PATIENT: Not too bad. It's been a bit sore.
PHYSIO: Do you want to take your shoes off and hop up onto the bed?

The patient takes off her shoes and sits on the examination couch with her feet up. She looks as though she is used to doing this. Whilst the patient gets ready, the physio reads through the patient file.

PATIENT: It's been more than a bit sore, really, it's been very painful again.
PHYSIO: Has anything in particular been setting it off?
PATIENT: Well, I've been looking after my neighbours' little girl, so I've been running around after her.

Whilst the conversation is going on, the physio examines the patient's feet, asking her to push against her hands or if a particular movement hurts.

PHYSIO: And how have the exercises been going?
PATIENT: Not too well. I've done them a few times, but it really hurt. I don't know if I'm doing something wrong.
PHYSIO: Did you speak to anyone in the physio team?
PATIENT: I phoned and left a message, but I don't know if it got through to anyone. I didn't get a call back.
PHYSIO: I'm really sorry about that, we've had a few people off sick. Your ankle is feeling stronger, so that's good news. Jump up and show me how you've been doing the exercises.

The patient stands up, holding on to the edge of the couch, and displays a heel dip and heel raise. She is very wobbly, but the physio gives her a lot of encouragement that she is doing it 'right' and 'well'.

References

Atkinson, P. et al. 2001. *Handbook of ethnography*. London: Sage.

Atkinson, P. 2015. *For ethnography*. London: Sage.

Atkinson, P. 2017. *Thinking ethnographically*. London: Sage.

Atkinson, P. and Coffey, A. 2010. Analysing documentary realities. In: Silverman, D. ed. *Qualitative research*. London: Sage, pp. 77–92.

Bambra, C. and Smith, K. 2010. No longer deserving? Sickness benefit reform and the politics of (ill) health. *Critical Public Health*: 20(1), pp. 71–83.

Barlow, C. 2016. Documents as 'risky' sources of data: a reflection on social and emotional positioning – a research note. *International Journal of Social Research Methodology*: 19(3), pp. 377–384.

Briant, E. et al. 2013. Reporting disability in the age of austerity: the changing face of media representation of disability and disabled people in the United Kingdom and the creation of new 'folk devils'. *Disability & Society*: 28(6), pp. 874–889.

Clifford, J. 2003. On ethnographic authority. In: Lincoln, Y. S. and Denzin, N. K. eds. *Turning points in qualitative research: tying knots in a handkerchief*. Walnut Creek, CA: AltaMira Press, p. 496.

Coffey, A. 1999. *The ethnographic self: fieldwork and the representation of identity*. London: Sage.

Coffey, A. 2009. Analysing documents. In: Flick, U. ed. *The SAGE handbook of qualitative data analysis*. London: Sage.

Cohen, S. 2002. *Folk devils and moral panics: the creation of the mods and rockers*. Hove: Psychology Press.

Creese, A. et al. 2008. Fieldnotes in team ethnography: researching complementary schools. *Qualitative Research*: 8(2), pp. 197–215.

Crisp, R. 2008. Motivation, morals and justice: discourses of worklessness in the Welfare Reform Green Paper. *People, Place & Policy Online*: 2/3, pp. 172–185.

Dunn, A. 2010. The 'Dole or Drudgery' dilemma: education, the work ethic and unemployment. *Social Policy & Administration*: 44(1), pp. 1–19.

Eastwood, L. 2014. Negotiating UN policy: activating texts in policy deliberations. In: Smith, D. and Turner, S. M. eds. *Incorporating texts into institutional ethnographies*. Toronto, ON: University of Toronto Press, pp. 64–92.

Fetterman, D.M. 1998. *Ethnography: step-by-step*. 2nd ed. London: Sage.

Fetterman, D.M. 2008. Ethnography. In: Given, L. ed. *The SAGE encyclopaedia of qualitative research methods*. London: Sage, pp. 288–292.

Gabbay, J. and le May, A. 2004. Evidence based guidelines or collectively constructed 'mindlines?' Ethnographic study of knowledge management in primary care. *British Medical Journal*: 329(7473), pp. 1013–1016A.

Gale, N.K. et al. 2013. Using the framework method for the analysis of qualitative data in multi-disciplinary health research. *BMC Medical Research Methodology*: 13(1), p. 117.

Grant, A. 2011a. Fear, confusion and participation: incapacity benefit claimants and (compulsory) work focused interviews. *Research, Policy and Planning*: 28(3), pp. 161–171.

Grant, A. 2011b. *New Labour, welfare reform and discretion: pathways to work for incapacity benefit claimants*. Cardiff: Cardiff University.

Grant, A. 2012. Barriers to work for incapacity benefit claimants in Wales. *Contemporary Wales*: 25, pp. 173–190.

Grant, A. 2013a. The effect of the use of discretion on occupational therapists' identity. *British Journal of Occupational Therapy*: 76(9), pp. 409–417.

Grant, A. 2013b. Welfare reform, increased conditionality and discretion: Jobcentre Plus advisers' experiences of targets and sanctions. *Journal of Poverty and Social Justice*: 21(2), pp. 165–176.

Grant, A. 2017. 'I Don't Want You Sitting Next to Me'. *International Journal of Qualitative Methods*: 16(1), p. 160940691771239.

Hammersley, M. 1992. *What's wrong with ethnography? Methodological explorations*. London: Routledge.

Hammersley, M. and Atkinson, P. 1995. *Ethnography: principles in practice*. Abingdon: Routledge.

Harper, R. 1998. *Inside the IMF: an ethnography of documents, technology, and organisational action*. London: Academic Press.

Hobbs, D. et al. 2003. *Bouncers: violence and governance in the night-time economy*. Oxford: Oxford University Press.

Hornberger, N.H. and Johnson, D.C. 2007. Slicing the onion ethnographically: layers and spaces in multilingual language education policy and practice. *Tesol Quarterly*: 41(3), pp. 509–532.

Hughes, D. and Griffiths, L. 1999. Access to public documents in a study of the NHS internal market: openness Vs secrecy in contracting for clinical services. *International Journal of Social Research Methodology*: 2(1), pp. 1–16.

Malinowski, B. 2004. *Argonauts of the western Pacific: an account of native enterprise and adventure in the archipelagoes of Melanesian New Guinea*. London: Taylor & Francis.

Mason, J. 2002. *Qualitative researching*. London: Sage.

Mead, M. 1935. *Sex and temperament in three primitive societies*. London: Harper Collins.

Meetoo, D. and Temple, B. 2003. Issues in multi-method research: constructing self-care. *International Journal of Qualitative Methods*: 2(3), pp. 1–12.

Miles, M.B. et al. 2014. *Qualitative data analysis: a methods sourcebook*. London: Sage.

Miles, M.B. and Huberman, A.M. 1994. *Qualitative data analysis: an expanded sourcebook*. London: Sage.

Pink, S. 2013. *Doing visual ethnography*. London: Sage.

Prior, L. 2003. *Using documents in social research*. London: Sage.

Rankin, J.M. and Campbell, M.L. 2014. 'Three in a bed': nurses and technologies of bed utlization in hospital. In: Smith, D. E. and Turner, S. M. eds. *Incorporating texts into institutional ethnographies*. Toronto, ON: University of Toronto Press, pp. 147–172.

Ritchie, J. and Spencer, L. 2002. Qualitative data analysis for applied policy research. In: Huberman, A. M. and Miles, M. B. eds. *The qualitative researcher's companion*. London: Sage, pp. 305–329.

Saldaña, J. 2013. *The coding manual for qualitative researchers*. London: SAGE.

Scourfield, J. et al. 2012. Sociological autopsy: an integrated approach to the study of suicide in men. *Social Science & Medicine*: 74(4), pp. 466–473.

Serber, D. 1981. The masking of social reality: ethnographic fieldwork in the bureaucracy. *Anthropologists at home in North America*: 1981, pp. 77–87.

Smith, D.E. 2005. *Institutional ethnography: a sociology for people*. Lanham, MD: AltaMira Press.

Smith, D.E. and Turner, S.M. 2014. *Incorporating texts into institutional ethnographies*. Toronto, ON: University of Toronto Press.

Spencer, L. et al. 2014. Analysis: principles and processes. In: Ritchie, J. et al. eds. *Qualitative research practice: a guide for social science students and researchers*. London: Sage, pp. 269–294.

Stewart, A. 1998. *The ethnographer's method*. London: Sage.

Taylor-Gooby, P. 2013. Why do people stigmatise the poor at a time of rapidly increasing inequality, and what can be done about it? *The Political Quarterly*: 84(1), pp. 31–42.

Thomas, W.I. et al. 1996. *The Polish peasant in Europe and America: a classic work in immigration history*. Champaign, IL: University of Illinois Press.

Thomas, W.I. 2015. *The unadjusted girl*. Montclair, NJ: Patterson Smith.

8

PARTICIPANT-CREATED DOCUMENTS AS AN ELICITATION TOOL

Things we might not have otherwise been told

Summary

Elicitation interviews are where participants are either shown items or asked to bring items to the interview in order to shape the direction of the conversation. This approach is often referred to as being part of '**visual methods**'. The chapter focuses in particular on when participants are asked to either bring everyday documents, such as photographs, or when they are asked to create a new document, with both sources serving as a 'topic guide' during interviews, which are directed by the participant. The advantage of this method over many documentary analysis methods is the presence of the **author** and the ability for the researcher to ask the author questions. This allows us to more easily establish **meaning** than in participant-absent documentary analysis. A detailed case study is presented of the research that aimed to understand health behaviours, such as smoking and drinking alcohol, during pregnancy. Ten women from deprived areas living on low incomes took part in **elicitation interviews**. Techniques of elicitation included life-history timelining (drawing a timeline of their life), collaging or using a paper template with thought bubbles to describe what it was like being pregnant, and sandboxing (that is, creating an image or scene using sand and a range of everyday items). Data was analysed using a **narrative analysis**, which is used to consider change over time. Guidance is provided on how to undertake **narrative analysis**. The findings highlighted a wide range of barriers and facilitators to abstain from alcohol and smoking during pregnancy, which were related to life circumstances. The key challenges of using such a method, including the ethical implications, are discussed. An exercise with additional data is provided to consolidate learning.

Key learning points

* How documents can be used as part of **elicitation interviews**, sometimes known as **'visual methods'**
* How the use of document **elicitation interviews** can reduce power imbalance between the researcher and participant, but does not automatically do this
* How to consider if a document **elicitation interview** is appropriate in your research study
* How to undertake **narrative analysis**

Background: using documents created by individuals during elicitation interviews

As discussed in Chapter 5, individually created documents can shed light on many phenomena within society. However, the most significant weakness in using this method, which we noted in Chapter 5, is the challenge in interpreting **meaning**. One way in which we can obtain the benefits of a participant-generated account, whilst also having a clear understanding of the **meaning**, is a document **elicitation interview**. When using this method, the participant will be provided with a brief by the researcher ahead of the interview to either create a new document or to bring existing documents to the interview. Here the purpose of the document is to help the researcher and participant create a shared understanding and to reduce the researchers' dominant position as an 'interviewer'. Unlike the use of documents in ethnographic settings, considerable attention has been paid to the value of this approach, and this is often linked to the term **'visual methods'** or to terms such as creative and participatory methods.

Prior to the twentieth century, researchers would have been the 'experts' creating documents, such as field notes and photographs, in the research field, when attempting to understand the behaviour of a group of people and bringing their own (often imperialist, white, middle-class) lens to interpret them (Mannay 2016). However, as has been made clear throughout this book, such an approach will not engender an understanding of **'meaning'** from the point of view of the people under study, which is important to truly understand the context behind these 'expert' documents (Scott 1990). For this reason, asking participants to create documents can enable them to define their own reality, albeit shaped by the researcher's brief. In this type of research, the site and context in which a document is produced has an impact on their content (Rose 2016).

A broad range of approaches can be used within document **elicitation interviews**. As with all research projects, the type of documents used in **elicitation interviews** should be carefully considered to ensure they are the most appropriate to fit with the **research question**. The first question to consider is whether you are interested in documents the participants already have, or if they should create something new for the research project. These two approaches are discussed in more detail next.

Use of existing documents in elicitation interviews

The use of pre-existing documents has been widely, and sometimes creatively, used in qualitative research. This approach has been discussed at length by Gillian Rose (2012) in her work on family photography. Rose conducted **elicitation interviews** with participants, to allow them to tell the story of their family through the images to which they had access. However, Rose noted that the types of events in photographs presented as part of the research project tended to depict leisure time, such as family holidays or festivals, in routinised ways. This excluded much of the everyday, ordinary, social and domestic life, highlighting that taking a photo is itself a social event, disrupting the event immediately preceding it (Banks 2001). That said, participants in photo **elicitation interviews** (using their pre-existing photographs) are able to construct meanings in similar ways, by discussing who took the photo, who was present, and providing lengthy accounts around some images, whilst skipping others (Rose 2012). Accordingly, the use of an **elicitation interview** is important to understanding the **meanings** behind photographs (Banks 2001). Whilst this approach may seem common sense, alternative approaches to understanding society through photography are advocated by Terence Heng (2017), who uses photography within **ethnography** to capture feelings and moods at events, and Marcus Banks (2001) who uses photographs that he has found or taken during interviews as elicitation tools. Thus it is important to note that there are many possible uses of any one type of document within elicitation-based research.

Although photos may easily come to mind as an elicitation document, other everyday objects and artefacts can provoke interesting accounts of society (Mitchell 2011). My own research, to understand intergenerational changes in infant feeding by working with new mothers and their own mothers (the grandmothers), raised the importance of context in designing methods for **elicitation interviews**. The likelihood that participants (who were new mothers) would have limited time to construct a new document was central in forming the research methods; as such, we asked participants to bring "everyday objects that make you think about infant feeding". Some participants brought traditional documents, such as leaflets given to them by health professionals and baby weight charts, whilst others brought objects used whilst feeding their infants, such as pumps (for expressing breast milk), bottles and shawls. The participant who brought a shawl used it to explain her fear of being thought of as sexual whilst breastfeeding (Grant et al. 2017). This issue may not have been established in a traditional interview, without the ability for participants to bring along objects and tell their own stories (Mannay et al. 2018).

More recently, as individuals document much of their life on social media, social media elicitation has been used as a form of narrative interview whilst "scrolling back" through Facebook profiles (Robards and Lincoln 2017, p. 1). In this study, the process of examining these participant-created digital documents allowed for participants to be 'co-analysts' of the data, reflecting on their mindset at the time of writing and how this varied from their present interpretation of the written account. In undertaking such research, important ethical questions must be answered; participants may not have considered the data in detail prior to the **elicitation interview**, and they may encounter elements that they would rather not discuss with a researcher. They may also have strong emotional reactions to documents that have not previously been considered in detail. Researchers should consider how to reduce the potential of harm to participants as part of their research design. In doing so, you should consult your professional body's Code of ethics prior to conducting such fieldwork (see, for example, British Sociological Association 2002) and review relevant literature on the use of **visual methods** (see, for example, Lomax 2015; Mannay 2016; Rose 2016). If you are undertaking research using social media as an elicitation tool, you should also refer to Chapter 5.

Creating new documents for research projects: a participatory approach?

The second approach to document **elicitation interviews** involves asking participants to create a new document which will be explicitly focused on the aims of the research. Participants may be asked to create a document in advance of or during the **elicitation interview**, depending on the research design. Elicitation tools include asking participants to draw, write or create content in some other way. A broad range of techniques have been used, such as diaries (which are discussed in Chapter 5) (Coxon 2006), collages (Mannay 2013), participant-collected photographs (Latham 2004; Rose 2012) and sandboxing (Mannay et al. 2017). The briefing document that participants are provided with will be key to ensuring they are able to help you answer your **research question**, by focusing their efforts on the area of enquiry (Rose 2016). They should also be considered as part of the **social construction** of creating the data and the **meanings** contained within it.

In undertaking an **elicitation interview**, there are a number of key points to remember. In advance of the interview, you should decide whether an interview can go ahead if the participant has not created a document. It may be that this adds extra challenges for a researcher, who might need to play a more active role in shaping the direction of the interview (Mannay et al. 2018). For this reason, it might be beneficial for researchers to have access to a topic guide, which can be used if no documents are provided (Phillips et al. 2018). When participants have created documents, it may be that they do not cover all aspects of interest to the researcher, and therefore it may be necessary to 'mop up' any uncovered areas of interest with some questions at the end. It should be decided in advance if this would fit within the ethos of the research, or if additional questions should not be asked.

Participatory approaches develop research agendas *with* the groups in the study, rather than in isolation from them. Within Participatory **Action Research** (PAR), the researcher or a practitioner guides and facilitates whilst aiming to empower the community to solve problems they have identified (Walter 2006). **Elicitation interviews** can be used within studies which are participatory or can be used in a partly participatory way to attempt to provide participants with agency (Lomax 2015; Mannay 2016). However, these documents and their site of production are often strongly shaped by the researcher; such research should not uncritically be classified as participatory, and other approaches may not be participatory at all (Sheridan et al. 2011). This may be, for example, because of the needs of project funders to focus on answering a relatively narrow **research question**, or because of the time constraints of completing a dissertation.

Quality and bias in document elicitation interviews

In considering quality in relation to documents in **elicitation interviews**, it is still relevant to consider criteria that are focused entirely on the quality and **biases** in documents. By using Scott's (1990) criteria (see Table 2.1), we can see that parts of **authenticity** are high, as we know that the document is original, and we usually know who created the document, but we cannot know what elements a participant has chosen to exclude. Likewise, the relationships between the researcher and participant will have a large impact on whether the participant felt comfortable enough or willing to provide a sincere and accurate account. Issues of **representativeness** in terms of the **sample** of participants are likely to be high, and the major way in which elicitation interviews score highly on Scott's criteria as compared to other documentary sources is that we are able to understand **meaning** through a dialogue with the author.

In analysing elicitation documents, areas of contrast between elicitation materials and the participants' spoken words should be given attention, such as the influence of others on the elicitation materials (Mannay 2013). A more thorough analysis of elicitation documents provided may occur in two ways: either alongside interview transcripts or in isolation from interview transcripts. In some studies, elicitation documents may be paid little attention during the analysis phase, as their purpose was viewed entirely as a way to encourage participants to talk about matters which were important to them. Prior to beginning your study, you should decide which approach is most suited to your research.

If you do decide to include the documents in your analysis, you may find it is difficult to decide whether to try to interpret the document yourself, or to provide an extract or the entire document in your output, to allow the **reader** to make their own interpretation. There is no generally accepted standard way of doing so (Banks 2001). One of the most basic ways in which elicitation materials can be analysed is through **content analysis** (Ball and Smith 1992), which is described in more detail in Chapter 6. Should you wish to interpret the **meaning** of the document you may wish to consider: the presence or absence of items (Mitchell 2011), the size of various aspects that are included (perhaps indicating their relative importance) (Banks 2001) and the colours present (Ball and Smith 1992).

Wider interpretation may focus on the portrayal of discourses, such as gender, place and portrayal of bodies (for a collection of examples, see Reavey 2011).

Health and wellbeing in pregnancy: detailed case study

In the final empirical case study of this book, this chapter moves on to consider the way in which documents can be used as a tool, instead of a topic guide, during an interview. The case study is based on a study in which I focused on health and wellbeing in pregnancy, and the context is briefly provided. Following this, the process of refining the **research question** and sampling participants is described. A detailed account of the four modes of data production – timelines, thought bubbles, collages and sandboxing – is provided. I then consider how to undertake **narrative analysis**, providing a reflective account of the process undertaken. Additional data is provided at the end of the chapter, to give you the chance to practise **narrative analysis** using a timeline and interview data.

Context

Three in four pregnant women in Wales, UK, either smoke, drink alcohol or are obese, and almost one-third of women experience more than one of these risk factors and thus, their babies are at increased risk for low birth weight, birth defects and Sudden Infant Death Syndrome (Reilly 2013). Women from poorer social backgrounds are most likely to engage in such behaviours (Health & Social Care Information Centre 2012). Considering this from a health services perspective, this has significant financial implications for the National Health Service, with a cost of up to £246M per year for smoking and obesity-related complications alone (Godfrey and Consortium 2011; Morgan et al. 2014). However, these health behaviours also exacerbate health inequalities throughout the life course, reinforcing social inequality. At the time of the research, it was a priority of the four UK governments to promote healthier pregnancies (see, for example, Welsh Government 2017). As such, considerable investment to encourage healthy behaviours during pregnancy has been evident in the UK. However, these programs often have low uptake and high dropout (Gamble et al. 2015) or do not produce the intended behaviour change (Robling et al. 2016). This is likely to be because such programmes fail to take account of the full, lived reality of people's lives. One approach that aims to consider health behaviour holistically is the socioecological model (Whitehead and Dahlgren 1991).

Research design

Research question

We aimed to develop an understanding of multiple health behaviours, including smoking, drinking alcohol and infant feeding, among pregnant women from deprived areas who lived on low incomes.

Population and defining a sample

From the very beginning, having reviewed existing qualitative work, it was clear that a single interview would be unlikely to allow the necessary rapport to develop that would uncover new insights. As such, we planned to speak to fewer women, but in a more detailed way. Within the budget available for the study, it was decided that a **sample** of ten women would be feasible within the resources, which was related to researcher time available to co-produce and analyse the data, but also a significant budget in terms of transcription (see Table 2.2).

As noted earlier, women from poorer social backgrounds are more likely to engage in risky health behaviours. Accordingly, we aimed to **purposively sample** women who lived in the most deprived areas of Wales, as measured by the Welsh Index of Multiple Deprivation (Stats Wales 2015), and who were in receipt of a means-tested benefit (welfare). We aimed to recruit participants in a way that would make them feel less concerned or stigmatised when disclosing a risky health behaviour, so decided to recruit participants away from the health service. We therefore created an advertisement which was shared through community groups in poorer areas, social media groups targeted at mothers and in local communities. Within the advert, we explicitly noted that participants would be thanked with a £25 shopping voucher for each phase of the research they participated in. The use of incentives is sometimes viewed contentiously; for example, in this study, the ethics committee who reviewed the research were reluctant to allow these incentives. However, the use of incentives is an important tool to reduce the inherent power balance between the researcher and participants, so if a broadly participatory approach is desired, incentives should be provided wherever possible.

Data production

As we were using an approach that aimed to be women-centred and as egalitarian as possible in terms of data generation, it is not appropriate to think of this data as having been 'collected' by the researcher. As such, unlike in other chapters of this book, this section is titled "data production" (Mannay 2016, p. 4). Data production occurred through three **elicitation interviews** per participant, with interviews two and three occurring on the same day following a short break. Nine of the ten participants contributed to all three interviews. One participant was unable to continue following the first interview. In the next section, I outline the four creative approaches utilised to produce data in this study.

Timeline elicitation interviews

Participants were sent a resource pack around a week before the interview. The pack included a simple timeline template (see Figure 8.1), which defined the time period of interest from the participants' "childhood and primary school"

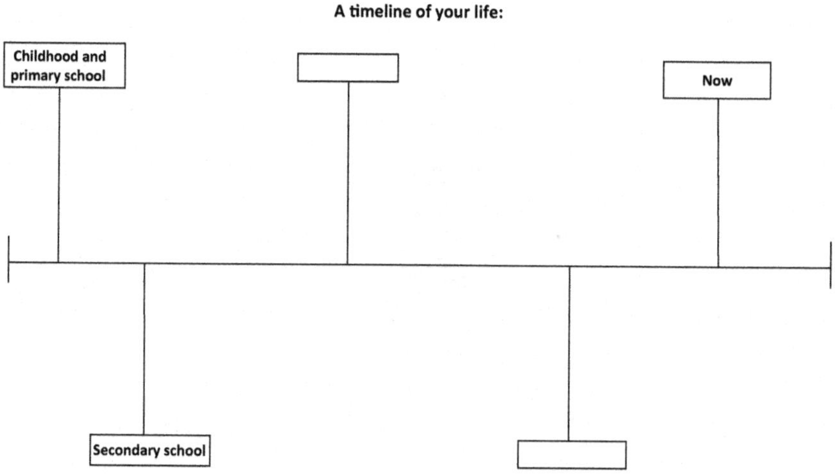

A timeline of your life:

FIGURE 8.1   Timeline template.

to "now". A range of alternative paper, and coloured stickers and pens were provided, which could be used to "represent emotions" (Gabb and Fink 2015). Guidance in the resource pack was reiterated during telephone calls and text message conversations prior to the interview. We asked participants to create a timeline of their life prior to the interview, but, in the spirit of an approach that aimed to reduce power imbalance, provided reassurance that they did not need to use the template and that the interview could go ahead without a timeline if participants did not want to create one. During **elicitation interviews**, the participants were asked to talk through their timeline and thus lead the interview.

Collage and thought bubble elicitation interviews

During the second data production period, participants were sent a second pre-interview kit that consisted of two activities: collaging and a thought bubble template. Materials for producing a collage included a range of coloured papers, stickers and glue. The thought bubble template featured a picture of a white pregnant woman's torso (with no head, to allow for ease of participant identification with the image; all participants were white) in the centre and thought bubbles around her. In this task, participants were asked to describe "how being pregnant impacts your everyday life" and were given the option to produce a collage or use the thought bubble template, or both, or neither (see Figure 8.2). Three participants only created a collage, five participants only used the thought bubble template and one participant did both. **Elicitation interviews** were undertaken, with participants using their pre-prepared collage or thought bubbles to direct the interview (Mannay 2013).

FIGURE 8.2 Thought bubble template.

Dyad sandbox elicitation interviews

The third interview included a dyad sandbox **elicitation interview**. Sandboxing is a **visual method** where participants select symbolic objects and ascribe **meaning** to them (see Mannay et al. 2017 for details and practical guidance). On the day of the interview, participants were provided with a sand tray and a range of 3D figures and objects[1] and were asked to create a scene, image or abstract design in relation to 'health and wellbeing in pregnancy' (see Figure 8.3). At the same time, but separately, the researcher created a 'sandbox' of their own experiences of health and wellbeing during pregnancy using a second set of equipment. When the sandboxes were complete, the researcher and

FIGURE 8.3 Sandboxing materials.

participant sat together for a third **elicitation interview**. First, the participant described their experiences of pregnancy through reference to their sandscape, and then the researcher described their own experiences, although there was an overlap in some of the accounts. Areas of similarity and difference were also discussed. Whilst a sandscape may not be considered a document in the traditional sense, the use of creative methods may work well with those who have created documents to inform previous elicitation interviews.

Analysis technique: narrative analysis

What is narrative analysis?

Narrative approaches consider change over time as the central element in analysis (Plummer 2001). Narratives may be structured around family, self or events in wider society. As with many approaches to qualitative analysis, there is no one standard definition of **narrative analysis**. For example, Kohler Riessman (2008, p. 539) states that **narrative analysis** is a group of approaches that analyse data presented in "storied form" around individual cases, which may include multiple data sources, such as interviews and documents. As well as considering 'stories', Plummer (2001) suggests that we may also pay attention to plots, characters, themes and structures. Broadly, Kohler Riessman (2008) argues that **narrative analysis** can be either thematic, focusing on the themes within the account, or structural, where the composition of the story is considered chronologically with attention paid to meanings ascribed. By contrast, Jane Elliott (2005) provides a comprehensive overview of narrative approaches to research, both within qualitative and quantitative paradigms. She states that "a narrative can be understood to organize a sequence of events into a whole so that the significance of each event can be understood through its relation to that whole. In this way a narrative conveys the meaning of events" (Elliott 2005, p. 3). As such, the significance of events, as described in a chronological fashion, is central to understanding the **meaning** in Elliott's **narrative analysis**. Moreover, if one is to adopt this position, a narrative approach to data collection should be adopted, with participants encouraged to describe events, rather than themes. Although **narrative analysis** may often be conducted on interview accounts, the method can also be used to make sense of reports (Kohler Riessman 2008) and other written documents (Elliott 2005).

How to do narrative analysis

As may be imagined, from the lack of shared definition, there is no one single type of **narrative analysis**, and researchers' particular interests in varying elements may shape the analysis strategy used (Elliott 2005). However, core elements may include empathetic understanding of life circumstances (Elliott 2005) and consideration of the telling of narrative to establish identity (Riessman 1990). It is relevant to note that the use of **narrative analysis** has come under criticism. It has been argued that in allowing ones analysis to focus on the narrative within data alone, the researcher may miss important details about the social context (Denzin 1997). Thus, researchers should not use narrative analysis within a **positivist** framework, but instead should be critical, seeing the data as a **social construction**. Box 8.1 provides a list of key stages within **narrative analysis**.

BOX 8.1 PROCEDURE TO UNDERTAKE NARRATIVE ANALYSIS (BASED ON ELLIOTT, 2005; RIESSMAN, 1990; KOHLER RIESSMAN, 2008)

1　Use a narrative data collection method
2　Audio-record the interviews and transcribe the recordings **verbatim**
3　Use **line-by-line** coding to code data into themes, chronological events or both
4　Consider the presentation of self and others in data extracts by creating reflective notes attached to data extracts
5　Repeat steps 1–4 for all other cases
6　Compare reflective notes to search for trends in the construction of self and others throughout the data set
7　Draw conclusions

Health and wellbeing in pregnancy: data analysis

Within this project, we wanted to consider both events over time (as in Elliott, 2005), but also themes relating to health risk behaviours, following the Kohler Riessman (2008) approach. As such, interviews were audio-recorded and transcribed **verbatim** by a professional transcription company (Stage 1 and 2 in Box 8.1). Following this, as part of Stage 3, we constructed an overview of the events presented during each life history interview. We used participant timelines and **line–by–line** coding to identify central events, with emotional and identity responses to the events written alongside them, in a simple Microsoft Office Word document (see Table 8.1 for an extract from one participant). It should be stated, however, that not all participants completed a timeline with 'events': one participant highlighted emotions and feelings at various points throughout her life. In this study, it was relatively simple to consider events over time, as the life history interview approach, facilitated by a timeline, encouraged participants to describe their lives chronologically.

Following the second phase of data production, full thematic coding occurred within **NVivo** 11 (the second element of Stage 3), using analytic memos to record researcher reflections alongside data extracts (Stage 4). Here, codes related to health and wellbeing (including smoking, alcohol, exercise, diet and infant feeding choice),

TABLE 8.1 Extract of narrative events and emotional responses from one participant

Age/time	Experience	Emotion
Primary school	Domestic violence (dad to mum), dad an alcoholic	Angry and upset
8	Parents separate; alongside this, family bereavement	Very upset
8–11	Lived with mum; had to move house a lot and didn't have many close friends	Alone, isolated, upset
[...]		
Late teens	Met partner at work	
Adulthood	Lots of family bereavements over a few years, including grandparents and dad	Very sad
Adulthood	Decided to get married and start a family	Content
First pregnancy	Suffered an accident and needed a lot of treatment for the injuries	Traumatised
	Lots of pregnancy-related sickness. The baby was OK	Happy
[...]		

as well as chronological life events, such as education and employment. Additional detail was added to the narrative accounts that had been created for each participant, based not only on insights from the second and third interviews, but also on the researchers' greater understanding of the participants' presentation of self.

The final stage of the analysis focused on drawing together findings from the ten participants (Stage 5). Due to the project funding, these focused on three core health behaviours (smoking during pregnancy, drinking alcohol during pregnancy and infant feeding) alongside the construction of a positive parenting identity, adopting an approach similar to that used by Riessman (1990). Participants described their own health as part of their life to date, including health behaviours of their family and social networks during the first interview. They reflected further on these during the second and third interviews, and all information was reviewed together. Here, comparisons were made between cases, by comparing quotations in relation to health behaviours between participants. Finally, we pooled all of the coding and analytic memos to draw conclusions (Stage 6), as can be seen in the next section.

Findings

Many of the participants felt very unwell during their pregnancies as a result of nausea, sickness and tiredness. However, these women did not see their pregnancy-related illness as a reason for rest and recuperation, as they had busy family lives and nine of the ten were already primary carers to children. The women avoided certain foods which they knew would increase their nausea symptoms and simply "got on with it". Several participants noted that the desirability of smoking a cigarette or drinking alcohol was severely reduced by their sickness and nausea.

As has been found in previous studies (see, for example, Grant et al. 2017), women reported that they felt that they were under surveillance when they were pregnant. This surveillance was tied to their (visibly pregnant) body and health behaviours. On one hand, the women said that they felt strongly that they should be able to make their own decisions, for example, regarding whether to smoke or drink alcohol. On the other hand, a high level of awareness of the potential judgements from others, and their own negative judgements regarding smoking outside of the home, meant that smoking and drinking alcohol were generally done in private at home, away from a public gaze. Partners played an interesting role at this time, with strong condemnation of smoking during pregnancy but subtle encouragement of drinking alcohol in the home.

The participants who smoked or drank alcohol during pregnancy performed identity work to maintain a 'good mother' self-identity in their narratives of events. They highlighted confusing and contradictory health advice from professionals, in relation to alcohol use and foods which should be avoided. Alongside this, participants noted examples from their own social network where mothers had smoked or consumed alcohol and their babies had gone on to be apparently healthy. In such an instance, participants were not considering a higher likelihood of symptoms associated with smoking during pregnancy, such as asthma or ear infections, but instead, focused on childhood deaths as the undesirable outcome, using phrases such as "I haven't killed them yet!" Women's strategy to reinforce their own good maternal identity was to follow their instincts, do what their own mothers had done or discuss their concerns with others, either face-to-face with their close social network or online via social media.

Women who did not partake in smoking or drinking alcohol during pregnancy reinforced their status as good mothers by highlighting how irresponsible mothers who smoke or drink alcohol. This practice, known as 'othering' (see Chapter 3), is a divisive strategy that serves to highlight the difference between social groups with which the participants could be associated with and ones which they felt might damage their reputation (Taylor-Gooby 2013).

Discussion

To conclude, overall women described many life circumstances that impacted their life and health choices. These factors, which the women often could not control, varied between their pregnant and non-pregnant lives. In the context of a society in which motherhood is strongly regulated, the women performed identity work through their narrative accounts in order to build and maintain a good maternal identity. This has impacts for providing care to pregnant women who smoke or drink alcohol, highlighting the need for non-judgemental care.

Challenges of undertaking document elicitation interviews

Gillian Rose, a leading methodologist, opens her seminal text by stating, "There's an awful lot of hype around 'the visual' these days" (Rose 2016 p1). Concern has grown regarding appropriate and ethical use of visual approaches to research (Lomax 2015; Mannay 2016), and as such, it is of vital importance to consider the appropriateness of research methods in relation to research questions and participants' likely engagement prior to study design. In much of my research a quasi-participatory stance is adopted: we aim to answer predefined research questions (often because I have been awarded funds to answer them), but to allow participants to give a reflective account of the issues as they experience them.

Using elicitation techniques in qualitative interviews requires interviewer confidence to allow participants to direct the interview. If you have not used these techniques before, it may be advisable to do a practice interview with a friend or family member about a topic that they would be able to discuss at length. Likewise, when undertaking analysis of **elicitation interview** transcripts, researchers should think with **reflexivity**, considering their role in shaping the data (Rose 2016). This includes through consideration of demographics and their physical and emotional presence in the research field (Coffey 1999). The safe dissemination of visual and documentary outputs, in terms of protecting participant anonymity (if desired), should also be considered (Mannay 2014).

Exercise: using narrative analysis with document elicitation interview data

The earlier analysis focused on how participants constructed narratives about their lives and health. In the next section, data is presented from a fictionalised 11th participant to allow you to practise **narrative analysis** of a timeline-facilitated interview.

Instructions

Using the timeline and the interview transcript extract, answer the following question:

How do events and relationships impact on identity and presentation of self?

I suggest that you consult Box 8.1 for guidance on how to conduct a **narrative analysis** (excluding Steps 5 and 6, as you only have one participant). You may wish to photocopy the data to facilitate your analysis.

Data

Source 1

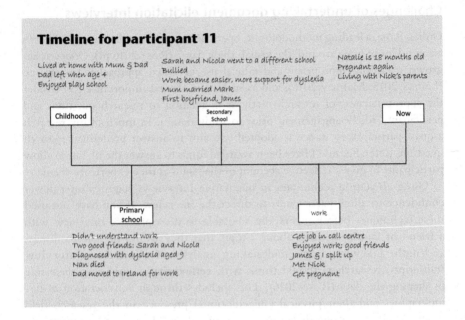

Timeline for participant 11

Lived at home with Mum & Dad
Dad left when age 4
Enjoyed play school

Sarah and Nicola went to a different school
Bullied
Work became easier, more support for dyslexia
Mum married Mark
First boyfriend, James

Natalie is 18 months old
Pregnant again
Living with Nick's parents

Childhood

Secondary School

Now

Primary school

work

Didn't understand work
Two good friends: Sarah and Nicola
Diagnosed with dyslexia aged 9
Nan died
Dad moved to Ireland for work

Got job in call centre
Enjoyed work; good friends
James & I split up
Met Nick
Got pregnant

Source 2

Selected extracts from interview with participant 11

I: Do you want to start off talking me through your timeline?

R: Okay. So in terms of my childhood, growing up, I lived at home with my mum and dad. It was pretty good, my mum and dad were so in love, always running around and hugging each other and laughing and kissing. There was always lots of fun, Mum didn't mind if I made a mess if I was painting or we were baking. We lived in a really nice place, with a park with a great slide only a few minutes from the house, which I used to go to most days. And my mum's sisters, my aunties, lived just around the corner. I don't have any brothers or sisters, but my cousins Jess, Kate and Jim and I were pretty close.

I: It sounds as though you enjoyed that part of your childhood?

R: Yes, definitely.

I: Did that change when your dad left?

R: No, not really. Things were calmer at home, and it was quieter, but it was okay. Dad told me I needed "to be mum's little helper", but looking back, I was already a really good kid. Mum and I always understood each other really easily: I could tell when she wanted help and when she'd rather be left alone. It did used to upset me when mum was sad, because I knew she missed him, but I think I was too young to properly understand. I was only four, and I still got to see dad in the evenings or the weekend. At about the same time, I started playschool. I really enjoyed having so many friends to play with, and my cousin Jim was in my class, which meant I got to see him every day. We're still good friends now.

I: OK.

R: I found it harder when I moved to primary school. At playschool everything felt really fun and easy; I really didn't understand the work at primary school. When everybody was making sentences and spelling words, I just couldn't do it. It made me really upset because I wanted to get the gold stars that the other children were getting. When I was nine I was diagnosed as being severely dyslexic, and then I got some help at school. Mrs Wiggins came to see me in the library twice a week. I found it really embarrassing at first having to leave lessons, but she understood how my brain worked and helped me to start to read as quickly as the other children in my class.

I: You mentioned some friends on your timeline?

R: Yes, Nicola and Sarah. We had to hang our coats next to each other on the first day of school, and Mrs Clemo, our first schoolteacher, told us that we had to look out for each other and be friends. So we did. Nicola lived close to my house – you just had to walk along the back lane, and there were no cars there – so at some point, I must have been about 8 or 9, my mum said that I could walk to Nicola's house by myself. I felt so grown up. I used to go there all the time – my mum used to joke that her mum would have to start charging me rent! Just before the end of primary school, my dad had to move away for work. It felt kind of weird, because it happened around the same sort of time that Nan died, and Dad had been living with her since he moved out. Thinking about it now, I've never really thought before – those two things are probably related, and maybe he didn't need to move away. He tried to talk to me on the phone, but he never really said very much, so we stopped speaking very often, but that's okay.

R: Things were different in secondary school. Sarah and Nicola had to go to a different school. I didn't get a place to go to their school because we lived just outside the catchment area. There were a few people from my primary school that went, including the school bully, a girl called Fiona, but it wasn't the same as having my friends there. I found it quite lonely and tried to hide away. Fiona joined up with a group of other bullies, and she made my life hell in that first year. I think I became known as someone you could easily bully – they'd all make fun of me being dys-lexic and because I didn't have the most expensive shoes or whatever.

I: Did you tell anyone?

R: I told my mum, and she tried really hard to sort things out. She spoke to the school, and when that didn't work, she went to Fiona's parents' house one evening and banged on the door until they let her in. I was completely mortified, but the bullying eased off after that.

[...]

R: And then (when I was 14) I met James, I had been going to trampolin-ing class on a Friday night at the community centre. It was the time that I always saw Nicola, and I loved trampolining, I was so good: I could do all of the somersaults. One evening there was a party, and Jo, the girl whose house it was, her older brother James was there too. I thought he was so cool, he was a bit older, and the lads my age all seemed so immature, you know – they still all thought girly stuff was stupid. He looked old enough that he was able to buy alcohol, and so we were all drinking cider at the party. We went out for the last two years of school, and then he decided to go into the army. I really didn't want him to do it, and we argued all of the time. I really loved him, but I just couldn't face him being away all of the time, so we split up.

[...]

R: I didn't do very well at school, even though in Year 8 I got some re-ally good help: they gave me a computer, and that made everything so much easier, but I just couldn't think when it came down to my GCSEs [exams]. Everything with James was just going on, and I couldn't think about anything else. Thinking about it now, I don't have a GCSE in English or maths, you know, above the grade C, so it meant that I couldn't go on the college course I wanted to. I think it's all worked out well now, in the end.

I: Do you want to tell me what happened after you left school?

R: I was really panicking, because I had always planned to go on and do hair and beauty college, you know, an NVQ, but they wouldn't take me un-less I agreed to redo my GCSE in English. After finding school so hard, I just didn't want to do any more exams, and I didn't want to lie to them about it. My cousin Jim always said he wasn't going to go to college – he wanted to get out and start work, he said. Before he even finished his exams, he had a job lined-up in a call centre where some of his friends worked. He said it would be a real laugh and that he could put in a good word for me. So he got me the job. I had to go for an interview, I felt so nervous, but he told me it would be okay that I had the job.

[...]

R: On a work night out, I met Nick. I hadn't really had another boyfriend since James – they'd all seemed to just be interested in one thing. Nick works on the evening shift, so I hadn't met him before. On our first date, I could tell he was different: he wore a shirt and everything. My mum told me then that she thought he was a keeper. We'd only been together about six months when I fell pregnant. I was absolutely terrified. I didn't know how mum would react, I thought dad would give me a right telling off, and I had no idea how I was going to be a mum to a tiny baby. But Nick was great. He told me we could do whatever I wanted – he made it seem like it would be easy.[...]

R: I had the worst morning sickness – I felt sick literally all of the time. Before I was pregnant, I'd go out drinking every Friday and Saturday with work people. We'd have such a laugh, but once I was pregnant I couldn't even bear the smell, so I had to stop going out. It felt really weird; I felt so different to everybody else. Luckily, I found out that Nicola was also pregnant, and that made it better – to know someone knew what I was going through. We both ended up going to this session run by the midwife where they tell you what you're supposed to do. It was so patronising, it's like, 'I'm young, not stupid'.

[...]

I: How have things been since Natalie was born?

R: It's been hard, people tell you that they don't sleep, and that you won't get to sleep, but you can't really understand it until it's happening. We are lucky that we live with Julie [Nick's mum] and Paul [Nick's stepdad], but... No one else is going to see this, are they?

I: No, nobody will know what you said.

R: It's just sometimes they can be really pushy. Like I wanted to try to breastfeed Natalie, but Julie kept on telling me to go to bed, to get some rest, but I think it was because she wanted to give Natalie a bottle. So she's been really kind, and I don't know what I'd do without her helping, but sometimes it's just difficult. I feel like I can't do what I want with my baby, but there wouldn't be space for us to go and live with mum and Mark (my stepdad).

[...]

R: It's like, now I'm pregnant again, I know I shouldn't be smoking, and I've tried so hard to stop. Nick tells me off for it, but in the evening when he's out at work I sit with Julie [his mum] and she lets me have one of her fags. I only ever have one, one a day, two at most. When I see the midwife, I have to blow into this tube and it says if you smoke, so I make sure I don't smoke the day before, and it says that I'm a non-smoker. I am definitely going to stop, but it's just so hard.

References

Ball, M.S. and Smith, G.W.H. 1992. *Analyzing visual data*. London: Sage.

Banks, M. 2001. *Visual methods in social research*. London: Sage.

British Sociological Association 2002. Statement of Ethical Practice for the British Sociological Association (March 2002). Available at: www.britsoc.co.uk/about/equality/statement-of-ethical-practice.aspx [Accessed: 31 May 2015].

Coffey, A. 1999. *The ethnographic self: fieldwork and the representation of identity*. London: Sage.

Coxon, T. 2006. 'Something Sensational...' The sexual diary as a tool for mapping detailed sexual behaviour. In: Scott, J. ed. *Documentary research*. London: Sage, pp. 181–194.

Denzin, N.K. 1997. *Interpretive ethnography: ethnographic practices for the 21st century*. London: Sage.

Elliott, J. 2005. *Using narrative in social research: qualitative and quantitative approaches*. London: Sage.

Gabb, J. and Fink, J. 2015. Telling moments and everyday experience: multiple methods research on couple relationships and personal lives. *Sociology*: 49(5), pp. 970–987.

Gamble, J. et al. 2015. Missed opportunities: a qualitative exploration of the experiences of smoking cessation interventions among socially disadvantaged pregnant women. *Women & Birth*: 28(1), pp. 8–15.

Godfrey, C. and Consortium, P.H.R. 2011. *Estimating the costs to the NHS of smoking in pregnancy for pregnant women and infants*. London: Public Health Research Consortium.

Grant, A. et al. 2017. 'People try and police your behaviour': the impact of surveillance on mothers' and grandmothers' perceptions and experiences of infant feeding. *Families, Relationships and Societies*: Online fir, p. DOI: 10.1332/204674317X148888 86530223.

Health & Social Care Information Centre 2012. Infant feeding survey - UK, 2010. Available at: www.hscic.gov.uk/catalogue/PUB08694 [Accessed: 7 October 2017].

Heng, T. 2017. *Visual methods in the field: photography for the social sciences*. Abingdon: Routledge.

Kohler Riessman, C. 2008. Narrative analysis. In: Given, L. ed. *The SAGE encyclopedia of qualitative research methods*. London: Sage, pp. 539–540.

Latham, A. 2004. Researching and writing everyday accounts of the city: an introduction to the diary-photo diary-interview method. In: Knowles, C. and Sweetman, P. eds. *Picturing the social landscape: visual methods and the sociological imagination*. London: Routledge, pp. 117–131.

Lomax, H. 2015. Seen and heard? Ethics and agency in participatory visual research with children, young people and families. *Families, Relationships and Societies*: 4(3), pp. 493–502.

Mannay, D. 2013. 'Who put that on there... why why why?' Power games and participatory techniques of visual data production. *Visual Studies*: 28(2), pp. 136–146.

Mannay, D. 2014. Story telling beyond the academy exploring roles, responsibilities and regulations in the open access dissemination of research outputs and visual data. *Journal of Corporate Citizenship*: 54, pp. 109–116.

Mannay, D. 2016. *Visual, narrative and creative research methods: application, reflection and ethics*. Abingdon: Routledge.

Mannay, D. et al. 2017. Visual methodologies, sand and psychoanalysis: employing creative participatory techniques to explore the educational experiences of mature students and children in care. *Visual Studies*: 32, pp. 348–358.

Mannay, D. et al. 2018. Negotiating closed doors and constraining deadlines: the potential of visual ethnography to effectually explore spaces of motherhood and mothering. *Journal of Contemporary Ethnography*: In press.

Mitchell, C. 2011. *Doing visual research*. London: Sage.Morgan, K.L. et al. 2014. Obesity in pregnancy: a retrospective prevalence-based study on health service utilisation and costs on the NHS. *BMJ Open*: 4, p. e003983.

Phillips, R. et al. (in press, 2018). Identifying the unmet information and support needs of women with autoimmune rheumatic diseases during pregnancy planning, pregnancy and early parenting: mixed-methods study. *BMC Rheumatology*.

Plummer, K. 2001. *Documents of life 2: an invitation to a critical humanism*. London: Sage.

Reavey, P. 2011. *Visual methods in psychology: using and interpreting images in qualitative research*. London: Routledge.

Reilly, R. 2013. *Multiple risk factors and adverse pregnancy outcomes - sata from the Welsh study of mothers and babies*. Cardiff: Wales Public Health Specialty Training Conference.

Riessman, C.K. 1990. Strategic uses of narrative in the presentation of self and illness: a research note. *Social Science and Medicine*: 30(11), pp. 1195–1200.

Robards, B. and Lincoln, S. 2017. Uncovering longitudinal life narratives: scrolling back on Facebook. *Qualitative Research*: 17(6), pp. 715–730.

Robling, M. et al. 2016. Effectiveness of a nurse-led intensive home-visitation programme for first-time teenage mothers (building blocks): a pragmatic randomised controlled trial. *The Lancet*: 387(10014), pp. 146–155.

Rose, G. 2012. *Doing family photography: the domestic, the public and the politics of sentiment*. Aldershot: Ashgate Publishing Ltd.

Rose, G. 2016. *Visual methodologies: an introduction to researching with visual materials*. London: Sage.

Scott, J. 1990. *A matter of record: documentary sources in social research*. London: John Wiley & Sons.

Sheridan, J. et al. 2011. Timelining: visualizing experience. *Qualitative Research*: 11(5), pp. 552–569.

Stats Wales 2015. Welsh index of multiple deprivation (WIMD) 2015. Available at: http://gov.wales/statistics-and-research/welsh-index-multiple-deprivation/?lang=en [Accessed: 4 December 2017].

Taylor-Gooby, P. 2013. Why do people stigmatise the poor at a time of rapidly increasing inequality, and what can be done about it? *The Political Quarterly*: 84(1), pp. 31–42.

Walter, M. 2006. Participatory action research. In: Walter, M. ed. *Social research methods*. Oxford: Oxford University Press, pp. 1–7.

Welsh Government 2017. Flying Start. Available at: http://gov.wales/topics/people-and-communities/people/children-and-young-people/parenting-support-guidance/help/flyingstart/?lang=en [Accessed: 4 December 2017].

Whitehead, M. and Dahlgren, G. 1991. What can be done about inequalities in health? *The Lancet*: 338(8774), pp. 1059–1063.

CONCLUSION

9

REVIEWING AND APPLYING CONCEPTS TO YOUR RESEARCH PROJECT

Summary

In this final chapter, the main lessons from across the chapters are brought together. In doing so, I highlight the opportunities to apply these in your own work. If you have read the entire book from cover to cover, these concepts will be familiar; if you have been in more of a hurry to start analysing your documents, this chapter should help you think critically when developing your proposal for a research project that uses them. The common challenges to undertaking documentary research are outlined. These are discussed in a chronological fashion throughout a study, in relation to the following:

- Sampling
- Ethical research conduct
- Consideration of authorship and readership
- Whether to triangulate your documentary research
- Data analysis
- Data management
- Write-up

Following this, critical questions to help you interrogate a range of data sources are provided. These sources of data are news articles; historical documents; **official documents**; individually created documents, such as diaries or social media; organisational case files; advertising materials; and documents created as part of research projects. The chapter ends with a comprehensive checklist for designing and carrying out your own research project with documents.

Key learning points

- What factors to take into account when designing your research protocol
- How to avoid the common pitfalls in documentary research
- How to avoid specific pitfalls associated with a range of methods, including:
  - News articles
  - Historical documents
  - Official documents
  - Individually created documents, like diaries or social media posts
  - Documents from organisations
  - Documents created to inform an **elicitation interview**

Are we nearly there yet?

Yes! We are very close to our destination: doing excellent research with documents. This conclusion draws together and reviews concepts that have been covered throughout the book. In bringing them together in this final chapter, it is hoped that they become greater than the sum of their parts dotted throughout the previous seven chapters. I hope that I have convinced you that using documents as data in your research projects can help you to understand society. I also hope that I have demystified the use of documentary analysis and made it seem like something that could be as easily achieved as an interview or survey-based study. (If I haven't, please do let me know why documentary research is still unappealing or confusing, and I will try to do better in the next book.) Another point that I hope has been impressed is that documents can be beneficial in triangulating other qualitative data.

Within Chapter 2, consideration was given to the process of designing a research project which used documents as data. Throughout the six case study chapters, these issues have been explored in detail. If you are unsure about any area of your research design, I suggest reading the section 'Practical tips for your research with documents' in Chapter 2 as well as the case study chapter most closely matching your source of data. In the next section, some of the common challenges encountered in documentary research are briefly recapped.

Common challenges when undertaking documentary analysis

It is not my intention to rehash the lessons on data quality and **bias** from Jennifer Platt (Platt 1981a, 1981b) and John Scott (Scott 1990) (see Chapter 2). However, they are important to consider in your own research. In this section, I consider seven key topics: **sampling**; ethical use of data; **authors, readers** and intended **meaning**; **triangulation**; analysis; data management; and dissemination.

How to select a suitable sample

A core challenge in all research projects is **sampling**. As discussed in Chapter 2 and in each of the subsequent case studies, there are two major concerns: selecting the right data and selecting the right quantity of data. First, in terms of selecting the right data, we need to consider how **representative** that data are, of all of the possible data you could have selected (Scott 1990). Access is related to theoretical issues such as do those documents still exist and, if yes, are they available to researchers? It is also influenced by pragmatic concerns: are the documents *really* available for your research project (see, for example, Hughes and Griffiths 1999)? Ensuring you select a **sample** that is a suitable size for the resources available to your project requires planning at the early stages. One way to plan adequately is to make a list of available resources (such as time and money) over a period of weeks, months or years and to consider how much time that gives you to collect data and to analyse it. A **Gantt chart** may be a useful tool in your planning (see Figure 2.2).

How to do ethical research with documents

A further issue we must carefully reflect on is whether it is ethical to use the documents you intend to without the explicit consent of the **authors**, or those who are being written about. Moreover, in some online spaces, **authors** request that their posts are not used by researchers, and this should be respected. Whilst other documents, including online content, may be freely available in the public domain, **authors** may be shocked by their materials being used by researchers. For this reason, it is important to consider your university departments' ethical code of practice and the codes of practice for your professional body, and to consider if you may be causing harm by undertaking the planned study and/or disseminating your research findings. If you are undertaking research using online data, helpful advice can be found via the Association of Internet Researchers (AoIR).

Critical consideration of the authorship and intended use of your document

As was discussed in the 'Documents and everyday life' section of Chapter 2, the type of data source and the **author**'s likely reason for creating the document can help to shed light on *why* it was constructed in the way it was. Throughout the case study chapters, I have discussed a very wide range of sources and their **authors**. I hope it has been made clear that the motivation for an **author** to write will affect what is written. For example, if we consider the motivation of a **journalist** writing about the use of a particular product (see Chapter 3), it will be very different from someone working in advertising trying to sell that product (see Chapter 6) or a user of that product sharing their experiences on social media (see Chapter 5). Likewise, when we, as researchers, ask our participants to create documents, we become part of the **social construction** which influences the document's contents (see Chapter 8).

In our analysis, we also need to consider the **authors**' likely perception of the intended **readers**. As we saw in our discussion of moral panics (see Chapter 3), sometimes particular words or images are chosen to say things that are 'unspeakable', for example, in relation to ethnicity, gender, sexuality and disability. Content may also be deliberately misleading, as in 'fake news' stories circulating the Internet at the time of writing. Likewise, in considering individually created documents, like diaries, **blogs** and social media, we need to consider the presentation of self. When documents are created by those working for organisations, we may also need to consider hierarchical relationships (see Chapter 4) and the legal status of documents (see Chapter 7). **Actor Network Theory** is a helpful mid range **theory** to interpret these document–human relationships (see Chapter 2).

Using triangulation in your research with documents

In Section II of this book, various forms of **triangulation** were presented. In your own research, it is worth considering if there is potential to triangulate your findings in some way. There are many forms of **triangulation** available to researchers using documents as data, including the following:

- Discussion (interviews or focus groups) with the actual **author**, or those who are similar to the **author** in some way
- Ethnographic observation of the creation and use of documents, alongside analysis of those documents
- Validation of your documentary analysis through discussion (interview or focus groups) with intended **readers**
- Detailed analysis of documentary sources to validate findings from discussion with intended **readers**

If you intend to triangulate your findings, you should consider the inherent biases in each of the sources of your data, and the way in which you plan to combine your findings when reporting your results. Here it is relevant to note that, as a **social constructionist**, I would not expect to find exactly the same results from multiple sources, and this variation is telling us something important about social life.

Doing 'documentary analysis'

Once you have secured your documents, it is often suggested that one does 'documentary analysis' in an unproblematic way. That is, of course, a fallacy and it is important to identify an analysis strategy at the outset. Your supervisor, colleagues or even rubber duck debugging[1] can help you to decide. Throughout the case study chapters, six analysis techniques have been described. Sometimes more than one approach to analysis has been used, where this could help to gain additional insights. In each of the case studies, I have explained why the analysis strategy was chosen, but often it would have been possible to use an alternative strategy. The more straightforward analysis strategies are **thematic analysis** (see Box 3.1) and **framework analysis** (see Box 7.2). If you have never done any analysis before, I would recommend these. For people who are more linear or visual in their thinking, the use of displaying data or summaries in matrices as part of **frame-work analysis** may be particularly helpful. In order to more critically consider the subtle **meanings** within documents, **discourse analysis** may be more appropriate (see Box 4.2 for information on one type of **discourse analysis**). Likewise, **semiotic analysis** examines text for signs and signifiers. A very basic approach to **semiotic analysis** is presented in Box 5.1; if you are intending to use this approach to its full potential, however, I suggest you consult Marcel (1994). A halfway house between the simpler strategies and the more critical strategies can be found in some types of qualitative **content analysis** (see Box 6.2).

Once you begin your analysis, it is good practice, to plan regular meetings with your supervisor or a colleague who is at least as experienced as you, where you can review your coding framework alongside data extracts to help develop your coding. To prepare for these 'data analysis meetings', it is most useful to have a copy of your up-to-date coding framework and some examples of codes that you have ascribed to each code. If you are encountering any particular problems, it is a good idea to have examples and to critically assess *why* you are finding that part of the analysis difficult in these meetings. In doing so, your analysis becomes more **robust**.

Planning your data management approach

On almost every project I have worked on or supervised, there has been an instance of data being lost or corrupted. On the projects where a suitable backup had been made, we were able to feel mildly irritated that up to a day's work had been lost, but were otherwise unaffected. When backups had not been made, this made for considerable difficulties: large sections of data had been lost or have had to be recoded and entire chapters have had to be rewritten. In Chapter 2, I provided some strategies to back up your data. I am not suggesting you have to use my strategies if you have your own that are working well for you, but you should use some form of regular backups. Losing your data, analysis or writing is horrible, and is a lesson you do not need to learn for yourself.

How to write up your documentary research

If you are a seasoned writer, you may skip this section. If you are not or you find writing difficult, read on. You may have noticed that throughout this book, I have been recommending that you keep notes and create tables showing parts of your sampling and analysis. This will help you when it comes to writing up (Delamont et al. 2000). However, some of the best advice I have ever been given is:

> Write early and write often

So, the notes based on your thinking regarding which documents should be in your **sample** and which should not can be collected together to form part of your methods section. Likewise, the notes that you make as you analyse your data can help you to understand some of the key points that you wish to make in displaying your results. Make sure you keep hold of all of these ideas. You also need to understand the conventions for writing the dissertation or article you will use to present your research. Find these out early in the process, and if possible, find a good example of this type of work. One big decision to make in writing your findings section is whether you should use any quantification of your findings (see Chapter 2 for further details). You should also consider if you will create any other outputs: will you write a summary for lay audiences, politicians or the third sector?

The specific challenges with different sources of documentary data

If you have read the detailed case studies (Chapters 3–8), you will have noticed that the specific challenges of using different data sources vary considerably. For this reason, I briefly reflect on these issues in this conclusion and have created a series of boxes containing critical questions which may help you reflect upon particular issues in the type of documents you are using in your research. These relate to news articles (Box 9.1); historical documents (Box 9.2); **official documents** (Box 9.3); individually created documents, like diaries or social media (Box 9.4); advertising materials (Box 9.5); organisational documents (Box 9.6); and documents created as part of research projects (Box 9.7). The boxes are not intended to be exhaustive of all issues but aim to help you make a start in considering the sources of **bias** within your documentary data.

In order to retain your early thoughts, if you are working on a project now, it is recommended that you make notes as you are running through these questions. This information will form part of your 'limitation' section, which is often found in the discussion of dissertations and journal articles.

News articles

In undertaking research using news sources as data, the inherent biases of the news source and/or the individual **journalist** are important to consider. Alongside this, the way that similar topics have been covered within that news source is of interest; sometimes it is even possible to see contradictory articles within the same day's issue. Likewise, images accompanying articles may tell a different story to the words and should be considered alongside them. Furthermore, journalism often results in 'black and white' reporting of issues, with a focus on a 'bad' issue and a 'good' victim, and **tabloid** sources tend to sensationalise content. Some questions to help you consider these issues are presented in Box 9.1.

BOX 9.1 CRITICAL QUESTIONS WHEN USING NEWS ARTICLES AS DATA

Answer these questions and consider what impact it might have on your data:

- Is the news source a **tabloid** or **broadsheet**?
- What stance do the news source(s) in your data set usually take?
  - For instance, are articles within this news source usually pro-government or more critical?
- What is the issue being reported on?
  - Is this type of issue one that other academics have written about with reference to news media sources? If so, consult their writing for key issues to consider.
- Who is the protagonist (the 'bad guy') and who is the victim?
  - How are they described in relation to demographics such as ethnicity, social class and age?
  - What language is used to describe those involved?
- Do the images that accompany articles seem to have the same meaning as the words, or do the images imply a different meaning?
- If you are using multiple news sources, how does reporting of the issue vary?

Historical documents

When using historical sources as data, it is important to consider the way that they came to be available for research, and which sources may not have come to light. The historical context is also highly relevant in informing why particular things may have been included in the document whilst others were excluded. If you are using historical documents in your own research, it would be beneficial to consider the critical questions found in Box 9.2 in relation to your data. Alongside being a historical document, the documents are also likely to fit into one of the other categories of document, such as being an official report or an individually created letter or diary. Accordingly, the critical questions in relation to the type of document should also be considered.

BOX 9.2 CRITICAL QUESTIONS WHEN USING HISTORICAL DOCUMENTS AS DATA

Consider these questions and the potential impact it might have on your data:

- How did these documents come to be found?
  - If they are in an archive, who donated them and when? Do you have reason to suspect that some documents were not included?

- Are the sources primary (from an observer of the phenomena) or secondary (from somebody who was not present)?
- What was society like in that geographical location at the time of writing, and how might this have affected the content of the documents?
- Have there been any important changes to language since the documents were written, which may change meanings?
- If your data include **official statistics**, how complete and accurate are they likely to be?

Official documents

Official documents also come in a range of formats, and their purpose will be important in terms of considering them as data. Alongside this, a wider reflection of the context is essential in your analysis. Key factors include which political party was in power and its stance towards the issue described in the data. The strength of the political opposition and its stance on the issue is also relevant. As with individually created documents, not all documents will be available to researchers, and changing terminology, including definitions in **official statistics**, may seek to conceal relevant information. In your own research using **official documents**, it may be beneficial to consider the questions in Box 9.3.

BOX 9.3 CRITICAL QUESTIONS WHEN USING OFFICIAL DOCUMENTS AS DATA

Answer these questions and think about what this means for the data in your study:

- Which political party was in power at the time the documents were written?
- What was the ruling party's general stance towards the issue you are investigating?
  - Is this document in line with the general stance, or are there areas of disconnect?
- Is it possible to identify a particular politician or civil servant who was likely to have overseen the writing of the document?
  - Does this document seem in line with their stance on the issue?
- Do you think that all relevant documents are accessible to you, or are some documents unavailable?
  - Would it be valuable to officially request copies of other relevant documents?
- If you are using **official statistics**, have there been any changes to definitions, missing data or changes to policy (or its enactment) which might affect trends?

Individually created documents (letters, diaries, social media)

A very broad range of individually created documents exist, and further details are provided in Chapter 5. Regardless of which type of individually created data you are using, you should determine the known limitations and reflect on if they are present in your data source. As the data are unlikely to have been intended for use by researchers, you should critically evaluate the impact of this on the data, but also reflect on what this means in terms of undertaking ethical research practice. Alongside this, the presentation of self is an important factor in the analysis of all individually created documents. These factors are noted in Box 9.4, which provides a range of questions to help you scrutinise your own documents.

BOX 9.4 CRITICAL QUESTIONS WHEN USING INDIVIDUALLY CREATED DOCUMENTS, LIKE DIARIES OR SOCIAL MEDIA, AS DATA

Consider these questions and the impact it might have on your data:
- Are there any known limitations of using the type of source you are relying on?
  - For example, there will be variations between online and offline data (see Chapter 5).
- Are there any ethical issues to consider?
  - For example, do you think the authors anticipated people using their documents for research?
- Is there any indication of why the document(s) were created?
- What 'sense of self' does the author appear to be portraying? Are there any areas of content that contradict this?
- Is it likely that anybody has influenced the content of the document(s), altered the document(s), or removed some of a collection?
- How long a period of time is covered by the documents, and can that reasonably be extended to cover other periods of time or not?
- Is it possible to consider the document(s) beyond surface meanings to provide an insight into social life?
  - If so, should this be undertaken as part of your project?

Advertising and marketing materials

The analysis of marketing materials is similar in some ways to the analysis of journalistic content. One major similarity is the use of images and metaphors to imply things that could not be written or said. Conversely, there is a different rationale between the organisations involved. The aim of a business is to make money, and advertising materials are designed to encourage purchases or to make a brand more desirable. In evaluating advertising materials, it is relevant to question the purpose of the company, for example, by understanding the relationship between parent and child companies, whether the company is in profit or loss and any political ties. Some products or types of advertisements will be bound by professional codes or regulatory bodies, and this will shape the content of such documents. However, if the regulation is weak, that is breaches go unpunished, businesses may disregard these rules. If you are undertaking research using advertising materials, the questions in Box 9.5 may help you to consider these issues in your own data.

BOX 9.5 CRITICAL QUESTIONS WHEN USING MARKETING MATERIALS AS DATA

Consider these questions and the impact it might have on your data:

- What is the overarching purpose of the company or organisation who created the materials?
- Is the company or organisation bound by any legislation, professional codes or regulatory bodies?
  - Have there been any recent legal challenges or other negative consequences for the organisation or competitors?
- Are the materials similar to those created by the company's competitors?
  - Are they particularly sensationalist?
- What can you tell about society beyond the obvious meanings?
- Will you be able to reproduce materials in your write-up, and if not, does this matter?

Organisational documents

If you are in the fortunate position of having access to organisational documents, well done for getting through the access challenges! In your critical consideration of the sources, there are some core issues to reflect on. These involve the nature of the organisation under study, including their purpose (as a public body or a private company), and their reputation for good or bad practice. In terms of the purpose of the actual documents, you may wish to consider whether they were planned to be internal or external, and if they are internal documents, who would have been able to access them? Likewise, for internal documents, it is always worth questioning if there is any potential for them to be involved in legal proceedings, for example, in the event of a client complaint. These factors are noted in Box 9.6 in the format of questions you can use to interrogate your own data.

BOX 9.6 CRITICAL QUESTIONS TO CONSIDER WHEN USING ORGANISATIONAL DOCUMENTS AS DATA

Answer these questions and think about what this means for the data in your study:

- What is the organisation under study?
  - Are they a public or private organisation?
- Has the organisation faced any scrutiny or criticism recently?
- What purpose(s) do the documents serve?
- Who has, or may reasonably be expected to have, access to the documents?
  - Does this include only those inside the organisation or those outside too?
- Is there potential for the documents to be included in any legal reviews or proceedings?
- Are there any particular words or phrases that might contain particular meanings within the organisation?
- Is it possible to observe the construction of these documents, or to interview the authors to help answer some of these questions?

Researcher-initiated documents

If you are undertaking research using researcher-initiated documents, there are a wide variety of excellent methodological sources you can consult (see Chapter 8). One major factor to consider is the influence of the research process and the researcher. This includes guidance provided to participants who were present when the document was created and those who conducted the **elicitation interview**. The sensitivity of the topic under study can combine with the characteristics of the interviewer or the research processes to produce wide variation in the data produced. Alongside this, the participants' competence, confidence and enthusiasm for producing the type of document you have requested will also affect the outputs. These issues are described through critical questions to assess your own research and data with in Box 9.7.

BOX 9.7 CRITICAL QUESTION TO CONSIDER WHEN USING DOCUMENTS CREATED DURING A RESEARCH ENCOUNTER

- Was the participant asked to create the document prior to the elicitation interview or alongside the researcher?
  - What guidance (including verbal) were participants provided?
- Was the topic under investigation sensitive or emotive?

- What were the demographics of the person facilitating data production?
- What were the demographics of the participants?
- Were there any barriers or facilitators for the participants regarding creating the document requested?
- How similar were participants and the researcher facilitating data production?
  - How might this have affected the data produced?
- Did anything of note happen during the elicitation interview which could have affected the data produced?
- Did you validate your initial results with participants to ensure accuracy?

So you've decided to do documentary analysis – what next?

In the next section, I present a detailed checklist that you can use to help develop your own research projects. This checklist is not designed to give you easy 'yes' or 'no' answers, as with qualitative research, such binary answers are rarely appropriate. Instead, it is designed to help you consider the issues that have been described in this book in the context of your own research study. You may feel that this checklist is missing elements that are vital in your research – do feel free to add them in to your own list, and to let me know if you feel that they may be relevant to others. It is my hope that this checklist will get stronger over time, as it is trialled by many researchers.

Checklist for designing studies which use documents as data

Stage 1: Research project design and protocol development

1. Broadly identify the time, resources and funding available
2. Identify your research topic and research team
3. Identify your broad research question
   Ensure it is interesting, relevant, feasible, ethical, concise and answerable (Green 2008)
4. Consider how you can generate impact, such as working with a third-sector organisation or public-sector body and if they should be involved in shaping your research design
5. Scope the potential available documentary sources
6. Describe the population or available data
7. Identify (and justify) sampling strategy and sample
8. Consider the potential to triangulate your data
9. Refine your research question if necessary
10. Identify and describe your data collection method

11. Consider how your research will need to be written-up
12. Identify and describe your data analysis method, ensuring it fits your research question
13. Consider whether any quantification of your findings will be valuable
14. Consider the ethical implications of your research
15. Consider any copyright issues in the reproduction of your data in a report or manuscript
16. In some disciplines, you will now write a protocol containing the aforementioned information

Stage 2: Collect your data

1. Having identified your **sample**, make a clear list of documents to be selected
2. If you are unable to access any of the documents you intended to, make a note of this, to refer to, as a limitation in your report
3. Ensure you have electronic copies of all data, scanning hard copy data where needed, unless it is explicitly forbidden
4. Give each document a unique Document Identification Number (**DIN**)
5. Where relevant, consult your ethical approval documentation to find out if you should retain any original unanonymised copies of data
6. **Anonymise** a copy of the data if necessary
7. If required, find safe storage for unanonymised data, and ensure it conforms to your university's policy
8. MAKE BACK UPS OF ALL DATA
9. Retain an unmarked copy of the data prior to Stage 3

Stage 3: Interrogate your data for intended use, quality and bias

1. Consider your documents' purpose, **authors** and intended **readers** and how this affects the content
2. Consider your documents in terms of sources of quality and **bias** (see Chapter 2)
3. Identify and critically consider variation within and between sources

Stage 4: Analyse your data

1. Use your predefined analysis strategy to analyse your data
2. Keep records of your coding structure and definitions for codes and if any of these change during analysis
3. Keep records of any changes to your analysis strategy, and why these changes were made
4. Write up your findings, in whichever way helps you to reflect on them, to assess coherence with your coding

Stage 5: Write-up, dissemination and impact

1. Confirm the guidance on word length and writing style for your write-up
2. Set out the structure of your document
3. Input the snippets of information you have been collecting along the way
4. Draft your report
5. Refine your report
6. Submit
7. Disseminate your findings more widely, if appropriate, including to policy makers and third sector organisations

Concluding remarks

Doing Excellent Research with Documents aimed to help **readers** understand how to do high-quality research with documents, and I hope I have gone some way towards meeting this aim. I have presented a review of existing literature, six empirical case studies and this final chapter, which provides practical guidance based on the previous eight chapters. I hope that you find this book useful in your own work or that of your students. As we know, documentary analysis is a flourishing field of research. In writing this book, however, I have become even more aware that there is a need for additional critical attention during research using documents; when we do research on documentary sources, we really must move beyond considering content outside of context. To facilitate this, there is a desperate need for high-quality methodological literature on doing research with documents. This would help both to break the assumption that this work is methodologically and ethically straightforward and to provide further guidance for novice researchers. For **readers** who are more experienced in research with documents, I urge you to help fill this gap. In turn, I have become further committed to my own exploration of positionality, quality and ethical issues in my research, both past and present. In my own research, I continue to regularly work with documents, often triangulating them with other sources of qualitative – and sometimes quantitative – data.

Note

1 The concept of rubber duck debugging is simply that by speaking out loud, we enable our brain to think in a different way. Accordingly, you do not need to talk to an actual person, but to any inanimate object to gain clarity of thought. See: www.rubberduckdebugging.com/

References

Delamont, S., Atkinson, P.A. and Odette, P. 2000. *The doctoral experience: success and failure in graduate school.* London: Falmer.

Green, N. 2008. Formulating and refining a research question. In: Gilbert, N. ed. *Researching social life.* 3rd ed. London: Sage, pp. 43–62.

Hughes, D. and Griffiths, L. 1999. Access to public documents in a study of the NHS internal market: openness Vs secrecy in contracting for clinical services. *International Journal of Social Research Methodology*: 2(1), pp. 1–16.

Marcel, D. 1994. *Messages and meanings: an introduction to semiotics*. Toronto, ON: Canadian Scholars' Press.

Platt, J. 1981a. Evidence and proof in documentary research: 1 some specific problems of documentary research. *The Sociological Review*: 29(1), pp. 31–52.

Platt, J. 1981b. Evidence and proof in documentary research: 2 some shared problems of documentary research. *The Sociological Review*: 29(1), pp. 53–66.

Scott, J. 1990. *A matter of record: documentary sources in social research*. London: John Wiley & Sons.

GLOSSARY

Action Research Research projects that aim to improve society or solve a specific problem. The researcher, who is often a practitioner, works in collaboration with an organisation or the people affected by the issue under study.

Actor Network Theory A theory that explains how human 'actors' are influenced by non-human 'actors', resulting in particular behaviours.

Anonymised This means data will be altered, for example, by removing names of individuals and places, so that nobody can tell who provided the data. Within research studies, anonymity is commonly promised to participants.

Application Programming Interface (API) A platform that allows communication between different applications (also known as 'apps'). In social media research, it may be used to collect data.

Archive(s) A collection of documents, often historical.

Archivist(s) A specialist worker in an **archive** who collects new documents and preserves, organises and arranges access to existing documents within the **archive**.

ATLAS.ti A computer programme that facilitates the coding and retrieval of qualitative data (see also **CAQDAS**).

Authenticity A document is authentic when it is an original or complete copy.

Author(s) An individual or group of people who have written a document.

Bias(es) Anything that changes the results of a research project. This can include issues within the researcher, data and within the analysis.

Blog(s) An online 'log', akin to a diary or journal.

Boolean operators A way of combining or excluding keywords in a database search. Commonly used Boolean operators include 'AND', 'OR' and 'NOT'.

Broadsheet (newspaper) Traditionally, broadsheets would have been printed on larger paper than **tabloid** newspapers; the content also varies, in that broadsheets are generally more serious.

Capitalism   An economic system where private businesses control trade and industry. **Capitalism** can be contrasted with socialism, where the state controls trade and industry.

CAQDAS   The abbreviation given to Computer Assisted Qualitative Data Analysis Software, including **ATLAS.ti** and **NVivo**. These programmes contain specific tools to enable researchers to code data and retrieve their coding.

Content analysis   An analysis strategy that requires the researcher to develop a coding framework, which is linked to the research question and used to code all data sources. See Box 6.2.

Credibility   A document has high levels of credibility when an author has reported their sincere views of events.

Critical Discourse Analysis (CDA)   A form of **discourse analysis** which assumes that written and spoken words have the power to reinforce, or change, attitudes and behaviour within society. See Box 4.2.

Deductive   A way of reasoning where data is used to test an existing theory. In qualitative research, this often involves using predefined codes to analyse data. The opposite of **inductive** reasoning.

Discourse analysis   A way of critically analysing data in order to consider language and power.

Document Identification Number (DIN)   A unique identification number given to each document in a sample to allow for ease of retrieval and to ensure any data loss is easily identifiable.

Editor(s)   An individual who has overall responsibility for a piece of writing and may make changes to its content and meaning.

Elicitation interview(s)   An approach to interviewing where participants are either shown items or asked to bring items to the interview in order to shape the direction of the conversation.

Emoji(s)   A small digital image used to either express an emotion (through a range of facial expressions) or to represent an everyday object.

Epistemology/epistemologies   A theory of how knowledge is created and its **validity**.

Error(s)   In **positivist** social research, error is the difference between an actual phenomenon and the findings of the research. **Bias** is one major element of **error** in qualitative research.

Ethnography   A form of qualitative inquiry that uses a range of methods, such as observation, interviews and analysis of documents, to understand a phenomenon.

Framework analysis   An analysis strategy that is similar to **thematic analysis**, but makes use of matrices (tables) to display data prior to drawing conclusions.

Gantt chart   A graphical representation of a project timetable. Time is usually displayed in the columns, with tasks represented by rows; shading is used to highlight the time when the task should occur. See Figure 2.2.

Heterogeneous/homogeneous   If all of the documents within a sample are very similar, they would be defined as having a high degree of homogeneity. By contrast, if the documents in the sample are very diverse in terms of content or style, they would be said to be heterogeneous.

Inductive   An approach to research that allows new theories and themes to emerge 'from the data' (although this will be affected by the researcher's existing knowledge and experiences).

Journalist(s)   A person who collects stories and shares them as part of the news.

Line-by-line (coding)   A term given to analysis that considers each individual line of text, rather than the overall meaning of larger segments of data

Marxism   A socio-economic theory based on the writings of Karl Marx that focuses on the role of money in influencing society.

Meaning   Whether the document can be easily read and the impact of the social context on content can be deciphered.

Narrative analysis   A form of analysis based on accounts given as stories, chronological events or changes over time.

Nexis®   A database for the storage and retrieval of news media articles.

Non-probability sample   A form of **sampling** that means that some documents in the **population** have a greater chance of being selected than others. This can be contrasted with **probability sampling**.

NVivo   A **CAQDAS** programme to facilitate qualitative data analysis.

Official document(s)   A type of document that has legal status of some sort.

Official statistics(s)   Numerical data published by a government or a public body.

Ontology   An approach to studying phenomena that can range from **positivist** to **social constructionist.**

Population   All of the documents that could answer your research question (including those that you may not be able to access).

Positivist ontology   An approach to studying society that assumes that a certain 'truth' can be found through rigorous scientific enquiry. Another **ontology** is **social constructionism.**

The Press   A news media organisation, including the printed press, who create newspapers, or a collective noun used to refer to a group of news media organisations.

Probability sample   A sampling technique where the whole **population** is identified and the cases to be included in analysis are randomly selected, with each case having an equal likelihood of being selected. Cases are usually selected either through use of a random number generator or by selecting every nth case.

Purposive sample   A sampling technique where documents are not **randomly** selected. Documents are selected because of predefined characteristics.

Random sample   See **probability sample.**

Reader(s)   Somebody who is consuming a document in some way.

Reflexivity   The process of critically considering one's own effect on the research, sometimes also referred to as positionality.

Representativeness A reference to whether the data was selected using **probability sampling** or **purposive sampling**. Missing data can also affect how representative a sample is.

Research question(s) A predefined question that a research project will attempt to answer.

Rigour An assessment of the quality of research design and processes. The definition of **rigour** varies between qualitative and quantitative inquiry.

Sample The documents that you include in your analysis.

Semiotic analysis The study of signs and signifiers and how they create meaning and understandings between **authors** and **readers**. See Box 5.2.

Social construction(ism) An approach to studying society that does not assume the existence of a single 'true' reality. Instead, realities are believed to be constructed between individuals using language and experience. The opposite of **positivist ontology**.

Stratified sample A sampling technique where the whole population is divided into groups (such as by gender or income level) and random samples are taken from these groups.

Tabloid (newspapers) These are smaller in size than **broadsheet** newspapers. The content is often less serious, and focused on sensationalising crime and celebrity gossip.

'The (ethnographic) field' A term used to describe the place ethnographic data collection occurs.

Thematic analysis An analysis strategy that involves either **inductively** or **deductively** identifying themes and then coding data for these themes to allow a comparison across the data set. See Box 3.1.

Theory A statement about how and/or why things occur in society.

Triangulation A way of combining two or more sets of data in order to gain a greater understanding of a phenomenon.

Validity The extent to which a research project is able to answer its **research question**.

Verbatim A way of recording somebody's exact words. **Verbatim** transcription is often required following qualitative interviews that have been audio-recorded.

Visual method(s) A range of artistic or creative research techniques, including the use of photographs, drawings and timelines. Visual data can be used alongside an **elicitation interview**.

INDEX